THE JACOBINS

THE JACOBINS

AN ESSAY IN THE NEW HISTORY

BY

CLARENCE CRANE BRINTON, Ph.D.

NEW YORK
RUSSELL & RUSSELL · INC
1961

To H. J. Laski
of
London University

PREFATORY NOTE

This study was made possible largely through a fellowship from the Social Science Research Council. The author wishes to thank that body, as well as the many archivists and librarians in France who have aided in this work. He is particularly indebted to M. Albert Mathiez, whose knowledge and willingness to help extend to the minutest details of revolutionary history; to M. Pierre Caron; and to M. Michel Lhéritier. In America he is especially grateful to Professor A. M. Schlesinger for his continued interest in a subject not properly his own, to Professor E. S. Mason and Dr. S. E. Harris, economists not in the least responsible for the gaps in the author's knowledge of economics, and to Professor Penfield Roberts, who has aided in the work from the beginning. Some of the material incorporated in this book has appeared in the *American Historical Review* and in the *Political Science Quarterly*. The author thanks the editors of these reviews for permission to use this material.

CRANE BRINTON

CAMBRIDGE, MASSACHUSETTS,
November, 1930.

CONTENTS

THE JACOBINS

THE JACOBINS
AN ESSAY IN THE NEW HISTORY

CHAPTER I

INTRODUCTION

Historians to-day seem pretty much agreed to leave kings and courtiers, statesmen and generals to the more graceful talents of the new biographers. History, as one of the social sciences, can no more than biology make the study of exceptional individuals an end in itself. The historian must study the behavior of many men in the past because he ultimately wishes to understand the behavior of many men in the present. The exceptional individual interests him therefore only as the freak interests the biologist, for the light he throws on the average man, for the extent to which he makes necessary a modification of the uniformities in human behavior already established by scientific investigation. For the historian, too, aspires to the discovery of uniformities, or laws, which will enable him to arrange the chaotic past in an order not merely chronological.

Now a scientific law is an instrument of prediction, and therefore potentially one of control. If we can, for instance, establish the laws under which revolutions run their course, we can possibly prevent revolutions, or make them less destructive, or at least protect ourselves in a measure from them. Does not a knowledge of meteorology allow us to take steps to lessen damage from drouth and from storm?

The historian with such scientific aspirations obviously

1

cannot content himself with describing events, with writing the older narrative history. All narration is unique,—the less unique, the less successful—and its characters exist and move about for their own sakes, or at very worst for the sake of the story. But the newer historian must eschew narration, and supplant the character with the unit. Danton is a character, and defies scientific generalization; the Jacobin is a unit, and will fit into statistics almost as well as a guinea-pig or a vitamin. It is true that this newer historian may seem to be hardly more than an economist, a sociologist or a philosopher with his attention turned rather more than usual to the past of his discipline. It is true also that the newer synthesis demands an almost journalistic omniscience of the historian. Yet the new history is upon us, and must be written. Who now would dare model himself on Thucydides —even without the speeches? That historian, indeed, though unquestionably a great figure in literature, failed to tell us anything about Athenian diet, Athenian industry, Athenian sanitation, and any number of other topics equally interesting to us and familiar to him.

Our new social history must, however, never lose sight of its ultimate goal, the discovery of generalizations which will have as much as possible of the force of scientific laws. Its newness depends entirely on this scientific purpose. Herodotus wrote social history, and social historians to-day run the risk of producing mere collections of odds and ends less amusing and less enlightening than his. The older narrative history, although, contrary to opinions apparently held by some teachers of history in the last century, it never was to be found fully written in the sources, was spared this particular difficulty. The historian had indeed to decide just what he was going to narrate, and he had to apply to the construction of the narrative, to the selection and rejection of material, principles genuinely critical and scientific. But his subject carried with it a certain unity, and set a problem which restrained him within certain limits. Just what went on in Paris and in St. Cloud on the 18th brumaire? What were the complete ramifications of the Hohenzollern candidacy? What did they talk about at Konopischt? In social history, however, the subject rarely carries within itself an adequate principle of unity. An account of social conditions in the New England colonies, for instance, might easily degenerate into a set of unconnected, if more or less picturesque details about the consumption of hard liquor, the blue laws, bundling, the codfish trade, peddlers and hawkers, and so on to a very great length. To save social history from mere rambling among details some specific problem must be set. The historian, like the natural scientist, must plunge into facts in search of an hypothesis, and, when he has found it, must test it upon those facts and others. The vast number of facts accessible to the social historian will thus acquire a meaning. In themselves, they have none, not even the meaning which attaches itself to the continuity of a single human life, for they never tell us enough about the separate Smiths and the separate Joneses of the past to allow us to reconstruct these obscure people as persons, as we can reconstruct Napoleon or Lincoln. But what we can find out about the lives of numerous men whose ultimate personality is forever lost, may be precisely what is necessary to answer the kind of question the social scientist must ask.

The subject of the following study does, one hopes, satisfy the requirements of the new history. In the first place, the documents are plentiful. The *Sociétés des Amis de la Constitution,* subsequently the *Sociétés populaires,* and in history simply the Jacobin clubs, were established all over France during the great revolution, and have left numerous traces of their doings. Practically all of them kept minutes in a form more or less parliamentary, and corresponded extensively with one another, and with public authorities. The larger ones printed pamphlets, issued addresses, published official organs, even subsidized theaters for propaganda.[1] Many of the records of this activity have disappeared, but French local historians have discovered and published an astonishing amount of material on these clubs, and still more remains in public archives, departmental and municipal, and in private possession.

Now, these clubs were clearly one of the means by which the French Revolution developed as it did. They were unofficial political groups, similar in many ways to the Anti-Corn Law League, the Anti-Saloon League, or the Ku Klux Klan. They got things done. They were, in short, the sort of agencies of political action made familiar by the studies of Bryce and Ostrogorski. About them many important questions can be asked, and answered modestly in the form of hypotheses. What sort of men joined these clubs? Were they rich or poor? failures or successes at their ordinary work before the revolution? old or young? calm or violent? Why did they join the clubs? What did they wish the clubs to do? In short, just what is a Jacobin? The question in that form is hardly new. Taine for instance clearly set himself to answer precisely that question. But though he searched in the obscurity of local history for instances of Jacobin cruelty and violence, the Jacobin he finally constructs is a creature curiously cerebral, made up of Descartes, Rousseau, Robespierre and St. Just. Taine may, of course, be right, and the best way to understand the average

Jacobin may be to study the exceptional one. But the
method made possible by the records of the Jacobin clubs
does at least afford us a chance of testing Taine's intui-
tions by a true induction. Moreover, these records get us
well outside of Paris, and show us the whole country in
revolution, from the Channel to the Mediterranean. It
may again be true that in the Revolution, Paris is France,
and that nothing important occurred in the provinces.
But that conclusion, too, we shall be able to test fairly
from the facts.

Ideally speaking, these records spread before us the
political consciousness and political behavior at a specific
moment of time of several thousands of Frenchmen. We
ought then to be able to study these men calmly, as the
naturalist might study a colony of ants, observe what
they were trying to do, how well they did it, perhaps
even why they wanted to do it. Indeed, we can find documents which will enable us to classify some of the observed characteristics of these Frenchmen statistically,
and thus apply the quantitative method to the study of
history.[2] We should be able to face this host of facts,
not indeed with a mind which merely sorts them automatically according to something orderly inherent in the
facts themselves (a process which, if possible at all, is
certainly not real thinking) but with a mind already
filled by experience with certain curiosities which seek
to sate themselves upon the facts. These curiosities have
no doubt a close relation with our desires. But if we use
our minds conscientiously, we can keep each term in the
long progression from subjective desire to objective fact
in its proper place, and approach what is called scientific
truth.

In reality it is hardly possible to attain in a study of
the Jacobins the rough but harmonious adjustment be-

tween the thinker's self and the external world he thinks about attainable by the natural scientist. In the first place, the records, rich though they are, are imperfect. Even the manuscript records have gaps, sessions omitted, speeches mentioned only by title, incomplete lists of members. But one could hardly consult all sources in the original, and still have time to write an account of the Jacobin clubs in general. Reliance must to a great extent be placed on local historians who have worked over the original material. And their work is very uneven. Some of them have written monographs more useful than the original records of the clubs, since they have gone to supplementary documents to add pertinent information. Others have contented themselves with bald and often inadequate summaries, or with arbitrarily chosen extracts.[3]

In the second place, there are certain logical difficulties inherent in the nature of the material and in the kind of question we are attempting to answer. Certain questions as to the social and economic status of the Jacobins can indeed be answered by a fairly simple process of counting. But the hundreds of examples of Jacobin political practice, Jacobin theory, Jacobin religion afforded by these records can be brought together only with difficulty. They cannot all be listed, all be related. But what is the norm under which they may be grouped? How much more important is a policy or a belief which appears in an important provincial center than a policy or belief which appears in a small market-town? If two Jacobins are found disagreeing in a given club, which is heretic? which orthodox? An infinite number of heterogeneous items must somehow be integrated, and this is a task which requires a feeling for values, a sense of judgment perhaps beyond logic.

Finally, the historian of any subject involving the

French Revolution can hardly flatter himself that he can really be free from prejudice, that the part of his emotions which normally responds to the stimulus of such abstractions as liberty, humanity, justice, and right, will in no way be affected. The historiography of the French Revolution is full of the names of writers who on one page announce their devotion to objectivity, to science, to truth, and on the next display the heartiest prejudices for or against the Revolution. The astonished reader may sometimes suspect the historian of insincerity; it is as though a man, while earnestly maintaining himself to be a complete teetotaler, should openly down glass after glass of whiskey. Nor is it to be expected that a foreigner should benefit by any aloofness from things particularly French, and so approach the study of the Revolution as the biologist approaches the study of guinea pigs. Not being a Frenchman helps a man in judging the French Revolution hardly more than not being a Jew helps a man in judging the life of Christ. All the important things in the French Revolution, as in Christianity—that is, the things men quarrel about—are now the common property of the western world.

It is something, however, to admit and recognize difficulties such as these. The task remains, lightened a bit by the knowledge that it must be imperfect. From the great mass of material about the Jacobins, we shall try to find answers to questions suggested by our modern interests in the French Revolution, and indeed in revolutions in general. Perhaps the most important of these is one from political psychology: Why do men revolt? Is the discontent that makes them want change economic or social? What place have the realities hidden in modern psychological terminology—frustration, inferiority complex, maladjustment—in political revolt? Then there are many other equally important questions. How numerous are the revolutionists? What are the relations between majority and minority in revolutionary action? What effect has revolutionary propaganda? What is the relation between ideas and wants in the consciousness of the revolutionists?

Now, we may hope to find some kind of answer to these and similar questions, as far as they apply to the French Revolution, from the records of the Jacobin clubs. These records are not, of course, résumés of the French Revolution; one could not write a political history of the Revolution from them alone. But they do provide the best possible means of getting at problems as purely sociological as those we have indicated. They do enable us us to generalize about very ordinary men, and even to enumerate and weigh some of their actions. Possibly similar studies of a sufficient number of other great revolutions would permit of generalizations, would enable us to work out laws for revolutions, establish a science of social dynamics. That, however, is another task. Whatever we may hope to establish from the present study is true of the first French Revolution. It may be true of other revolutions, but that the present study cannot hope to decide.

Even if these ambitious excursions into sociology should prove failures, we may still succeed in giving some sort of an answer to the question, what is a Jacobin? Not the least of the services within the power of the new history is an added precision, a new concreteness, in our definitions of the abstractions with which the past is unfortunately almost as filled as the present. There is something behind the abstraction Jacobinism, as, indeed, there is behind most "isms." That something is, obviously, common to all good Jacobins. It may, indeed, be nothing more than a string of minor "isms." But Jacobinism has perhaps endured too long to be quite that sort of humbug. Few studies would be more interesting than an account of what Jacobinism meant to the generations of the nineteenth century. No one has yet traced the growth of the Jacobin legend, less crudely dramatic, but possibly even more influential, than the Napoleonic legend.

Our task, however, will be to define the words Jacobin and Jacobinism from the words and deeds of the ordinary members of the Jacobin clubs. The problem is essentially the very old one of universals. It is to be doubted if this generation possesses logical tools for its solution in particular cases much superior to those of preceding generations. Wherever possible—wherever, indeed, the method does not seem too ludicrous,—we shall have recourse to counting, and make the universal arrived at a statistical universal. Elsewhere, we may be obliged to arrive at the universal by a process suspiciously akin to that of the artist; that is, by an intuitive condensing of hundreds of experiences, or of examples, into one typical experience or example. And thus the Jacobin, though he fail to provide us with a grand theory of revolutionary action, may at least turn out to be a fact.

CHAPTER II

ORGANIZATION

I

Language is sometimes a most treacherous guide for the historian. It might seem that, since the French borrowed the word "club" from England, they borrowed the thing as well; and essayists have often brought forward this detail to help contrast the ease and frequency with which the Anglo-Saxon creates all sorts of voluntary groups and the social poverty of the Frenchman, with only the family between himself and the state. But any attempt to discover the origins of the Jacobin clubs will soon show that this sort of association was quite indigenous to eighteenth century France. It is not unlikely that a Frenchman spoke of "le club," when he might have spoken of "le cercle," "la chambre" or "la société," much as the Englishman might say "rendezvous" for "appointment" or "assignation," because it sounded distinguished and a trifle romantic.

The Jacobin clubs, though their proliferation in 1790 and 1791 seems at first a new thing, had very clear antecedents in French social life before the Revolution. The various groups in which it is possible to see forerunners of the Jacobins are not, however, on the surface political clubs, for such clubs could hardly have a place in a polity molded by Louis XIV. Broadly, these groups are of two kinds, the "literary societies," called by Augustin Cochin

10

the "sociétés de pensée" [1] and the secret societies, mostly masonic.

The "chambres littéraires," established in great numbers in French provincial towns in the latter part of the eighteenth century, are themselves ultimately derived from the learned academies of the Renaissance. They show how far intellectual activity had penetrated down into ordinary middle class circles by 1789. The great French academy was a creation of Richelieu. The provincial academies which followed, and which by the early eighteenth century were in full activity, were still composed of the locally distinguished, and set for themselves scholarly ends. Then came various societies for agricultural improvement, and for the spreading of enlightenment in other ways. These societies were definitely ceasing to be academies. Their membership was larger, though still limited to the active class of intellectual reformers, and their aim was obviously propaganda. Finally, beginning about 1760 and continuing up to the Revolution, the literary societies were founded in almost all towns with pretensions to a social life—centers of the complicated administration of the old régime, capitals of the historic local division known as the *pays*, ports and even important market towns. These societies included representatives of all the branches of the middle class, merchants, lawyers, doctors, *rentiers*, and not merely men of scholarly leanings.

The societies were definitely social clubs in the full English sense of the word. The "société de Moulins" was founded in 1787 to "bring together a number of citizens of all orders of society, to procure them respectable diversion, to enable them to communicate to one another their knowledge and their talents." It had four rooms used respectively for reading, conversation, billiards, and cards and other games. It subscribed to the leading newspapers, and increased its library from new books as fast as its means would permit. Its dues, thirty-six livres per year, would correspond to at least that many dollars to-day.[2] The "cercle littéraire" of Castres was founded in 1782 to enable its members to "rest from their daily work, to read the latest political and literary publications, to talk about the news and learn the chief events in Europe, to amuse themselves at legitimate games, and finally, to enjoy the delights of conversation as praiseworthy as decent." [3]

Augustin Cochin made an extremely exhaustive study of these literary societies in Brittany.[4] He concluded that their literary character was an unconscious sham, and that they really were political clubs, and as such prepared for the calling of the States General, and engineered the elections to that body. So thoroughly filled were these respectable *bourgeois* with the abstract political philosophy of their time, a philosophy which was disseminated largely through the literature of the *salon*, that they cannot be accused of masking their political activities under the name of literature. Cochin goes on and submits the political program and the political ideas of these societies to a criticism whose principles are obviously derived from Taine on the Jacobins. To this criticism we shall later revert. But, at least for Brittany, Cochin's thorough research has certainly proved his point: that the literary societies, closely organized by committees of correspondence, and united by a central committee, did by propaganda, caucuses, electioneering and public manifestations influence political events. It must, however, be added, first, that in Brittany this political machine formed by the literary societies seems to have been much more complete than anywhere else in

France (the Breton delegation to the States General was notoriously radical) and second, that Cochin deliberately neglects the social and cultural side of club life. Many a good citizen must have gone to his club to enjoy a "legitimate game" of cards.

As to the continuity between these clubs and the various "Sociétés des Amis de la Constitution" which, following the lead of Paris, began to spring up in the provinces in the late autumn of 1789, there can be in general no doubt. Many of the members of the Breton literary societies identified themselves later with the local Jacobin clubs. But in many instances the literary society itself continued as body, merely assuming the name of "Friends of the Constitution" and securing affiliation with the Paris Jacobins. The society at Colmar continued, with a certain expansion in membership, the *Tabagie Littérairé* of 1785.[5] So the societies at Moulins, Castres, Avranches,[6] Nantes,[7] Sisteron [8] are clearly derived from previously formed literary societies. Even at Mainz, in a part of Germany very open to French influence, we find a "Lesegesellschaft" as precursor of the "Gesellschaft der Freunde der Freiheit und Gleichheit." [9] There was a period of transition, when it was hardly clear to the founders of new societies what sort of title they should take. A society founded at Cherbourg in April, 1790 took the title of "Société littéraire des Amis de la Constitution" and only dropped the "littéraire" in October.[10] At Nancy, the "Cabinet littéraire national" founded in December 1789 did not take on the orthodox title until February 1790.[11] No analysis in statistical form can at present be made to show how many Jacobin clubs had had a previous existence as literary clubs. But it can be safely said that in most towns a minority at least—and that the most cultured and most prosperous minority—of the lo-

cal Jacobin club had enjoyed the benefits of association
with friends of similar tastes in literary societies where
talk of politics was certainly not banished. How indeed
could it have been, when every man of letters in France
was a sociologist?

The other chief antecedent of the Jacobin clubs is certainly to be found in the secret societies, and especially
in the freemasons. Such a subject, however, is one which
the newer historian must approach with trembling, and
dispose of as quickly as possible. There is something romantic about any secret society, something of the "back-
stairs" history which hardly fits into science. There is the
inescapable impossibility of getting reliable information
from men sworn to secrecy. There is the cheap fear of
such societies, from which writers like Mrs. Nesta Webster have constructed philosophical melodramas. Yet it is
unquestionable that many freemasons were among the
founders of the first Jacobin clubs in various parts of
France. According to Labroue, two-thirds of the freemasons of Bergerac joined the club in 1791; and of the
fifty-eight members of the *société mesmérienne* (a title
which shows its connection with the Enlightenment)
forty-two joined the club.[12] Brégail thinks that at Auch
and in the Gers the clubs were founded by freemasons,
and establishes definitely that the leaders of the clubs
had also been leaders in the lodges.[13] In the north, the
same would seem true for Lille.[14] And in general, those
who have used documents emanating from the clubs—
petitions, addresses, letters—can testify that the three
masonic dots are not infrequently to be found accom-
panying signatures. Yet these masonic signatures are
rarely in a majority. The register of the society of Toulouse, for instance, founded in May, 1790, has only four
such signatures out of thirty-eight.[15]

Moreover, certain practices which appear very early in the clubs point to masonic origins. Such are the fraternal embrace with which the presiding officer greets his guests, the universal use of the word "brother"—in the early minutes many of the speakers are referred to as "brother so-and-so"—the admission of new members by a secret vote with the use of blackballs, and occasionally, the existence of a *master of ceremonies*.[16] Not infrequently, after the manner of friendly societies the world over, the society delegates two of its members to visit a brother's sick-bed, and sometimes provision for this is made in the rules.[17] Finally, freemasonry itself dies out with the Revolution, and the lodges are not revived until the Empire.

The extent to which freemasons in eighteenth century France are to be regarded as plotters of revolution can scarcely be estimated objectively. M. Gaston Martin has studied the problem thoroughly and his conclusions seem fair.[18] The typical eighteenth-century mason was a cultivated *bourgeois* or nobleman. The lodges were certainly centers of active propaganda, or enlightenment, as they would doubtless have had it. Masons undoubtedly worked through the press and the literary societies to prepare for the Revolution, to draw up the *cahiers,* to get people aware that political change was possible and desirable. But of organized plot in the melodramatic sense there is no proof. Too many non-masons were obviously active in the early societies.

Many Jacobin clubs, however, even in the first years of the Revolution, cannot be traced at the moment of actual establishment either to literary societies or to masonic lodges. The circumstances of their origin vary greatly, and afford an instance—and by no means the last we shall notice—of the extraordinary diversity of French provincial life, a diversity which even the centralizing government of the Terror was never wholly able to destroy. It was not uncommon for the club to be formed by the electors chosen in 1789 to elect deputies to the States General, or more particularly from Committees of the electoral college of the local Third Estate which had continued to meet after the formal business of election was over.[19] At Tours, the club was founded by disgruntled radicals who had failed to dislodge a conservative city government by ballot or by rioting.[20] At Troyes, it was founded by the radical city-government, which, finding it could not as a governing body affiliate itself with the Paris Jacobins, turned itself into a club.[21] At Saverne, the club was formed in April, 1791, by two agents, members of the club of Strasbourg, sent out by the department of the Bas Rhin to depose the conservative town government, and introduce a little revolutionary leaven in the very clerical and royalist Alsatian town.[22] Later, when the revolutionary government was in full swing, there was little pretense of local spontaneity, and clubs were artificially foisted from above on towns which obviously ought not to be without such precious auxiliaries of self-government.

Yet in the beginnings of the Revolution the clubs seem a spontaneous, if not undirected, growth. The rest of the country may have imitated Paris, but the imitation was voluntary, like the imitation of a fashion. Just how much of the habits of the old régime, and therefore of naturalness still guided these budding revolutionists is evident from the rules and regulations of the "Club littéraire et patriotique de cent" founded in Toulouse in May, 1790 by sixteen "citoyens actifs," all prosperous petty tradesmen and eventually filling its membership to one hundred.[23] The preamble states that "in the assemblies of the

society Religion, the Nation, the Law and the King must
not be spoken of save with respect and veneration." The
oldest member of the society became automatically its
head, under the name of "père patriote." He could appoint a chancellor to do the actual work of presiding for
him, and was assisted by a board of four "ephors" who
prepared the business to come before the club. All acts of
the club were to be preceded by the letters E. F. P.
(Egalité, Fraternité, Patriotisme) and concluded by
V. M. D. N. L. R. (Vaincre ou mourir pour Dieu, pour la
Nation, pour la Loi et pour le Roi). There was an elaborate secret code, by which the members were to recognize each other. "There will be four signs of recognition,
of which the first will be the raising of the eyes towards
heaven, without affectation, to show that the love of God
came first into the spirit of the society, the second the
placing of the fingers of one hand gently to the eyes, to
show that the eyes have shared in the light which il-
lumines the Nation, the third the placing of one finger on
the forehead, to indicate that from the mind comes the
new law which relights the sacred fire of the Fatherland,
and the fourth, the placing of the hand skillfully on the
heart, to show that Louis XVI, the restorer of liberty,
has there established the seat of his empire." The "père
patriote" is a significant survival of the rule of the father
so characteristic of the ancien régime.[24] The respect for
the throne cannot be wholly hypocritical. And the rather
juvenile love of secrecy and brotherhood ritual needs
hardly any subtler explanation than a well-worn reference to human nature.

II

With the election of the States General in the spring
of 1789, and with its transformation by early summer

into a national assembly self-charged with the task of giving France some kind of representative government, the earnest talkers of the literary and patriotic societies throughout the country began to realize that France was theirs to govern. In a surprisingly short time there appeared two institutions almost unknown to the old monarchy, a newspaper press and modern political parties. With the former we are not immediately concerned; but the great organization which grew out of the simple caucus of radical deputies at Versailles known as the *Club Breton*,[25] and which became one of the most effective party machines in history, is the whole subject of this study.

Nothing could be more natural than the establishment of the *Club Breton*. A deliberative body of twelve hundred members was set up suddenly, without organization, without precedents, without a parliamentary procedure. The assembly was, as regards other assemblies, in what the eighteenth century would have called a state of nature. According to the fashionable philosophical beliefs held by a majority of its members, it ought, indeed, to have listened patiently and open-mindedly to any proposals brought before it, and to have made its decisions freely in accordance with the dictates of reason. Actually, members of a like turn of mind, and of like political desires, soon found that by getting together before the sessions of the assembly, by agreeing to vote a certain way no matter how eloquent and how reasonable upholders of another way might be, and by pledging as many others as possible to vote with them, they could get what they wanted. Of the groups thus formed, the caucus of Breton deputies which met in a café near the assembly hall soon proved to be one of the best knit. Gradually deputies from other provinces, who agreed with the Bretons in wanting strongly democratic measures, joined the group. It soon became clear, however, that, in an assembly where the nobles and clergy had a representation equal to that of the Third Estate, even a well organized radical party could not command a majority. Recruits must be found outside the assembly; at the next election, more of the radical party could thus be returned, and in the meantime a "public opinion" could be created, private individuals could petition the assembly, local government units could be won over, newspapers could keep the necessary issues warm. Even before the assembly left Versailles to go to Paris—as early, indeed, as June 10—outsiders, men who were not deputies, appear to have been admitted to the *Club Breton*.[26] After the October Days the members of the *Club Breton* came together again in Paris, took in new members, and launched the Society of Friends of the Constitution. They met at first in a room rented from the monks of a Jacobin convent in the rue St. Honoré conveniently near the meeting place of the National Assembly. Their official name was much too long for current use, and not the least of historical ironies has forever fastened upon these violent anti-clericals the popular French name for their landlords, friars of the Order of St. Dominic.

Throughout the country in 1790 and 1791, local Societies of Friends of the Constitution were founded, and formally affiliated with the mother society at Paris. To the relations of these societies with one another and with the Paris society we shall later return; but first we must describe the internal structure of the typical society. There is abundant material for such a description in the minutes, and more especially in the pompous rules and regulations, which have survived in great numbers. Here a caution is necessary, one that will have to be repeated

later. The rules and regulations governing the Paris club
served as a pattern for the provincial clubs, but any examination of the details of provincial organization re-
veals a hundred differences born of genuine variations in
temperament and in tradition. The relation between
Paris and the provinces is something subtler than wholesale imitation. The Jacobins of Marseilles or of Lille are
never quite the Jacobins of Paris.[27]

The rules and regulations of the clubs almost always
begin with a philosophical preamble in which the local
intelligentsia rewrite the *Contrat social*. Then follows
an elaborate scheme of organization, based obviously on
English parliamentary procedure, already somewhat
transmuted by fashionable French usages. The members
took an obvious delight in the exercise of parliamentary
formalities, in moving the previous question, referring
proposals to committees, tabling motions. They had
talked about politics, and read about politics for years,
but until this blessed Revolution they had never been able
to give themselves the illusion that they were in politics,
that they were governing themselves. But now they had
not only chosen a States General; thanks to the Jacobins, they were not limited to this silent and unspec-
tacular exercise of a franchise to choose their representatives, but could voice their opinions on all things at the
tribune of the club. Each little town was a new Athens,
at least as far as political opportunities go. In the earlier
records of the clubs there is an unmistakable delight in
the game of politics, in posturing before the public, in
going through the ordinary rites of collective action—not
an ignominious nor a puerile delight, though it seem so
at first sight, for it was a part of a genuine and as yet
almost unembittered freshness of emotion real enough,
surely, in the pages of the *Prelude,* though it disappear

into unreality beneath subsequent sociological terminology as mass-contagion.

The clubs then, whatever is left in them of masonic ritual and of the informalities of social gatherings, are at bottom debating clubs with parliamentary organization and parliamentary ambitions. A speaker is recognized, makes a motion, defends it, yields the floor, sees his motion referred to committee, passed as a resolution, or defeated. Rules govern recognition of speakers, order of debate, and the other details of procedure. Set speeches are almost always made not from the floor, but from the *tribune,* a sort of pulpit usually raised opposite the president's desk. French inexperience in political life comes out, as it does even in Paris, by the frequency of written speeches, and the absence of genuine debate, save when personal and local issues crop up. Not infrequently the sessions of the clubs, at least in the early years, are dull and barren for lack of real things to quarrel about, and of skilled improvisers to heat the quarrel. The club of Senlis in 1791 was reduced to filling a whole session with reading aloud speeches already delivered in Paris by Isnard and Condorcet, supplemented by a catechism on the rights of man.[28]

The officers of even the smallest club were numerous, and as far as the more distinguished officers went, elected for very short periods. The presidency, a position much coveted by ambitious leaders in local politics, was usually held for two weeks, and hardly ever for more than a month. Reëlection was usually possible only after an interval. Rotation in office was sound democratic theory, and made the game more interesting. Some clubs had vice-presidents to preside in the absence of the president, but at first the commoner practice was to have the oldest member present—the *doyen d'age*—take the chair in de-

fault of the president, a trace of that patriarchal theory
which the Revolution was so completely to destroy. The
number of lesser officers varied greatly with the different
clubs, but in general there seems to have been no deliberate multiplication of honors and offices such as is common in American friendly societies, for instance. The
club at Toulon had a president, vice-president, four secretaries, two inspectors of the hall (whose duty was to
keep order), two inspectors charged with issuing membership cards, and seeing that they were not transferred
to outsiders, a treasurer (who took charge of the collection of dues) an *économe* (who directed the expenditure
of the club's money, and kept the books), an archivist
and a vice-archivist.[29] All of these officers, however,
clearly had work to do, and the reason why there were so
many of them is apparently that there was a great deal
to do, and that most of the officers were inefficient and
inexperienced. As the clubs grew from debating societies
to petty local assemblies charged with part of the work
of governing France during the Terror, their organization
became a bit less top-heavy, though it can rarely be said
to have been efficient. At Rodez, during the Terror, the
club had a president, two secretaries, five readers (apparently secretaries in charge of correspondence and an-
nouncements), two censors to preserve order in the
ladies' gallery, four to preserve order among the men, a
treasurer and an "agent de la société" (apparently a liai-
son officer between the society and government officials).[30] Judging from the records they have left behind
them, the secretaries were rather inattentive and careless. The clubs would have two, four, and even six of
them in the hope that one at least would always be
present. This hope was not always realized. The register
at Perpignan reads in one place as follows:

25 brumaire an II. There having been no secretary, there were no minutes.

26 brumaire an II. Same observation as for the previous meeting.

27 brumaire an II. The secretaries being still absent, it was decided they would be severely censured if they missed the next meeting.

On the 28th brumaire a secretary finally turned up, and the minutes were written.[31]

The clubs were not, of course, usually as badly served as this. They seem to have had much better luck with their treasurers, most of whom served for long terms. At Montauban, indeed, the same treasurer held office from the birth to the death of the society, from 1790 to 1795— a period during which the external political allegiances of the club went through extraordinary changes.[32] Nor do there seem to have been many serious examples of malversation in office on the part of these treasurers. Graft there undoubtedly was during the Revolution, but it has left almost no traces in the finances of the clubs. It must be remembered that the clubs, even during the terror, were not official bodies. They always retained something of the voluntary association. Their records are far from perfect, but on the whole their officers seem to have worked fairly hard at work that was neither public nor private, and certainly brought most of them no direct financial reward.

In the matter of election to membership, the clubs show a definite change in policy as the Revolution develops. In the beginning, elections are made by black and white balls, with all the apparatus of election into a secret society. Then for a while in 1792 and 1793, and especially in country towns and villages, election is by open vote, and not very difficult. Finally, during the Terror, election, though still public, is extremely difficult,

and like so many other Jacobin acts, though based in
theory on majority vote, demands in practice something
very like unanimity. The admission requirements at
Limoges in June 1790 may be taken as typical of the earlier societies:

The admission of a member will depend on the following conditions:

1. It must be proposed by one member and seconded by four
others;

2. it will not be voted upon until the third meeting after this
proposal;

3. during this interval it may be discussed at any time, and the
names of the candidate and his sponsors will be posted on a board
designed for such purposes;

4. it must be accepted by the society by a favorable vote of at
least five-sixths of those present;

5. it cannot be voted upon at all in a session when half the
membership of the society is not present, unless the session has
been especially called for the election of new members.[33]

At Artonne the society declared "the number of members will not be restrained. Any individual who shall
unite love of country with moral purity shall be eligible"; but it required a three-fourths majority of white
beans in favor of the candidate.[34] The majority necessary
for election varied greatly; at Paris, even in 1790, after
certain formalities only a bare majority was required; [35]
at St. Etienne it was seven-eighths; [36] at Rouen, two-
thirds was required.[37] There is an interesting variant in
the little town of Sauveterre in Rouergue, one which
shows how much the methods of the secret societies of
the Enlightenment influenced the clubs. Election to
membership required unanimity. If there was a single
black ball, the candidate had to leave the room, and
those who voted against him were obliged to acknowl-

edge the fact, and to explain their reasons. If the society by a majority vote approved of these reasons, the candidate was excluded. If the society failed to approve these reasons, the original black balls were counted out, and the candidate "unanimously" elected.[38] At Lunéville it was harder for non-residents of the town to get into the club than for residents; at Tulle the reverse seems to have been true.[39]

When later the clubs became more militantly and more religiously a body of the elect, entrance was more difficult in reality, though not always in form. One common solution was to have a committee on elections, with secret proceedings, to examine rigorously into the political past of a candidate, and to turn him down or accept him. The public vote of the club itself thus became a mere formality. The *comité de présentation* at Dreux in 1794, was to have a register, "on which was to be kept the names of all candidates, their surnames, professions, residences, how they have conducted themselves since the Revolution, their lives and their morals." [40] With such information the committee itself could make a final decision. The society at Beauvais used another method for keeping out the unfit. A candidate was voted on by the whole society, but if he was refused by a majority, his sponsors were reprimanded by the president and suspended for one month "for having sought to introduce into the sanctuary of liberty a member who could not breathe its pure air." [41] Finally, entrance to some of the perfunctorily organized village societies seems at all times to have been fairly simple. One joined the society at Castelnau-Rivière-Basse even in 1793 simply by inscribing one's self on the list of members and paying one's dues.[42]

There are in these regulations surprisingly few provisions concerning a minimum age-limit for membership. Many clubs later made 18, 20, or 21 years necessary for a full voting membership, but permitted a sort of associate membership for younger men, especially for sons of members. Yet, as we shall see, the clubs were never filled with young men, and if their actions seem to sober conservative critics the work of immature persons, the immaturity is certainly not a physical one.

As parliamentary bodies, the clubs had of course to have a committee system. These committees, moreover, were simply the expression of the normal tendency of large bodies to slough off work—and power—to smaller and more manageable ones. There is again a great variety in these committees; in general, they tend to multiply in number as the societies take more and more part in work that is partially administrative, while at the same time one of them, usually a kind of steering committee, assumes more and more the ultimate decision in all important matters. This committee is called variously *comité de surveillance* (often undistinguishable from the legal town committee of the same name instituted as part of the revolutionary government outlined by the decree of 14 frimaire an II), *comité de recherches, comité central.* The *comité de recherches* appears quite early in many clubs. It was bitterly attacked in the Paris club in March, 1791.[43] It was clearly one of the instruments by which the Terror was prepared.

The club of Poitiers is a good example of one of the older and stabler clubs. In 1791, it had eight committees, averaging five to seven members each, and appointed by the president. There were committees on correspondence, on relations with governing bodies, on agriculture and commerce, on the public good, on mendicity, and finally the *comité de surveillance.*[44] Such committees were at first renewed in personnel at monthly or quarterly intervals.[45] Clearly much of this sort of committee work must have been mere catering to the vanity of members by giving them the illusion that they had something to do. Such committees as those on agriculture, on public good, on commerce occasionally produced schemes for improving something, but there was too much else to be done, or at least to be said, for concrete improvements to stand much chance. Nevertheless, whatever the clubs accomplished in social service was usually the work of these committees, and its sum total is not unimportant. As a portent of the future, of course, it is extremely important.

As the revolution went on, the clubs fell more and more into the control of the more active minority of their members. The characteristic method of exercising that control was the committee. In this, the clubs follow the same course as French government during the Revolution. Dictators, bosses, even leaders are singularly uncommon even in French local history during the Revolution. Power tends to take refuge in commission. Several hundred men are soon seen, in spite of fashionable theories, to be unable to arrive at any decision; but enough force is left to the theories to prevent undisguised personal leadership, and even undisguised oligarchy. The groups, usually varying between five and fifteen, which controlled most of the *sociétés populaires* during the Terror had occasionally no official status whatever in the clubs. In general, however, they were a committee constituted for some particular function, and which gradually assumed direction of the clubs' policies. At Coutances, the Terror was the work of an informal "Comité des cinq" of the club.[46] The "comité de six" of Treignac, which had complete charge of admission to the club, seems to have

turned into a kind of steering committee.[47] Other clubs
erected central committees, which were divided into sub-
committees, and which controlled completely all the
business of the club. Such a committee was chosen in
1793 at Lons-le-Saunier; its twenty-four members took
over all the work of the five separate committees previously charged with correspondence, admission, surveillance, agriculture and commerce.[48] At Nice the central
committee of 42 was unusually large, but it was divided
into seven sub-committees, one of which had charge of
membership and procedure.[49]

There can be no doubt that such committees, under
whatever name they were erected, did a great deal quite
independently of their society as a whole. This is true,
not merely of the central committees in which were
grouped the natural leaders of the society, but even of
the lesser and more specialized committees. Even as
early as February, 1792, we find Robespierre at the Paris
club protesting against a circular issued by the committee of correspondence without consulting the club. He
asks that in the future "no committee may send out letters and circulars unless the whole society has heard them
read." [50] At Perpignan the central committee, beginning
early in 1791, kept its own series of registers, and clearly
acted towards the whole body in a relation something
like that of a cabinet to a parliament—except that a
very great deal of business was done by orders in council.[51] This comes out even more clearly from the papers
of the society of Toulouse.[52] The more active members
of the club were all attached to various committees,
which, as can be seen from what is left of their registers,
were monopolizing much of the activity of the club as a
body. The *comité de bienfaisance, économique et d'admission* (an awkward accumulation of functions, gram-

matically as well as politically) distributed bread to the poor, intervened in labor difficulties between employers and employees, supervised hospital sanitation, presented several virtuous and republican ladies with enough of a dowry to allow them to marry, and did much else, most of it without consulting the society. Finally the silent members seem to have revolted, and in germinal of the year II. an attempt was made to set the committee system in order. The society was even obliged to send delegates from itself to certain of its own committees in order to get authentic lists of the membership of each committee.[53] It was decreed that each committee was to have a membership of eleven, that no office-holders should be allowed to sit on a committee, that committee members should sit as long as they had the confidence of the society, but that no one could sit on more than one committee, and finally, that committees should not be allowed to meet together and telescope their functions. That there should be need for such a measure is in itself the best possible light on the way the committee system worked in the clubs.

To judge from what is left of their records, the finances of these clubs were not as badly managed as the pessimistic critic of democratic methods might hope. As we have noticed before, there is little trace of corruption in club finances, partly, perhaps, because the sums handled were rarely very great, at least as long as the societies remained unsubsidized by the government. Rent, furniture, heat, postage and printing were the chief necessary outlays of the earlier clubs, with charity, public celebrations, prize contests and other fairly expensive propaganda for the richer clubs. The club at Montauban paid 26,000 livres in 1791 for its headquarters; at Paris, the yearly dues alone in 1791 must have been nearly 30,000 livres.[54]

After 1793, the clubs took to improving their assembly-halls, and increased their interference with actual government. The committee of public safety and the representatives on mission often found it worth while to subsidize the important societies. The following decree is typical: "The committee of public safety decrees that there shall be delivered to the *société populaire* of Le Havre an order on the national treasury for 5,000 livres to be taken from the 50 millions put at the disposition of the committee by the Convention; which sum shall serve for the propagation of public spirit, for watching the enemies of the Republic in the port, and chiefly for establishing the society in the hall of the *ci-devant* Capucins, situated in the city of Le Havre."[55] So Bentabole on mission granted the club at Dreux 4,000 livres for a new hall.[56] The club of Thonon got 1,500 livres for propaganda from the representative on mission.[57] Even the lesser societies cut some of this melon. At Bourgoin the club got 800 livres from departmental commissioners to put the church in shape for its meetings, the money to come from a "revolutionary tax" on the rich.[58] The village club of Eymoutiers got 1,200 livres for the same purpose, the product of a revolutionary tax on the marquis de la Bachelerie de Châteauneuf granted by the representative of the people Lanot.[59] Yet with all this the signs of deliberate waste are few. The society at Pont-à Mousson received 15,000 livres from representative Bar, and raised 6,736 livres by public subscription; it spent 16,055 livres on its new meeting place (galleries for the audience formed here as elsewhere the chief expense) and 7,833 livres for public festivals. Expenses were 23,888 livres and income 21,736 livres; the resultant deficit was finally filled by members of the society.[60] When the treasurer of the committee of charity of the club of Toulouse left office late in 1794, he handed over 31,820 livres to his successor, 2,234 livres 12 sous of which was in specie.[61]

Even the dues, on which the societies were always somewhat dependent, and at first wholly so, came in fairly well. The registers have nothing like as many complaints of non-payment of dues as they have of absences and disorder. The club at Lons-le Saunier indeed was obliged to decree that "the concierge shall visit the houses of members of the society who have not paid their dues, so that they may pay their share towards getting the club out of debt, and he shall keep a record of their contributions." [62] At Le Havre there seems to have been trouble with members who failed to pay their dues, and one virtuous, paid-up member proposed to hail those who failed to pay their dues before the justice of the peace. That this could happen in May, 1792 is an interesting example of how far the Jacobins had already identified themselves with the state, and of course with its police powers.[63] But these complaints are not numerous, and for voluntary societies the dues seem to have come in pretty well. At Breteuil, on 30 thermidor year II. 107 out of 132 members were paid up; at Cherbourg, in March, 1793, only 56 members out of some four or five hundred were in arrears.[64]

These dues usually amounted in the early days of the societies of friends of the constitution to 24 livres per year, no doubt in imitation of the Paris club,[65] plus an entrance fee varying from 3 to 12 livres or so. The definitely upper-middle class character of the clubs at the beginning of the revolution should be clear from this fact alone. Fewer problems of history are more difficult than an estimation of the value of money in the past, for no matter how scientifically the economist goes about it, what he must do to be clear to his contemporaries amounts to estimating the psychological value of money in the past. Probably to the modern American the dues above described would weigh about as heavily as a sum of between fifty and eighty dollars. Certain clubs were more democratic from the start. At Montauban, where the radical protestant capitalists needed as many of the catholic workmen as they could win over, dues were 24, 18, 12, 6 livres or nothing at all, dependent on the capacity of the member to pay.[66] At St. Servan as early as 1790 the dues were only 9 livres, and workmen (*ouvriers*) were allowed to pay only 3 livres.[67] And in general in smaller towns the dues were not so great.

There is a general lowering of dues as the revolution goes on, as the Jacobins feel more and more the need of allies in the lower classes. Sometimes clubs attempt to manage on a purely voluntary basis, and members are urged to give what they can; but this is rarely successful.[68] Almost always, however, provision is made that those too poor to afford regular dues shall be excused; as the rules of the club of Montignac put it, "indigent *sans-culottes* pay with their patriotism." [69] For the others, dues vary greatly, as the following yearly dues, chosen more or less at random from societies in 1793-1794, will show: 5 livres, 6 livres, 12 livres, 12 livres, 8 livres.[70] The little rural society at Callas was able to get on with special assessments on everybody from time to time as need arose.[71] Another method was to have graduated dues. At Caussade the finance committee drew up a list of members, with their incomes, as estimated from their tax bills, apparent expenditures, etc., and assessed them as follows; incomes of 1,500 livres per year or more, annual dues 30 livres; 1,200 to 1,500 livres, dues 24 livres; 900 to 1,200 livres, dues 18 livres; 600 to 900 livres, dues 12 livres; 300 to 600 livres, dues 6 livres; 100 to 300 livres, dues 3 livres; below 100 livres, no dues need be paid.[72] Similar systems were in force at Auch, at Vouneuil-sur-Vienne, at Romans, and certainly at many other places.[73] Societies so organized can hardly be said to have flirted with communism.

The problem of preserving order in the meetings of these clubs was one which continued to vex their officers and rule-makers throughout the revolution. Very early almost all the clubs threw their meetings open to the public—that is to say, they had separate parts of the hall fitted up to hold spectators who, not being members of the club, could not of course take part in its proceedings. Order thus had to be kept not only among the club members, anxious to be heard in debate, but also among the audience, many of whom had clearly come to scoff. Furthermore, most of the clubs insisted on admitting children to their meetings, on the ground that these future citizens could not too soon begin to learn the art of self-government. No doubt too a Gallic excitability, which, if it be regarded as penetrating into every part of a Frenchman's life, is just another national myth, has in such matters as public debate a certain reality.

The records, then, are full of mention of disorder. The society itself, as distinct from the spectators, "l'assemblée" as distinct from "le peuple des tribunes" is at times turbulent enough, and the president must have special powers to suspend debate if need be. The rules of the club of Chablis provide that "as republican brothers and as brothers sufficiently friends to be above politeness, the members will keep their hats on, except that the president shall remove his, if need be, to bring the assembly back to order." [74] At Lille it was suggested that to restore order in debate the president place his hand respectfully on the head of Marat, for a bust of

that hero always stood on the presidential desk; though
this proposal was rejected it was finally decided that the
prescribed gesture should be the placing of the president's hands on the Declaration of Rights, of which a
framed copy was hung at the back of the desk.[75] Moreover, apart from crises of debate, the members do not
seem always to have been very considerate of the dignity
of their assembly. At Montauban, even before the public
was admitted, there was much disorder. Members would
call to one another, move their chairs about (the chairs
had finally to be nailed down) hurry in and out, and
hang about the entrance-way.[76] A sitting of the municipal council of a little Alpine town having been disturbed
by some petitioners "the mayor calls them to order, and
would have them observe, that a sitting of the general
council of the town is not a Jacobin club, and that in such
a sitting all ought to pass peacefully." [77] Then there was
always a certain amount of difficulty with drunken members. The rules of the club at Dieuze provide: "Members
shall recall that the first attribute of the free man is
the complete exercise of his reason, that therefore none
should present himself to the assembly in a state of
drunkenness, nor trouble its order by improper acts."
To any one contravening this rule the president must
use this formula; "Citizen ———, you forget your dignity,
you have outraged the decencies; the respect due the
sovereign people requires that you leave this hall." [78]

With their audiences the clubs had much the same sort
of trouble, complicated by the presence of women and
children. We have already seen how special officers were
elected to preserve order in the tribunes.[79] As a good
brother of the society at Chablis said, "it is of the greatest interest that children should be present at these meetings, for it is here that these young Republicans will

absorb the principles of true sans-culottism; it is here
that they will learn to recognize their rights."[80] Yet once
admitted, the children failed to live up to their opportunities, at least as far as political philosophy went.
Something had to be done, and the society finally decided not to let in children under the age of twelve; but
as they still managed to slip in, the society was finally
obliged to hire a door-man.[81] At Beauvais, the society
had to put children in the separate part of the hall under
the eye of a special commissioner, and added the surprising provision "children between the ages of twelve
and sixteen shall not be allowed to vote."[82] At Toul, the
children having "failed of respect for the sovereign
majesty of the people by improper acts" were put together right underneath the president's desk.[83] One club
had reluctantly to decide that mothers who brought with
them children *less than six years old* should be sent back
home.[84] The presence of women was even more disturbing. One by one practically all the clubs abandoned the
practice of throwing open their balconies to both sexes,
and set off separate sections for women. At Mayenne, a
member protested that young people of both sexes were
coming to the club, "not to listen to political discussions, but for quite other purposes."[85] A member in a
little Norman club was actually expelled for a somewhat
too definite flirtation during a meeting.[86] At Pau, even
after the introduction of separate galleries for men and
women, there was trouble. Complaints were made that
prostitutes kept coming in and sitting with the men, and
in general it was difficult to maintain the separation of
the sexes.[87] The Jacobins, apparently, had wider interests than their enemies among historians have always
been willing to admit.

The culminating point of Jacobin organization is the

system of affiliation. The regulations of all the clubs provide for affiliation with any similar club of approved and obvious orthodoxy, usually after a favorable majority vote of the club whose affiliation is solicited. The Paris Jacobins, affiliation with whom was the final consecration of any provincial club,[88] directed the spreading of a network over all France. It accepted direct affiliation from the large provincial centers, and then charged these latter with the responsibility for the smaller clubs in their regions. The Paris club kept a firm hand on the machine. It insisted that no club should have other affiliations at Paris. The Lille Jacobins, already affiliated with the Cordeliers of Paris, the famous club of Danton and Hébert, were obliged to drop relations with them at the behest of the Paris Jacobins.[89] Nor would the mother society permit more than one Jacobin club in any given town. A deputation from the Society of Social Virtue of Versailles appearing before the Paris Jacobins in 1793 were told in reply to their request for affiliation that they ought, if they were patriots, to unite with the Jacobins of Versailles.[90] So solid was this organization that the Paris club could levy a small sum per member on each of the affiliated societies to help pay for postage and printing of its numerous circulars.[91] Affiliation with the Paris club, at first fairly easy, became harder as the political orthodoxy of the club stiffened. As early as May 1792 there are complaints that *feuillants* and other doubtful people fill many supposedly Jacobin societies. Collot d'Herbois remarked, "it is not having many affiliated societies that is important: your strength consists in tightening the bonds which hold Jacobins together, not in extending, and thus loosening them." [92] On his motion, affiliations were suspended while a more exacting method for testing demands for affiliation was worked out.

The relations between the provincial center and the smaller towns repeats the relationship between Paris and the provincial centers. The society at Beauvais writes to Paris: "We shall improve, friends and brothers, if your correspondence with us is renewed. Revolutionary sans-culottes, without you we are nothing. By attaching ourselves to your principles, we are everything."[93] In turn the society of Ons-en-Bray writes to Beauvais "we confess to you that, without help, we may lose ourselves on that stormy sea which we do not fear to face, but whose reefs we do not yet know. . . . The lights and experience which you possess belong to us as brothers in the great family of Frenchmen." [94] The society of Sézanne refuses to affiliate the society of Villenauxe-la-Grande until the latter has abolished secret voting for admission, which is contrary to republican frankness, has restored complete freedom of religious discussion, and has removed the provision in its regulations sending a greater number o. delegates to a president's funeral than to that of an ordinary member, a provision obviously contrary to the principle of equality.[95] So, too, the society of the cantonal town of Ars-en-Ré reprimands and brings to order the society of a nearby village for an unrepublican measure on grain consumption.[96] The society of Crest went in a body to Aouste and turned out the unworthy members of that village society, and then reported the whole matter to the local center, Valence, for approval.[97] The clubs are in a sort of hierarchy according to their geographical importance.

The business of keeping up communication between the members of this informal federation was in each club the concern of a committee of correspondence, which was usually obliged to work very hard. From Paris alone a deluge of circulars descended on the provinces; and each club would reply, consult others, send out all over France great packages of propaganda, usually with postage collect. Complaints are frequent from clubs receiving literature that it wasn't worth the postage. Much traveling about too, took place, and communication between clubs of the same region was kept up by interchange of visits. We find at Tulle in 1790 present at one meeting: "MM. Laborde, père et fils, le premier membre de la Société de Souilhac, le second de celle de Toulouse; M. M. Pérédieux père, électeur, et son fils, membres du club de Meyssac; M. Verdier, membre du club d'Argentat."[98] In August and September 1791, on the sole subject of the schism between the Jacobins and the Feuillants at Paris, this same club received letters from nineteen clubs in all parts of France.[99] In the papers of the society at Le Havre, there is a register for visitors from other societies covering a period of about five months in the spring and summer of 1794. It has 113 signatures from twenty-nine different societies.[100] Some of the functions of modern conventions and trades-meetings must have been fulfilled by these Jacobin clubs, whose activities on close inspection bear less and less of the stamp of the abstract, inhuman closet-philosophy of the 18th century so insisted upon by Taine.

III

How many of these Jacobin societies made up the network over France? The question provides an interesting problem in research, but an exact answer, even if it could be given, would not be of first importance to the historian eager to make sound generalizations of sociological importance. A society of such slight influence that its name can only with difficulty be dug up from revolutionary archives can hardly have affected the course of history. We know there were societies in all towns of importance. Additions to the number of known societies can only come from small farming villages, and these societies, as the slightest investigations of their records will show, were often pathetically formal and empty institutions foisted on the peasants by outsiders. Their existence proves that certain peasants in these villages were willing to accept, without knowing much about it, the revolution as directed in Paris. It does not prove that these peasants were Jacobins. More important is the question, what proportion of the population of a town joined the club? Equally important, too, is the question, what proportion of the enrolled membership of a club was genuinely interested in and active in its affairs? Some attempt must now be made to give a rough answer to each of these three questions.

The question as to the total number of societies at the time of their greatest multiplication (which was undoubtedly in 1794) has recently been renewed by the studies of M. Chobaut in the *Annales historiques de la Révolution française*. By exhaustive search in municipal as well as in departmental archives of the series L, M. Chobaut has been able to list for six departments of the southeast 825 societies out of a total of 1409 townships (*communes*).[101] The same proportion for the whole of France would give the surprising figure of 23,600 societies, far above any previous estimate. M. de Cardenal, who has long been studying the societies all over France, has personally listed but 2,997.[102] Taking random estimates from various sources for five scattered departments, and working with population figures of 1802, it has been possible for the present writer to arrive at an estimate of 6,800 for all France.[103]

Now, M. Chobaut himself found many fewer societies

in the Ardèche, the Lozère and the Hautes Alpes—only three or four, indeed, in the latter. He is inclined to think that the fondness of the southerner for political debate brought about the undue multiplication of societies in the region studied, and that the same ratio would not hold for all France. Moreover, certain parts of La Vendée and Brittany can hardly be considered as belonging to the republic in 1794. But detailed researches in other departments would probably increase the total number of societies now actually known. Perhaps the truth lies somewhere between 5,000 and 8,000 for all France, so that from one out of five to one out of eight communes possessed a Jacobin club.[104] This ratio varies greatly over France, and is probably most favorable to the clubs in Provence and parts of Languedoc. Whether the clubs were thicker in prosperous or in poor regions cannot be determined. For the Gard, M. Chobaut finds proportionately more societies in the rich plain than in the poorer mountain country; for the Drôme, the reverse is true.[105] One thing, however, is certain, and it is the most important thing for us. The centers of administrative, political, and economic life—the *chefs-lieux de département et de district*—had practically without exception Jacobin clubs in 1794.[106]

To answer fully the second question, what proportion of the population were enrolled Jacobins, one would have to know the answer to the first. We have, however, quite satisfactory figures for the larger towns, and enough from villages scattered about France to hazard an estimate. Taking clubs in thirteen typical towns, and including every name found on their books over the whole period of their existence, we find that out of a population of 201,959 (Table I), the club members numbered 9,400, or 4.2%. This means that about one adult male in six was a Jacobin.[107] But this estimate exaggerates greatly the numbers of the Jacobins at any given time, since in all clubs many members were dropped during the Terror, and often others were added. Moreover, most of the clubs in the years 1789 to 1792 were established in provincial centers, and were the only clubs in their districts. Their membership included many radicals from outlying districts, who subsequently contented themselves with their own local clubs. Then too, many of these early clubs admitted soldiers garrisoned in their towns, and admitted them in wholesale lots. Thus the club at Colmar, for instance, though it has 1,037 names on its books, cannot have had much ever 600 at any one time, and of those hardly more than 400 residents of Colmar city proper.[108]

It is necessary therefore to have recourse to a special period in the life of a given society. Table II is based on lists of membership between 1793 and 1795, a period when the revolution was at its height, and when the Jacobin clubs were most characteristic in composition and most powerful in practical politics. The twenty-five towns there studied (of which six were included in Table I) had a population of 334,733, and a club enrollment of 7,439, making 2.2% of the population Jacobins, or about one adult male in twelve.[109] This proportion is reasonably consistent in the towns studied, for the highest percentage of Jacobins is 8.5% and the lowest 0.9%.

Village societies present a somewhat different problem. Apparently when a club exists at all in a village, it is likely to contain a larger proportion of the population than a town club. The fourteen villages considered in Table III, with a population of 16,364 have a club membership of 1,392, so that 8.5% of the population, or one man out of every three is a Jacobin.[110] In certain villages in the Gard, in the southeast, and in the Haute-Saône,

in the east, the percentage of members is so high that the
club seems to have contained representatives of almost
every family in the village. At Beauvoisin, 19.2% of the
total population, or nearly 4 men out of five were members; at Fleurey-les-Faverney, 15%, or 3 men out of five;
at Faverney, 11%, or nearly every other man. In other
rural societies, however, as Charost in Berry or Gaillefontaine in Normandy, the percentage is much lower,
and more like that of town clubs.[111] A thorough study of
village clubs all over France would probably show much
this same sort of regional variation. It is not as important as it might seem at first to be. Of course, the existence of numerous village clubs with large membership
proves that a given farming region was not royalist, nor
violently clerical, but it hardly proves more than that.
The peasants were too illiterate, too immune from ideas,
and too attached to the principle of private property
ever to have been good Jacobins in 1794. Probably the
existence of more and larger rural societies in some regions than others is above all a tribute to the organizing
powers of the representative on mission sent out from
Paris, or the zeal of the society in the departmental capital. The rural societies have a certain interest in themselves, and we shall later return to them, but they need
not here disturb our calculations very seriously.

Assuming then that the proportion of roughly 2% of
the entire population obtained from Table II is just, and
that the lack of rural societies in many regions will make
up for the proportionally larger size of their enrollment,
we may hazard an estimate of 500,000 for the number of
enrolled Jacobins in France during the Terror. This, of
course, includes only the pure ones, the followers of the
Mountain. If one wishes to include all who at one time
or another identified themselves with the clubs (and

these would all be quite radical, for even back in 1790
the Jacobin clubs can hardly be accused of conservatism)
then Table I would be a fairer basis, and one might risk
something like 1,000,000 as the top limit of the total
club membership.[112]

To Taine as to other nineteenth century writers, the
number of enrolled Jacobins seemed shockingly small;
to us, more skeptical, and yet perhaps more tolerant, of
the ways of democracy, it may seem amazingly large.
That one man in twelve, perhaps even one man in six,
should spend a very great part of his time—in many cases
the greater part—upon public business argues an heroic,
an Attic, age.

Frenchmen of the revolutionary period were not, however, as assiduously political as the enrollment of the
clubs would suggest. When we come to investigate our
third question, what proportion of the Jacobins were
really active in the clubs, we find a steady series of complaints about poor attendance, early departures, unwill-
ingness to serve on committees, and general failure to
measure up to the "hauteur des circonstances." A few
examples only need be cited. At a time when the enrollment was about 150 we find at Avallon 23 members present on the 20th brumaire year II, 28 on the 25th, 26 on
the 28th.[113] At Nuits-St.-Georges, with over 100 members, there were present on the 8th of December 1791
24 members; on the 12th, 19; on the 14th, 27; on the
16th, 25.[114] At Montbard, with a membership of about
70, only 13 were present on the 1st of September, 1793,
and these 13 decided to write to their brothers and wake
them up, and to add to the rules a provision making absence at three successive meetings without legitimate excuse bring about automatic expulsion from the society.[115]
The society of Senlis had in May, 1792 a membership of

about 120; attendance was taken at meetings beginning the 9th of May, with the following results: 12, 8, 11, 12, 19, 7, 10, 8, 26 (this was a special visit of the constitutional bishop Massieu) 11, 17, 10, 11, 7.[116] At Le Havre, when according to the records there were 797 members eligible to vote, only 146 voted in the election of a president. With about 350 members early in 1794, only 92 voted in the election of a committee of *épuration.*[117] Such instances could be multiplied indefinitely. The visitors in the galleries, too, began to find the proceedings dull. The club at Le Havre went so far as to reject twice the proposal that the sexes be separated in their galleries, for the quite evident reason that it would hurt the attendance.[118]

This is of course no fair description of the whole course of Jacobin history. It merely shows that, lacking some special excitement or purpose, the greater part of the membership stayed away from the meetings. There was a small nucleus of the faithful, and a larger number available only in extraordinary circumstances. These latter were not, however, necessarily bad Jacobins. Probably most of them must be classed as honest Jacobins, just as in the modern world great numbers of people who habitually do not go to church must none the less be classed as good Christians. Certainly the insincere Jacobins, the royalists in disguise, would be the last people to stay at home. They would come to the club for its protection. The enrollment of the clubs does, then, on the whole, represent men willing to accept the Jacobin point of view, if unwilling to accept Jacobin responsibilities. That only a small proportion of those enrolled actually did the essential work of the clubs is quite what one might have expected. In all political bodies, from committees to nations, the leadership, and also the labor, tend inevitably to devolve upon a minority. Moreover, active personal participation in government does not, in modern times. even interest the majority of men. The Jacobins were proportionately far more numerous than any voluntary political society in modern America, with the possible exception of such societies as the Anti-Saloon League; and certainly the average Jacobin had more actual political responsibility than an Anti-Saloon Leaguer, a Ku Klux Klansman, or even a Tammany man.

CHAPTER III

MEMBERSHIP

I

Statistics will do more for us than count the Jacobins by head. Existing documents are complete enough to permit statistical treatment of Jacobin wealth, occupation, birthplace, residence, and age.[1] It is true that these characteristics are in a sense external, that they do not necessarily enter into Jacobinism as a state of mind. But states of mind cannot be counted; and a man's wealth, occupation, birthplace, residence and age go far to make up the man as a political animal—not so far, perhaps, as the economic interpretation of history would have them go, but so far that no reasonable historian would neglect them. From these documents, then, we ought to be able to place the normal Jacobin in an economic and social "class"—decide whether he is upper class, middle class, or lower class, noble, bourgeois, or proletarian.

But we can perhaps go further, and use this statistical method to investigate a sociological question not wholly outside our search for a definition of Jacobinism. There is a current theory—or better, a current opinion—that all violent revolutions are the work of men who are discontented with the society from which they rebel almost wholly because they are failures in that society. They are victims of maladjustment, and this maladjustment, save for a few "misguided superiors," usually shows itself in economic inferiority. Violent revolutionaries are poor men, at the very least failures in their life work. Revolutions are essentially risings of the unfit against the fit. These sociological opinions are not limited to writers like Mr. Lothrop Stoddard. They are discernible in Taine, who, however, thought the government of the *ancien régime* a bad government; and in the work of Augustin Cochin, and still more in that of M. Pierre Gaxotte, who finds the *ancien régime* essentially sound, they appear full-fledged. At any rate, the maladjustment theory is sufficiently widespread to be worth testing. If then we ask ourselves, were the rank and file of the Jacobin clubs failures or successes in their chosen professions, we can, for the French Revolution at least, give this theory a test.

Our sources of information are adequate enough to permit a statistical answer to this question. Once equipped with information as to the names, residence, age and profession of individual Jacobins in a given club, it is possible to search out these men on the rolls of direct taxes for this locality at the very end of the *ancien régime,* and find out how much they were taxed. By comparing the average Jacobin tax with the average tax paid by non-Jacobins on the same roll, one can place the Jacobins pretty exactly in the common life of their community. Tax rolls of the revolutionary period itself were not always drawn up; and those which have survived are usually hidden away in uncatalogued municipal archives. But millions of francs worth of confiscated property was sold by the government, and lists of buyers of this property are almost everywhere available. We can easily find out how much of this property our Jacobins bought and thus learn how many had surplus funds for such investments.

Such information will not, of course, have even the relative accuracy possible in a study of contemporary demography. Its limitations come out clearly when we attempt to classify the Jacobins by profession. In the first place, the occupation of some is not given at all. Some of these were too young to have a gainful occupation, for the clubs frequently admitted sons of their members from sixteen, and even from twelve years of age. Some were *rentiers,* already in the eighteenth century a familiar French figure. Other omissions are to be explained by the carelessness of secretaries in drawing up lists which, after all, are not quite official. At any rate, it is safe to conclude that the category "no occupation given" does not represent a jobless and irresponsible set of poor men. It is not very risky to assume that it includes much the same sort of men as the other groups, and that it can therefore be neglected. But even where occupations are given, all is not clear. The word *négociant,* like the American "business man" implies wealth and social standing greater than that of the *marchand,* best translated by the English "shopkeeper." The difference is between the upper middle class and the lower middle class, and is worth noting; yet the two words are very loosely used, and many a listed *négociant* is merely an aspiring *marchand.* Revolutionary leveling would have none of the old distinctions between *avocat, procureur,* and *notaire,* and the successful barrister and the humble notary are often listed alike as *hommes de loi.* So too an *officier de santé* may be a great surgeon or a mere barber. But the most serious difficulty is with the peasants. Obviously what is most important to know about a peasant is whether he is a landowner, a tenant farmer or a landless agricultural laborer. This it is unfortunately almost impossible to learn from these lists.

Propriétaire, métayer and *journalier* are perfectly clearly owner, tenant and laborer; but these terms are used much less often than the ambiguous *laboureur, agriculteur,* and *cultivateur,* of which the first usually implies ownership, the last either landlessness or very small property, and the middle nothing at all for our purpose. Thus our classification of the peasantry into owners and non-owners will be very tentative, and best not attempted save for certain localities.

There is still another difficulty. Over the whole course of the Revolution, the personnel of the clubs varied to a considerable degree with the proscription or resignation of moderates and the recruiting of radicals. While it is not true that 1793, the year of the Girondin defeat, marks a complete change in personnel, there certainly was in most clubs a period of renewed energy in the autumn of 1793 which corresponds to a partly renewed membership. We shall then, do well to consider the clubs for which we have statistics in three groups: (1) a group in which all names appearing on the records from the foundation of the clubs to their extinction are included; (2) a group in which only members during the years 1789-1792 are included; (3) a group in which only members during the years 1793-1795 are included.[2] A comparison of the distribution of professions in these groups will afford a rough means of estimating the extent to which, as the Revolution progressed, it recruited its adherents in lower social strata. We must say *rough means,* for in addition to difficulties of identification and classification mentioned before, it has not been possible to include every club in all three groups. So defective are the records, especially on the membership before 1793, that the investigator must be content with a miscellaneous assortment of clubs. Fortunately, the third group, covering the years 1793-1795 is most numerous, for in these years the Revolution attained its maximum of *social* as opposed to merely *political,* action.

Now, simply from a study of these tables of occupation, certain conclusions may be made as to the social standing of the Jacobins. A few—a very few—of those without occupation were ex-nobles. Study of the proceedings of individual clubs not infrequently discloses the presence even in 1794 of a few noblemen who had succeeded in living down their birth. In Saverne, indeed, the local boss was a noble. When, at the height of the Terror priests and nobles were excluded by law from the clubs, he resigned amid the regrets of his fellow members, and ran the club quite adequately from behind the scenes.[3] But nobles were certainly an exception among the Jacobins, even from the start. For our purposes, they may be dismissed. What really matters is whether, judged by their occupations, the Jacobins deserve to be labeled *bourgeois* or workingmen, whether they were predominantly professional men, merchants, artisans, or laborers. Let us, then, arbitrarily decide that lawyers, priests, teachers, artists and other followers of the liberal professions, business men, shopkeepers and officers are *bourgeois;* that cobblers, masons, carpenters, locksmiths and other artisans, as well as plain soldiers, are members of the working class; and that peasants, since in most clubs they cannot be sorted into landed and landless, should be counted apart. We shall also disregard the category "No profession given," since there is no reason to suppose it comprises men of different social standing from those whose professions are given. The twelve clubs of group I (1789-1795) would then include 62% *bourgeois,* 28% working class, and 10% peasantry; the twelve clubs of group II (1789-1792)—of which six are also in group

I—would include 66% *bourgeois,* 26% working class, and
8% peasantry; the forty-two clubs of group III (1793-
1795), a period when the social revolution was at its
height, would include 57% *bourgeois,* 32% working class,
and 11% peasantry. Shopkeepers (grocers, drapers, mil-
lers, tailors and such small retail tradesmen) number
12%, 10% and 17% in each group respectively; business men (*négociants*), 7%, 9%, and 8%; professional
men, 19%, 24% and 18%. As for the peasants, in ten
villages where some sort of line can be drawn between
owners of property and non-owners, the proportion is
about six to four in favor of the owners, who were no
doubt chiefly small proprietors.[4]

This classification must, of course, ignore failure and
success. Yet surely a poor lawyer considers himself as
much a gentleman, as much a member of the *bourgeoisie*
as a rich one. We may safely reckon the professional men
and the business men as members of the middle class,
many of them, no doubt, as members of the upper middle
class. As for the shopkeepers, they are middle class if not
in fact at least in aspiration. So, too, are the civil servants and the officers. The land-owning peasantry, as the
nineteenth century was to show, are politically members
of the middle class. There remain only artisans, landless
peasants and common soldiers who can perhaps be said
to be politically out of sympathy with *bourgeois* aims.
Yet even here, many a man listed as a carpenter or a
weaver is really a master craftsman, an employer of
workmen, and often more prosperous than many definitely middle-class lawyers.

This weakness our next tables will remedy.[5] If the
mason is really a contractor, for instance, and a rich man,
he will be taxed accordingly.[6] Yet even here, our statistics cannot aspire to accuracy. First, on the side of the tax

rolls, it is well known that the direct taxes of the *ancien régime* were not apportioned strictly according to income. Yet the unfairness of the system has probably been exaggerated by nineteenth century historians who mistook the confusion of the *ancien régime* for injustice; and certainly even though the very rich were relatively more lightly taxed than the poor, they paid absolutely greater sums. Of the taxes used in constructing these tables, the *vingtième,* a tax on real property, was paid by *roturiers* and *privilégiés* alike, and is generally admitted to have been a fair tax, and hence a good standard of the relative wealth of those who paid it; the *capitation,* originally a graduated poll-tax, was sometimes evaded by the nobility, or at least not paid in due proportion to income; the *taille,* a direct tax on personal income or on real estate, depending on the region, was not paid by nobles, priests or privileged *bourgeois.* Wherever possible, the *vingtième* has been used. Yet even where other taxes are used, the result need not be considered untrustworthy. In the first place, tax rolls of 1790, even though they retain the old names of the taxes, have been fairly assessed under the new régime which began in 1789; secondly, where the new taxes have been used, as for Beauvais and Grenoble, objections to the inequalities of the older ones no longer hold. Again, even for the *taille,* where property owned by nobles was commercially exploited, it was taxed just as ordinary property, landed or not. Usually the tenant paid the tax, even though it was listed in the noble's name on the roll. Yet nobles did actually sometimes pay the *taille* themselves. See for instance at Rodez, where a record of payments appears on the roll.[7] Finally, the sort of omission from rolls of *capitation* and *taille* in 1789 and earlier years are precisely the sort that will leave the prosperity of the Jacobins underestimated rather than overestimated. For from these rolls the *privilégiés* are omitted [8] and the average payment made by the Jacobins will be the less by our inability to trace the payments of privileged Jacobins.

On the side of the lists of members, too, there are difficulties. Many members are not sufficiently identified to be traced further, since neither Christian name nor professions are always given. Many members had moved into the town since the tax roll was drawn up, and cannot therefore be found on it. Many were too young when the roll was made, or not heads of families or owners of property in their own right. Finally, errors of identification are easily possible, though these are in some way compensating—that is to say, as many Jacobins would normally be mistaken for non-Jacobins as non-Jacobins for Jacobins.

The result of a study of these tax rolls is to confirm what was already indicated by Jacobin occupations. In many towns, a list of the poor and incapacitated fellows the tax roll; in others, the poor are listed with their fellow citizens, but their names are followed by the entry "no tax" (*néant*). The names of Jacobins are almost never found among these poor.[9]

For those who did pay taxes, the documents permit two ways of comparing Jacobin assessments with assessments of non-Jacobins.[10] First, the total assessment of all Jacobins traceable on the tax roll can be divided by the total number of members on the club books, *those who were assessed the tax as well as those who were not*. Then the sum total assessed on the town can be divided by the total number of adult males in the town, *those who were assessed the tax as well as those who were not*. Thus the average for the Jacobin club as a whole may be compared with the average for the town as a whole. By this method, a definite cross-section of both the smaller and larger groups is obtained, and we avoid the reproach that no account has been taken of the large number of Jacobins (about one-half) not traceable on the rolls. This method gives, for eight clubs considered over the whole period 1789 to 1795, an average payment of 32.12 livres for the Jacobins, and an average payment of 17.02 livres for all the male citizens of the town; for twenty-six clubs considered over the period 1793 to 1795, an average payment of 19.94 livres for the Jacobins, and 14.45 livres for all the male citizens.

Secondly, the amount paid by Jacobins can be divided by the number of Jacobins actually paying the tax. Then the amount paid by non-Jacobins can be divided by the number of non-Jacobins on the roll. The resulting comparison is not unfair, if one may assume that privilege, youth, non-residence before 1790, residence of unmarried sons with the father, errors of identification, and similar reasons, rather than poverty, explain the absence of certain Jacobins from the roll. As a matter of fact, this second method yields results almost identical with the first. For sixteen towns, of which membership in the years 1793 to 1795 is taken, the average payment of club-members is 14.47 livres; for non-members, 10.79 livres.

One tax deserves special consideration.[11] This is the *vingtième d'industrie,* a small but very fair tax assessed on all save civil servants who pursued a gainful occupation. Naturally, this excluded the nobles and the priests. The tax was so small that the total assessed does not vary greatly, ranging usually from one livre to twelve or so. But the apprentice or journeyman always pays a minimum, the master more, the merchant and business man still more. Unfortunately rolls giving individual names are rare, for the various guilds usually subscribed

for a definite sum, and then apportioned this sum themselves among their members. These guild rolls are very
hard to find. But Table X covers all occupations, or certain trades, in eight typical provincial towns, and does
give a certain basis for conclusions. It shows that the
average Jacobin paid 4.47 livres as his *vingtième d'industrie,* the average non-Jacobin, 2.49 livres. Clearly, then,
among the shopkeepers and artisans, the more prosperous
ones were the ones who were active revolutionists. The
Jacobin carpenter was not a poor carpenter, but a good
one; the steady master workmen outnumber the wild
young apprentices in the clubs.

Too much is not to be concluded from our next table,[12]
based on purchases of the *biens nationaux.* The Jacobins
who bought property—mostly land—confiscated from
nobleman and priests had perhaps enriched themselves
in ways familiar to politicians, revolutionary or not. Still,
they appear to have been a bit too numerous to have
been grafters to a man; and we can at least be sure that
men who invested money in land are not likely to have
been communists at heart. Moreover, these tables have
a certain interest for students of the disposition of the
biens nationaux, for they help to show how far the buyers
actively identified themselves with the Revolution. In
thirteen towns, 763 Jacobins—over one-fifth of the total
club membership—bought on an average property to
the amount of 14,181 livres. Non-Jacobins to the number
of 817 bought an average property of 5,650 livres. In four
towns—Colmar, Noviant-aux-Prés, Perpignan, Toul—
the number of non-Jacobin buyers exceeded that of Jacobin buyers. Only in one, however—Vesoul—did the
average sum expended by the non-Jacobins exceed that
expended by the Jacobins. And in Vesoul the non-Jacobin average is high because of the very great purchases of

a single buyer, whose name does not appear on the list of members in 1795, but who almost certainly was a member in the early years of the club's existence. Table XII, finally, shows that 517 members out of a total membership of 2,160 in six towns bought property, the amount of which could not be estimated conveniently from existing records. Thus, for the nineteen clubs included in Tables XI and XII, 22% of the membership were buyers of *biens nationaux*. This again confirms the economic prosperity of the Jacobins.

Finally, there are two other bits of information available which serve to indicate the social responsibilities of the group of Jacobins. The first is the age of their members. For ten clubs considered [13] the average age varies very little, from 38.3 years to 45.4 years. The average for the group of ten was 41.8 years. There were some boys in each club, but almost always the sons of prominent members. As can be seen from the average age, the young were quite balanced by the old. In no sense can these clubs be considered a collection of foolhardy young men. The second bit of information concerns the birthplace and actual residence of the members. For twenty-three clubs,[14] the lists of memberships, drawn up mostly at the very end of 1794 show that 2,359 were born in the town in which they were living, and that 1,456 were born elsewhere; for fifteen of these clubs [15] the lists show that 2,571 were resident in the same place before and after 1789, and that 378 had moved into their actual place of residence after 1789—that is, since the Revolution. Too much again must not be concluded from this fragmentary evidence. We do not know for just what proportion of the population of eighteenth century France birthplace and residence coincided, but it would seem that the 3,815 members of the Jacobin clubs above studied

numbered rather more immigrants (38%) than the towns
in which they were established. No doubt most of these
immigrants came from nearby places, and were often
country people who had moved to town; but the point
is that they had moved. Sociologists may still dispute
as to whether emigration indicates initiative or irresponsibility, but to judge from evidence of tax-lists, these
emigrants had been successful. As to the second item,
the fact that only 378 out of 2,949, or 13%, had moved
into the towns since 1789 would show that the Revolution was not fathered largely by itinerant and more or
less professional trouble-makers, but by men who knew
the surroundings in which they worked.

II

The extent to which the personnel of the clubs was
changed at different periods of the Revolution is an important, but extremely difficult, problem. The best lists
of the clubs, lists giving names, professions, age and
birthplace, are the lists aforementioned, lists drawn up
late in 1794—in accordance with the law of 25 vendémiaire an III, that is, after thermidor.[16] Such lists usually
lack the more violent terrorists. As a matter of fact, however, this lacuna can be filled by lists of terrorists later
disarmed.[17] These club lists of vendémiaire may sometimes also include surviving moderates welcomed back
into the fold. For other periods we have to depend on
chance lists drawn up for secretaries' convenience, or on
the actual minutes which usually mention by name members elected at any given session. But these latter list-
ings are frequently very vague—sometimes merely a surname, at best a surname and a profession.

Yet if we are to test the economic interpretation of

history as applied to these clubs, we must make some attempt to find out whether their membership became to a pronounced degree proletarian as the Revolution went on. The statistical treatment attempted on this problem is, for reasons given above, even more inadequate than that employed in the previous section of this chapter. But it may at least point out a possible approach to the problem, and indicate the tremendous amount of spade work in the archives necessary to any exact knowledge of this point.

Any study of the minutes of a typical club, filled as they are with *épurations,* resignations of members, proscriptions of members, sometimes actual schisms (as that of the *feuillants* of Paris) makes it evident that the variation in personnel is great. Existing information would make the task of settling the exact figures for each year extremely difficult, if not impossible. But the really significant point of departure is that between the "société des amis de la constitution" and that of the "société populaire"—between the club under the monarchy and the club under the republic. Inasmuch as it is not always possible to learn the exact date within a given year when a member is chosen, January 1, 1793 makes a fairly suitable point at which to make the division. The following tables then contrast the membership of certain clubs first, at some time before January 1793, and second, at some time after that date.

Table XIII [18] gives for six clubs an answer to the question, how far was the membership in these two periods identical? It shows that 987 members out of a total of 3,208 appearing on the books during the whole lives of the clubs maintained their membership in both periods. That is, 31% of the membership were Jacobins throughout the Revolution. Table XIV [19] is based on the membership of eleven clubs as it is listed during the Republic—usually at the very end of 1794 (vendémiaire an III). Of that membership 1,870, or 57%, had been elected prior to January 1793, and 1,395, or 43%, had been elected after that date. Table XV,[20] also based on lists of members drawn up after January 1793 classifies the Jacobins into four groups: 1) those elected to membership *before* January 1793 who, to judge from their occupations, belong to the middle class; 2) those elected to membership *before* January 1793 who, to judge from their occupations, belong to the working class; 3) those elected to membership *after* January 1793 who, from their occupations, belong to the middle class; 4) those who, elected *after* January 1793, from their occupations, belong to the working classes. Here, as in Tables IV, V, and VI, those whose occupations are not given are neglected, as are also the peasants. The totals show that prior to January 1793, more middle class members than working class members were chosen (523 middle class, 443 working class) and that after January 1793 only slightly fewer middle class members than working class members were chosen—(417 middle class, 433 working class). Finally, Table XVI[21] contrasts the average tax paid by samples of the membership of nine clubs, again from lists drawn up after January 1793. In seven of these nine towns, members chosen before January 1793 averaged a higher tax payment than those chosen after that date. Only in one, Nîmes, do the Jacobins enrolled in the years 1793 and 1794 pay a much higher tax than those enrolled previously (15.3 livres as opposed to 5.5 livres). The explanation here is doubtless this: At Nîmes, a workingman's club was founded in 1791, as a rival to the *bourgeois* Friends of the Constitution. Eventually this workingman's club won out, and the club of the Terror reckoned itself, as a *corporation,* identical with this earlier workman's club. But the more radical *bourgeois* were also admitted after the fall of the monarchy, thus actually raising the economic level of the club.

These tables suggest the complexity of the question. There is undoubtedly a great regional variation. In industrial towns, workmen's clubs sometimes were the true parents of the *société populaire,* as at Nîmes. In some towns, the *bourgeois* Friends of the Constitution were almost wholly displaced by a new set of men, much less prosperous and less distinguished, as at Beauvais. Yet the prevalent opinion that the personnel of the societies was wholly changed after the fall of the monarchy is obviously not true, nor can we even be sure that the newer recruits were predominately proletarians.[22] At most, it would seem that for the larger towns, an increasing number of shopkeepers and artisans—the lower middle class, if you like—were admitted after the fall of the monarchy, and even before; and that many of the richer *bourgeois*—though by no means all—drop out befor the Terror.

III

These statistics are not in themselves an adequate explanation of the rôle played by the Jacobin clubs in the Revolution. The minutes and correspondence of the clubs, local history and local biography must be studied before any final conclusions can be reached. No doubt many of the prosperous members of the clubs kept their membership during the Terror precisely in order to moderate Jacobin political action, and tame their wilder fellowmembers. No doubt many rich Jacobins were simply grafters who used their membership to cover stock speculation and land-grabbing. Many of the rural clubs (Faverney, Beauvoisin, etc.), include most of the male population of the village. This may mean that in these sections the people were whole-heartedly in favor of the revolution; or it may mean that these societies were skillfully organized by the *représentants en mission* and their agents in order to put a good front on their work and that they really represent no unanimity of opinion at all. At any rate, it is obvious that statistics alone are not sufficient to settle these and many other questions necessary to an understanding of the clubs.

Yet other methods of approach to the problem of the social and economic position of the Jacobin personnel yield substantially the same result. It may be protested that the foregoing study, concerned as it has been with the total membership of the clubs, includes many who were Jacobins out of fear or policy. The real leaders, the hotheads, the Terrorists, could hardly have had such respectable origins. Now, by the law of germinal III, the disarmament of *terroristes* all over France was ordained, and carried out by local authorities. These authorities gave very diverse interpretations to the word terrorist. In some large cities, like Rouen, where the sections drew up tentative lists, neighborhood rancors produced enormous lists. On the other hand at Beauvais the municipality, pressed from above, finally produced four names. Little villages in the Haute Garonne discovered a dozen or so terrorists apiece. Still, these lists are as nearly complete lists of local extremists as can be found. Applying to some of them the methods we have previously used, we can sort them according to profession and income judged by tax assessments. Twenty towns and villages [23] with a total of 637 terrorists, give, according to profession, 61% middle class and 39% artisans and peasants. Of these,

16% were of the liberal professions, 7% business men, 15% shopkeepers. Sixteen towns and villages [24] with 456 terrorists, show that the average terrorist paid a tax of 6.2 livres, the average townsman a tax of 3.4 livres. Even the terrorists, then, are definitely middle-class people.[25]

Still another approach lies through the individual biographies of the local leaders, the Robespierres and the Dantons of the provinces. From the records of almost any club it is possible to distinguish the names of three or four men who stand out at least as leaders, if not bosses in the American sense. Local historians have often provided supplementary details as to the lives of these men. Here the statistical method is impossible, and we must proceed by the method of sampling.

At Bergerac, the names that stand out are those of Ponterie-Escot, rich *bourgeois*, Boissière, physician, d'Esmartis, former captain in the navy, Bourson and Dommenget, *petits bourgeois*, and Boyer, barber.[26] At Limoges, there were the two Gay-Vernons and Foucaud, priests, Imbert, monk and pamphleteer, and Pedon, journalist and man of letters.[27] At Lons-le-Saunier, Buchot, former regent of the college and Dumas, also an ecclesiastic.[28] The leaders at Nantes were Goullin, of good *bourgeois* family, Chaux, a merchant, once accused of fraudulent bankruptcy, and Bachelier, solicitor, and of course, the famous Oratorien Fouché.[29] At Lunéville, the list of presidents—a good test of leadership—includes four lawyers, two business men, one *rentier*, one clerk, one postmaster, and one tax-receiver.[30] Jacob, "vrai montagnard," leader at Toul, would appear in a biographical dictionary as follows: born Nancy, 1735; advocate before the *présidial* of Toul to 1789; city councilor, 1790; mayor, 1791; president of the district tribunal, 1792; deputy to the Convention, 1793; judge of the *tribunal de cassation,* 1796; receiver for the public domains at Toul, 1799; died at Toul, 1809. Here is the biography of Carez, Joseph, another leader at Toul: born at Toul, 1752; master printer, invented the method of printing called stereotyping; city councilor, 1790; deputy to the Legislative Assembly, 1791; mayor in the auxiliary battalion of Toul, 1793; city councilor, 1798; sub-prefect of Toul, 1800; died at Toul, 1801.[31]

The leaders at Orthez in 1793 were d'Arnaudat, mayor, ex-noble; Vidal, rich *bourgeois,* Paraige, barrister.[32] In the little village of Gerberoy, in the Oise, the leaders were Fégneux, aged 57, formerly chief forester for the vidame of Gerberoy; Dubois, aged 44, land-owning peasant; Girard, aged 26, former student of the liberal arts, notary's clerk; Desbart, aged 51, physician; Dumesnil, aged 30, notary; Gromas, aged 72, veteran soldier; Delapierre, aged 28, scrivener.[33] Jean Tanqueray, president of the club of Bayeux in 1794, was a former barrister, had drawn up the *cahier* for the Third Estate of Bayeux, and had held to the Revolution throughout its most radical period. Another leader, Mutel, was a solicitor; a third, Laboussaye, had been lieutenant-general of police under the *ancien régime.*[34] Even at Nancy, where the club was led during the Terror by strangers to the city, men of much less than the average respectability, one hardly finds genuine proletarians. Philip, the tyrant of the club, was a former sea-captain more than suspected of piracy (did even Taine number pirates among the Jacobins?) and Glasson-Brisse was an actor; but Febvé was a respectable *bourgeois* of Lunéville, Montrolle a physician, Durozet an ex-noble, Arsant an artist (not a good one).[35] If Dufresse at Lille was an actor, and hence in eighteenth century France not respectable, La Valette was a gentleman, an army officer before the Revolution, and Duhem a successful lawyer.[36] At Mainz, Wedekind was an excellent physician and professor of therapy, Hofmann a professor of philosophy, Mathias Metternich a professor of mathematics, and George Forster a savant, man-of-letters, scientist and companion of Cook.[37] Prieur, called the "Pére Duchesne of Beauvais" owned real estate worth 568 livres a year in 1789, and invested in *biens nationaux* to the extent of 6,000 livres.[38] The leaders of the *Société montagnarde* of the little Gascon town of Fleurance were Bigourdan, physician, Larée, schoolteacher, Margoët, justice of the peace, Larrey, barrister, Coué, carpenter, Carbonniau, tilemaker, Domingue, shoemaker.[39] The village club of Charnècles in Dauphiné was led by a notary from nearby Voreppe; and the only active members in this little rural community were members of the *petite bourgeoisie* more or less well read in eighteenth century literature.[40] The officers of the club of Toulouse number two functionaries of the *ancien régime,* two business men, five lawyers, two physicians, one judge, one *professeur de collège,* one draper, one tailor, and six whose professions are not given.[41] The presidents of the club of Moulins include four civil servants, two *bourgeois,* two lawyers, two physicians, two ex-priests, one apothecary and one watchman.[42] The brothers Bonac, one a lawyer, the other a physician, and the leading men of the little town of Pellegrue (Gironde) were the very life of the local club, even in the Terror.[43]

Here again, the mere repetition of disparate details will hardly get us nearer proof. The gap between intuition and statistics will never be filled by instances, piled ever so high.[44] But in the records of club after club it is clear that the leaders are men of the middle classes, and men of a certain amount of education. These are certainly not as a rule lawyers, nor are lawyers even in a majority. Many were priests or ex-priests. As M. Mathiez has pointed out[45] the clubs were very frequently founded, in 1790-1791, at the initiative of constitutional priests anxious to defend themselves against the nonjuring priests, and as our tables show, many of these constitutionalists continued in the clubs after 1793, at the cost usually of abjuring their orders.[46] Within the limits of the normal occupations of literate men of the time, these local leaders cover a range quite as great as that of the rank and file. At most, there is perhaps a slight tendency towards the intellectuals. It is noticeable that, in cathedral towns like Rodez, for instance, the faculty of the college—who were of course, priests—are very well represented in the club, while the cathedral chapter has but one representative.[47] Yet that familiar figure, the radical physician, is extremely common; and medicine, even in the eighteenth century, was not an abstract science.

The leaders, then, are substantially of the same social standing as the rank and file. Possibly there are, among the leaders during the Terror, more men who seem definitely, in 1789, failures, or at least at odds with their environment. Yet the proportion of these village Marats is not striking. Again and again one comes upon instances like that of the boarding-house keeper of Blois, a violent radical, but whose boarding-house, by the admission even of royalists, was very well conducted, and morally irreproachable.[48] These men have left behind them in local tradition—and therefore in the work of local historians— a reputation for violence and political extremism which has easily been turned into a reputation for immorality and irresponsibility. But the genuine scoundrels, like Lacombe of Bordeaux and Philip of Nancy are very few indeed. From hundreds of these brief *cursus vitae* of revolutionary leaders, the impression very clearly arises that they fitted their old environment, that to an observer in 1788 or 1789 they would appear essentially normal in thought and action. In 1794, most of them talked nonsense and some of them acted it. In 1794, then, they are to be distinguished from the normal respectable *bourgeois*. Yet as their social origins are essentially the same as those of the normal respectable *bourgeois*, one may perhaps be pardoned for doubting if the explanation of their conduct in 1794 lies in their social origins.

Still another approach to the problem is possible by accumulating bits of evidence as to the social standing of the Jacobins, odd phrases, motions, decrees of the clubs that throw light on their membership. This method, used alone, might be reproached as too unsystematic. But as a supplement to our previous study, it may not be altogether useless.

The Friends of the Constitution of the early years of the Revolution were invariably men of wealth and standing. The founders in almost any town, from great cities to country market-towns, are *bourgeois*, lawyers, priests, business men, physicians. The list of members of the club of Bordeaux in 1790, for instance, is filled with names of famous Bordelais of the 18th century. With their strong admixture of foreign names, they suggest the commercial greatness of the place, its liberalism and its interest in new ideas—Balguerie, Boyer-Fonfrède, Baour, Dubergier, Johnston, Journu, Lafond, Vandoren, Duranton, Grangeneuve, Garat, Muller, Lavau, Werthamon, Beck.[49] But, although very soon after their foundation, the clubs ceased to be purely, or even largely, upper middle class, they never wholly lost this element in their membership. Indications of this fact are numerous. The club of Moulins protests that, in the spring of 1794, the

club of Hérisson is presided over by a nobleman, and has
two priests as secretaries.[50] The club of Toulouse got
around the law forbidding membership to nobles and
priests by decreeing that nine nobles and four priests
were good citizens, and would be members if the law permitted.[51] At Blaye, the general staff of the garrison was
elected to membership in a body late in 1793—the officers, not the men, were made members of this democratic
club.[52] In the list of members of the club at Dijon a
dozen or so names are listed as *bourgeois* (i. e. men living
on their income, without specific profession) before 1789,
and *citoyens* after 1789.[53] At Paris, in April 1794, a member, to prove his patriotism, said that "he had sent fifteen
of his workmen to the front." It is true that Collot took
him up, and protested that "we are all of us workmen
now; there are no masters"; but his words failed to alter
the fact that the original speaker was a capitalist, a large
employer of labor.[54] Many of these rich Jacobins were of
course *nouveaux riches*. At Rodez, a certain Sompayrac,
négociant, was an active Jacobin, bought several hundred
thousand of livres' worth of *biens nationaux*, but spelled
badly and wrote little better, as a testimonial of his in
favor of some terrorists proves.[55] At La Garde-Freinet,
among villagers of roughly the same economic status,
there stands out a rich cork manufacturer, evidently the
capitalist of the place, and of course a member of the
club.[56] The club of Toulouse was rich enough to endow
fifteen young women of virtue willing to marry virtuous
young republicans, and to provide bonuses for the first
ones to "produce little Republicans for the fatherland."[57]
The adherence to Jacobinism of the leaders of the new—
and old—industrialism is obvious from membership lists
in all sorts of towns, in Lille, Ste.-Marie-aux-Mines, Grenoble, Nîmes, Romans. And certainly the *industriel*, the

selfmade man is not to be accounted a failure, maladjusted to any normal Christian environment.

Yet, very soon after their foundation [58] the clubs began to recruit themselves among petty tradesmen, artisans, and others whom the French label *petits bourgeois*. Hence the clubs during the Terror number people of all sorts of professions, masters as well as men, and give a complete cross-section of French society, with the old court aristocracy, and the recent industrial proletariat, left out. Yet, as we have already indicated in our statistical study of the problem, it must be insisted that these *petits bourgeois* were the most prosperous and most enlightened of their class.[59] For a time under the monarchy, and in certain places, workmen's clubs were formed separately from the expensive upper-class Friends of the Constitution.[60] In Paris, already ripened to nineteenth century social complexity, these workmen's clubs deserve to be called proletarian. But the *Enragés,* however important in the history of the Revolution, need not enter into a definition of Jacobinism. In the provinces, these workmen's clubs eventually coalesced with the bourgeois clubs; and their union established the orthodox Jacobins, the sole club of the town.

A good example of these clubs of rather humbler personnel than the Friends of the Constitution is the *Société patriotique siégeant à la Mercy,* of Bordeaux.[61] This was a neighborhood club, founded in September 1790 by respectable artisans of St. Rémy. One reads their professions—watchmaker, goldsmith, glazier, joiner, engraver and so on, and is hardly prepared for such formalities as "Tous ces respectables Messieurs, étant connu de tous les membres de la société par leur patriotisme, ont été reçu avec empressement." [62] Yet there is a certain overformality in diction, an exaggerated absorption in Rousseau and other intellectual fashions of the day, and an occasional error in spelling to indicate the aspiring and self-taught workman.[63] A club like this corresponds pretty exactly to A. Cochin's *chambres littéraires,* save that it is recruited from the *petite,* not the *haute, bourgeoisie.* There is no trace in its minutes of genuine economic grievances. Language, theory, ritual, is exactly that of the upper classes. Finally, it must be noted that these artisans are the best of their class, all active citizens and qualified voters (that is paying direct taxes to the amount of three days wages) sober, steady men.

In fact, such is the overwhelming social respectability of the majority of these clubs, even during the Terror that their occasional championing of the poor, their glib references to equality, even their use of the sacred word "sans-culottes" may seem hypocrisy.[64] When the revolutionary tax on the rich was decreed, the society of Lunéville decided that its committee "will limit itself to a simple invitation in the case of wealthy *sans-culottes,* and will requisition aristocrats." [65] The club at Artonne decreed concerning this same tax: "According to the report of the committee named to make up the list of the rich, it is decreed that members of the society shall be exempt from this tax." [66] Yet this club was composed of lawyers, doctors, the *bourgeois* of Artonne, and had shown great contempt for the simple farmers round about them: "almost all the town officers are farmers, who don't even know what a decree or a law is." [67] The truth is probably that words like "sans-culottes," "virtuous poor," "Jacobins," "aristocrats," had in the minds of these people no exact meaning—certainly no meaning translatable into economic terms—and that at most "sans-culottes" meant to them "the right people, people like us, people with whom we sympathise." Therefore the

phrase "wealthy sans-culottes" is not a contradiction, as
to the economist "wealthy poor" would be; the poor in
this sense, like the poor in spirit, are blessed. Nor was a
club selfish, illogical, or hypocritical when it exempted its
members from a revolutionary tax on the rich; this tax
was really a levy against the enemy; and the enemy was
not an enemy because of his money, but because of his
principles.

IV

The sum of what we have been able to find out about
the externals of the Jacobin—his social standing, his
wealth, his occupation—is hardly more than this: the
Jacobin was neither noble nor beggar—though most considerable clubs have a sprinkling of both of these—but
almost anything in between. Our statistics will show that,
if the mathematical average of Jacobin wealth is just a
bit above that of the communities they live in, it is not
because all Jacobins are near that average, but because
they represent a complete cross-section of their community. At Romans, where dues were graded according to the
wealth of the members, we find 32 members paying 10
livres apiece, 52 paying 5 livres, 37 paying 2½ livres, 36
paying 1½ livres.[68] But deciles, taken from clubs chosen
at random from those studied in tables VIII and IX of
appendix III are even more convincing.

Dijon, 1795 (*vingtièmes*). Maximum 249 l., minimum 3 l., deciles
11-18-22-26-30-35-45-59-78.

Grenoble, 1795 (*capitation*). Maximum 63 l., minimum ½ l., deciles 2-3-3-4-6-6-9-12-18.

Libourne, 1790-1794 (*taille* and *capitation*). Maximum 189 l.,
minimum ½ l., deciles 2-5-8-15-26-35-48-75-127.

Moulins, 1794 (*capitation*). Maximum 71 l., minimum 1 l., deciles 1-2-3-5-6-8-10-13-19.

Perpignan, 1794 (*vingtièmes*). Maximum 132 l., minimum ½ l.,
deciles 1-2-3-4-6-7-11-19-31.

The range of incomes shown in these five clubs is typical enough. Any given club might count among its members representatives of the very rich and the very poor, although the bulk of its membership was no doubt middle-class. It is hard to see what purely economic interests a man taxed 189 l. and one taxed ½ l. on a graduated poll-tax (the *capitation*) could have in common.

The range of occupation is as great as the range of incomes. If the Jacobins were held together as a community by the fact that they were mostly intellectuals, *philosophes*, nourished on the great encyclopedia, certainly there is nothing in their occupations to show it. The intellectual professions do not even possess a monopoly among the leaders. Nor do the Jacobins have even maladjustment to their environment as a common, external bond. Though the Jacobins were of the most diverse occupations, they might get on very well together if they were all failures at their occupations, and hence discontented and eager for a social Revolution. But the statistical method, the method of sampling, even random bits of Jacobin records, all confirm the respectability of the bulk of these revolutionists, their success at their life work. The lower one goes in social ranking, the more this is true. The Jacobin cobbler was almost certain to be a good cobbler; the Jacobin lawyer might have been a briefless barrister before the Revolution.

We have learned enough, then of the membership of these clubs to realize that what held them together was no class-feeling in the ordinary sense. The Revolution began no doubt partly as a rising of the middle class against the nobility, of the class-conscious Third Estate against the privileged orders. The Friends of Liberty and Equality of 1794 hated aristocrats even more violently than the Friends of the Constitution of 1790 had hated them. But the Terror made plebeian victims as well as aristocratic; the Jacobin revolutionary tribunals were occupied with servants, prostitutes, tradesmen at least as much as with dukes and duchesses.[69] The Jacobins of 1794 were not a class, and their enemies the "aristocrats" were not a class; the Terror was not chiefly then a phase of the class-struggle, but even more a civil war, a religious war. For if the term "class" is to have usefulness at all, it must mean a group of persons having a common social standing and social background, a common standard of life, and common economic interests. These the Jacobins did not have.

CHAPTER IV

TACTICS

The Jacobins were never quite a party in the modern sense. They were from the start much more than a voluntary organization for influencing public opinion and lobbying for particular measures. They were too numerous to be political conspirators. Their clubs, as corporate bodies, never quite became identical with the government of France. Yet in part all these statements are true: the Jacobins were partisans, electioneers, propagandists, lobbyists, conspirators, rulers of France. We must, in this chapter, try to disentangle these activities, to measure them, to distinguish just what part the clubs, as organized bodies, played in revolutionary politics. Our main theme, then, will be Jacobinism as a form of political tactics. First, however, it may be well to review very briefly the legislation officially governing the clubs between 1789 and 1795.[1]

I

Political societies, like newspapers, sprang up in France in 1789 without express authorization: and though the first two assemblies attempted a mild and decent measure of control over both press and clubs, they never succeeded in imposing any serious restraint. The Convention, with the Terror to aid it, was more successful.

By a law of 14 December 1789, right to assemble peacefully for political purposes was limited to "active" citizens—that is, to those who by paying direct taxes equivalent to three day's labor qualified as voters under the new constitution. By another law of May 1790, the clubs were forbidden to petition in their collective name; by the laws of 1 May 1790 and 19 September 1790 they were forbidden to interfere with the soldiery quartered in their towns. Now, the slightest investigation into the records of almost any club will show that these laws were very generally violated. "Passive" citizens were admitted, though not in great numbers, for the poor never really flocked into the clubs.[2] Soldiers garrisoned in the towns were freely invited to the clubs, feasted, pampered, urged to disobey their royalist officers if necessary.[3] As for the provision about petitioning in the name of the club, it was avoided by having every interested member sign his own name to the petition, which was represented in the text as coming from a "body of citizens" or "patriotic citizens of X."[4] But all the world knew the club was petitioning. At the very end of the first assembly the decree of 29 and 30 September 1791 summed up this previous legislation, and tried to set definite penalties for violation of the provisions forbidding collective petitioning and admission of passive citizens. Under the succeeding assembly, the clubs continued to disregard the law.

Once the monarchy had been overthrown, and the Jacobins had come fully into power, the relations of the government and the clubs took a new turn. The clubs were taken up into the government and were adopted as quasi-official units of administration. Hence a law of 25 July 1793, providing that: "Any authority, any individual, who shall permit himself, under whatsoever pretext, to place obstacles in the way of the meeting of the *sociétés populaires*, or to attempt to dissolve them, shall be pursued as guilty of a criminal attempt against liberty, and punished as such." The penalty was ten years in irons for an official, five years for a private citizen. This law, during the Terror at least, was thoroughly respected. Women were excluded from the clubs by law on 9 brumaire II (30 October 1793) and forbidden to form clubs of their own. By the same law, all sessions of the clubs were required to be public. Both these provisions really consecrated a *fait accompli*.

After the fall of Robespierre, the clubs began to decline. Their membership fell away, the central club at Paris was shut by order of the Convention (21 brumaire an III), exact registration of the membership of provincial societies was required, and finally, by the new constitution of the Directory, political assemblies under the name of *sociétés populaires* were expressly forbidden. After the *coup d'état* of 18 fructidor an V. (4 September 1797) the clubs were permitted a temporary revival, and under such names as *cercles constitutionnels* struggled on until under Fouché, Napoleon's minister of police, they were driven completely underground.

II

In July 1789 Arthur Young complained that there was no way of getting news in provincial towns like Besançon. By the next year, however, there was a Jacobin club in Besançon, a reading room with all the newspapers and pamphlets—at least all the patriotic ones—and plenty of other works to enlighten the people.[5] All the clubs without exception subscribed to as big a list of newspapers as they could afford.[6] Sometimes, perhaps usually, the reading of these papers was a privilege reserved to club members. Sometimes public reading rooms were maintained.[7] Very frequently the important news was read publicly by club members, in special sessions, to unfortunate but virtuous citizens kept illiterate by the wickedness of the old government.

A study of Jacobin political action may then well begin with a study of the clubs as agents for propaganda, since in point of time, at least, their first achievement was a thorough stirring-up of the political consciousness of Frenchmen. It is sometimes too readily assumed, both by its enemies and its friends, that the art of advertisement was very primitive until quite recent times. This is quite false, like so many other assumptions based on the dogma that men were never ingenious before the industrial revolution. Jacobin propaganda is so extensive, and so good—that is, so suited to its purpose—that even so modern a word as ballyhoo hardly flatters it.

In the first place, its quantity was surprisingly large for a civilization without rotary presses and dependent on stagecoaches for carrying the mails. An inventory of the archives of the society at Toulouse shows that it received 827 separate packages, containing over 1,000 pamphlets, mostly from other clubs, during a single year (1790).[8] The secretary of the society at Chablis in the summer of 1794 reported the forty-first package received from the Paris club in the last two or three months.[9] A provincial society sent out in one month in 1791 eight pamphlets, mostly reprints of speeches by its members on taxes, loans, obeying the law, the national guard, the new constitutional bishop, trading licenses, and non-juring priests.[10] Over one-half the revenues of the club of Montauban under the monarchy, was employed for printing alone; the printer's bill for the club in this little provincial town of some 25,000 inhabitants was in our money to-day something like $5,000 in a single year.[11]

Where a club has left any documents at all behind it, a
large part is sure to be composed of circulars, pamphlets,
letters from other clubs.

The club at Paris was the source of most of this literature. It regularly sent out printed circulars on the state
of the nation to its daughter-societies, and these circulars
were important in building up the Jacobin machine. They
recur regularly in the pages of Aulard's *Société des
Jacobins*. A good example of the vaguer sort of propaganda sometimes used by the Jacobins is afforded by a
circular sent out from Paris on 9 July 1791, addressed to
the "peoples of the universe." [12] Foreigners are urged to
disavow the *émigrés* and make common cause with the
French for the good of mankind in general. This was to
be translated into various tongues, and sent out by individuals to friends abroad. An example of more specific
and more effective propaganda is the well-known pro-
war circular sent out on 11 January 1792.[13] "Let us form
a barrier of free countries between us and the tyrants
of Europe" says the circular, since it is clear that, through
the stupidity of princes, war is made inevitable. The king
cannot be trusted; this must be a national, not a dynastic,
war. The clubs must prepare this popular movement:
"We urge you especially to maintain the soldiers (garrisoned with you) in their love of liberty." Jacobins can
see to it that pikes are manufactured for the people, who
have hitherto been deprived of arms by a tyrannous governmental monopoly. The circular closes by giving a list
of newspapers, readings from which to the public should
be given by the local clubs. Such examples could be
multiplied indefinitely. These circulars, like so much else
the Jacobins produced, show a curious mixture of abstract
flamboyancy and shrewd practical sense. The Jacobins
were certainly aware that their mission, however pure,

needed advertising. An orator, though he apologized for the expression, proposed to "jacobinize" Savoy, and added, "we have, it is true renounced conquest; but surely we did not mean to renounce the conquests of liberty, our idol, and the empire of the unprescriptible rights of man." [14] Propaganda meant peaceful conquest. The Jacobins felt quite justified in trying to anticipate the tastes of their readers. Dufourny protested early in 1793 against a pamphlet in the style of Hébert to be sent out by the club "which would compromise itself, perhaps, by speaking the language of *Père Duchesne.*" But the pamphlet was sent out none the less.[15]

Very early indeed the Paris club began sending out packages to provincial societies, which in turn were to spread their contents throughout their district. Several packages arrived for the club at Toul, before any such club had been formed. They were handed over to the city government, which was so delighted by their contents that it solicited from the Paris club a continuation of this correspondence.[16] The records of the club of Bergerac give us a list of the contents of two of these packages, sent out somehow under the frank of the National Assembly. Here follows the list, long but illuminating: 1) Address of the Society of Friends of the Constitution of Paris to the National Assembly; 2) Speech delivered on 12 September, second year of freedom (1790) at the Society of Paris by M. Dumas, member of the Society of Corbeil, at the head of a deputation; 3) Resolutions made by citizens of the *section de la Halle aux blés,* read at the Society of Paris, 26 January 1791; 4) Address on the means of developing the prosperity of commerce and on the aid to be afforded it, presented by M. Papion jeune, of Paris; 5) Speech delivered at the Society of Paris by a deputation from the

Society of Young Friends of Liberty, established in the rue du Bac; 6) Speech on taxation, delivered at meetings of the Friends of the Constitution on 11 and 15 October 1790; 7) Prospectus of the *Mercure Universelle;* 8) Speech delivered before the Society . . . . . of Paris by M. Lebihan, officer of the national guard, at the head of the battalion of the Val-de-Grace, 19 September 1790; 9) Letter from the Society . . . . . of Strasbourg, 13 January 1791; 10) Reply to an article of the new plan for a Constitution for the medical profession in France, by the medical society of Paris; 11) Speech on the theatre delivered by M. de la Harpe, 17 December 1790 to the Society of Friends of the Constitution; 12) Letter from M. Cussac, printer and bookseller to the Society . . . . . of Paris.[17]

The newspaper is the simplest form taken by this propaganda. Good Jacobins were urged to read and promote the circulation of certain patriotic papers.[18] They soon, however, had their own organs. A *Journal des Clubs ou Sociétés patriotiques* was established in Paris in November 1790 to give accounts of the meetings of the Jacobins, their correspondence, and the meetings of other Parisian clubs. At the same time Choderlos de Laclos founded his *Journal des Amis de la Constitution,* a weekly published under the direct authorization of the Paris club, and designed to act as a sort of clearing house for correspondence between the different clubs. It was a very useful instrument of propaganda in the provinces. Finally, under the title of *Journal des débats de la Société des Amis de la Constitution séante à Paris,* and later of *Journal de la Montagne,* the club allowed certain of its members to publish semi-official accounts of its debates. These journals, organs of the Paris club, make it possible to reconstruct its history, though its documentary records have mysteriously and completely disappeared.[19] Many provincial clubs extended their patronage to newspapers, or even set up definite organs of their own. The *Journal Toulousain* was founded in November 1790 by the local club.[20] The society at Limoges published a semi-weekly organ, the *Journal du département de la Haute Vienne,* which managed to make a good deal of trouble for the more moderate departmental government.[21] At Nantes, at Châlons-sur-Marne, the societies published papers; [22] at Besançon, the local *Vedette* profited by the express approval of the club.[23] Provincial journalism, indeed, came more and more to be a function limited to orthodox members of the clubs, often subsidized by the clubs as corporate bodies.

As for pamphlets, they are almost countless. Vanity played its usual innocent, and here unusually naïve, part, for now the pleasure of seeing one's self in print had overnight come within the reach of almost anyone. Most of these pamphlets are incredibly dull, and hardly worth the efforts even of the historian of thought. But like the now unreadable sermons of previous centuries, they once had an effect. They were good propaganda, as a whole, if only because each one repeated its predecessors. The list given above [24] of pamphlets sent out from Paris will do as a sample. More—617 separate titles, in fact—can be found listed under the *Amis de la Constitution* in Tourneux's repertory of printed works for revolutionary Paris.[25]

The clubs did not, however, rest contented with the printed word. They carried on an extensive campaign for public education—education in the rights of man, the sovereignty of the people, and other Jacobin dogmas. This zeal for education frequently took the form of

prizes to be awarded to school children for reciting the
Rights of Man,[26] or for writing out this new gospel in
the fairest hand.[27] This method of arousing attention by
prize-giving sometimes went beyond the bounds of pure
education. The club at Limoges announced that it would
present a civic crown to the first priest in the department courageous enough to take a wife.[28] Even at sophis-
ticated Paris, the club personally shared in the task of
bringing the young up to be good citizens. On 29 November 1791 "M. Machenaud read to the Society the
list of members who are undertaking the noble task of
instructing children and giving them the catechism of
the Constitution." [29] At Mende a commissioner was
named "to go into the classrooms and find out what
sort of works young people are made to read, and invite
school teachers to have their pupils read and learn by
heart the Rights of Man and the heroic deeds of French
republicans." [30] Nor did the clubs limit themselves to
the education of the young. The club at Montpellier had
six commissioners who shared the labor of explaining,
on special Sunday and holiday meetings, the decrees of
the national assembly to "the good national guardsmen
and other good illiterate patriots." [31] The club at Coutances, recognizing that "ignorance is . . . the source
of the greater part of the ills that afflict humanity"
worked up an elaborate scheme for adult education in
what we should now call civics.[32]

The theatre was for the Jacobins another instrument
of propaganda. The club at Limoges backed up the civic
theatre, distributed tickets free-of-charge among the
poor, and encouraged its members to take part in the
productions.[33] Of course, the plays given were all patriotic, "exalting republican sentiments or ridiculing the
vices of the old régime." [34] Or as a representative of the

society of Metz told the city council "the theatre ought, given back its proper dignity, to become a school of morals and a burning hearth where souls can constantly be re-tempered in republicanism." [35] The connection between club and theatre was not always as close as at Limoges, but during the Terror, at any rate, managers of whatever theatres there were took good care to join a club. The Jacobins of Rouen made use of the theatre, but very subtly, so that their tracks were almost covered. In December 1790, they decided to persuade the manager of the theatre to give *Brutus,* partly for the subject, and partly for the famous lines

> Je suis fils de Brutus, et je porte en mon coeur
> La liberté gravée, et les rois en horreur.

But the manager was warned not to disclose the fact that the initiative for giving this republican drama came from the club. As a good public servant, he complied to pressure as evidently originating with the public.[36]

The constant intercourse of Jacobins with one another all over France helped greatly with the main purpose of propaganda, which is less to gain converts than to keep up one's own spirits. Much of this visiting about in nearby towns, sending of delegations to departmental meetings, joint-meetings of societies, commissions to form societies in smaller towns, really amounts to what we should call junketing at the expense of the society as a whole.[37] The records of the clubs are full of examples of professional patriots going the rounds of the important clubs for purposes of publicity. Such no doubt was the brave Marseillais who appeared before the club of Bordeaux in 1792, exhibiting the stump of a sword he had broken "fighting the satellites of despotism." And the minutes continue "this worthy citizen is given a seat beside the president to the unanimous applause of the society and the galleries and receives 100 francs for his trouble." There is no indication that this Marseillais had any other business in Bordeaux.[38] So too professional orators crop up from time to time, men who seem to act as traveling salesmen for the Revolution. Such was the eloquent stranger who electrified the small Provençal club at Trets, and who seems to have made similar speeches at other clubs.[39] One of these men, who attained a certain subordinate prominence in the Revolution, was the "sieur Dorfeuille" who appeared before the Jacobins of Bergerac in January 1792, equipped with "several recommendations extremely flattering to himself from several Societies of Friends of the Constitution at Paris, Bordeaux, Montauban, Agen, etc., and especially a letter from Ste. Foy." Ste. Foy was the nearest town, and one can easily plot out Dorfeuille's territory and route from this information. Before he left Bergerac, this agent succeeded in persuading the club to send a petition to Paris asking for the confiscation of the property of emigrant nobles.[40]

The clubs were almost from the beginning concerned with a particularly difficult bit of propaganda, the process usually described in their records as "enlightening the inhabitants of the countryside." Almost every club at one time or other composed, printed and distributed, as did the club of Noyon, an "Address from the *Société populaire* to its brothers the country people." [41] The clubs of the Yonne, led by that of Auxerre, formed a central committee, which issued a broadside of 15 articles, two of which were concerned with rural propaganda.

Art. VIII. The societies will make every effort to persuade the inhabitants of the countryside to plant trees of Liberty, and the members of the societies, who shall be present at inauguration

ceremonies, shall explain to the people the meaning of this
patriotic symbol.

Art. IX. The Societies shall be invited to employ all legal means
towards multiplying the number of civic festivals and celebrations
of noble deeds.[42]

The club at Larche was founded in June 1793, for the express purpose of guiding public opinion in this agricultural canton. As M. Thouzy, *bourgeois*, explained, "the
Farmer, that useful and dear portion of humanity, cannot save himself by his own strength and good will; he
lacks enlightenment and knowledge of things." This lack
the club will supply, point out to him true patriots from
false, and guide him in his civic duties.[43] The club of
Epinal told the simple farmers, "when you are sent a letter or a pamphlet, examine carefully whether it tends
to make you love the Constitution. If it does not, it certainly comes from an impure source. Send it to some
society of Friends of the Constitution, and soon the society will tell you what you ought to think of it."[44] Later
"apostles" and "missionaries" sent out by town societies
to convert the country became a common feature of that
religious outbreak commonly known as the Terror.[45]

The Jacobins profited by the confusion between public
and private authority so common throughout the Revolution to further the dissemination of their principles. The
club at Avallon acted as distributing center for revolutionary literature in the district, and sent out pamphlets,
not only to clubs and individuals, but to the local village
governments.[46] At Limoges, in 1793, the society appointed commissioners in charge of propaganda for each
district of the department, and these commissioners were
to report to and work under the official administrative
council of the department.[47] Lacoste, on mission in the
Bas Rhin, decreed in November 1793 that "the city of

Saverne be divided into 8 quarters, that the citizens of each quarter should attend in turn a session of the *Société populaire* to learn the catechism of the constitution and to listen to the development of the principles of liberty and equality; that a roll-call be made at each session of the citizens required to attend—and those whose third successive absence is noted be expelled from the city." [48] Few propagandists enjoy an audience compelled to listen. But the Jacobins in the end went even farther, and silenced all opposing opinions. During the Terror, freedom of speech and freedom of the press did not exist. Signs of the Terror, however, in this matter as in so many others, can be seen quite early, long before the foreign pressure republican historians make responsible for the whole Terror had begun to have any reality. The club at Honfleur decreed in June 1791 that its members should "stop or buy up all incendiary writings (i.e. royalist or clerical) that should come to their knowledge, but always taking care not to be detected in so doing." [49]

III

The Jacobins, true to their origins as a caucus of the National Assembly, always busied themselves with elections. In a day when, even in parliamentary countries like England and the United States, party was synonymous with faction, and regarded as a corruption of political instincts, the Jacobins could hardly come out as a party with platform and organization in the modern style. Their influence on elections was therefore complicated, exercised now by open propaganda, now by intrigue, now by pressure of official or unofficial police power, but in the long run always preponderant. Jacobin methods in elections, like Jacobin methods in propaganda, come at times very near to what may pass for the permanent in human political behavior.

One obvious remark must be made at the start. A great deal of Jacobin success in elections is due to the simple fact that they were organized and disciplined, that they voted as a unit. The club at Strasbourg decided in November 1791 that any member who failed to vote in any public election—and such elections were very numerous in the doctrinaire constitution of 1791—should be expelled from the society. Similar resolutions are common among the societies.[50] At the first public session of the society at Blaye, the president had club and guests alike take oath "to sacrifice their dearest interests in order to be present at the primary (electoral) assemblies." [51]

The excellence of the Jacobin organization allowed them to draw up better and more complete lists of candidates for the various offices. This practice, although it is perhaps hardly in accord with Rousseauistic principles, appears quite early. The club at Toulouse circulated a list of candidates for city and departmental offices in November 1790, and brought out thereby a protest from one of its own more idealistic members. "It is useless for ordinary citizens to go to these (primary) assemblies. The clubs monopolize them and control all the votes; the city is inundated with lists hawked about in every ward, and presented publicly in the name of the clubs and the general staff (of the National Guard, a citizen militia whose membership was largely identical with that of the clubs)." [52] The club of St. Geniez proposed in July 1790 the following scheme for the whole department of the Aveyron: "1) Invite all the patriotic societies in the department to get the list of eligible electors (in the second degree) in their cantons; 2) designate in this list the citizens most worthy of public confidence; 3) send this list to all the societies in the department; 4) ask the society of Rodez (the capital) to make a general departmental list." The society at Rodez thought this scheme a bit too neat and turned it down; but it is obviously equivalent to the kind of list produced by modern French parties under the *scrutin de liste*.[53] In the little village of Lucy-le-bois in the Avallonais, the head of the local club writes to the club of Avallon: "We have drawn up a list of candidates worthy of renewing our municipality, and have sworn to give to them alone our votes at the next election. We read in the latest news from Paris that the patriotic societies were very generally busying themselves with such matters." [54]

The election pamphlets with which the clubs usually accompanied such lists contain much good advice to citizens armed for the first time with the vote. Democracy must choose the best; but how recognize the best? After the platitudes, the pamphlets come down with surprising unanimity to asserting that no one associated with the old régime should be chosen. Robespierre himself drew up such a pamphlet for the Paris club. "In general," he begins,. "virtue presumes or carries with itself enough talent to be fitting in a representative of the people. The energy of a pure and well-intentioned soul is the principal source of sane political ideas." [55] He continues by giving simple enough rules to detect virtue; they come down in practice to not having held a good position in the old régime. So too in an election pamphlet of the club of Bordeaux issued in July 1790 the real point is contained in the phrases, "Citizens, do you think these functions (of the new government) can be confided to men imbued from their childhood with ideas contrary to the Revolution, avid for honors, exemptions, privileges?—Would you call to the administration of the commonwealth citizens bound by vows to the Catholic church?—We must have new men for a regenerated government." [56] The new men were at hand, in the clubs.

Such practices, if not worthy of what the eighteenth century thought to be true democracy, are none the less perfectly legal. The Jacobins, in spite of their friendship for the constitution, were not men to be bound by a strict interpretation of the law. Sometimes, their maneuvering seems harmless enough. The Jacobins of Montauban succeeded in getting the loyalist regiment of *Royal-Pologne* sent away from their town before the municipal elections and the patriotic regiment of *Touraine* left as the only guardian of order. This not only enabled them to hinder the publication and distribution of the opposing newspaper, but left many monarchists afraid to vote, since their regiment no longer protected them. [57] When the electors of Paris formed a *Club des électeurs patriotes,* led by Cerutti, Kersaint, Brissot and others, and thus were enabled to unite the various secondary assemblies in Paris into one, and elect 30 Jacobin judges in one assembly, instead of taking their chances in six, convenience, if not the law, was served. [58] The society at Bergerac was perhaps not intentionally conniving at electoral corruption when it took up a subscription to send electors to Périgueux to vote for a new constitutional bishop, or when it tried to take up another collection to pay traveling expenses of electors chosen by primary assemblies. But when it drew up a list of electors who were present, and another of those who were absent, at the election of a priest for Bergerac, it must have been aware that it was beginning a system of political blackmail. [59] As time goes on, the pressure exercised by the clubs on the electoral assemblies is hardly disguised. At Nice—in conquered territory, it is true—the club sent one hundred of its members to the primary assemblies to "guard against the influence of intriguers with the people." [60] Naturally, in the absence of the secret ballot, such methods got results. At Orthez, after a speech on the necessity of electing good men as justices of the peace, the club decided to vote at once as to who were good men. The electoral assembly ratified their choice.[61] It is with very little surprise that one finds the president of the primary electoral assembly of Villedieu in Poitou writing to the society of Poitiers simply that he "has done as he was told by the society." [62] The surprising thing is that the society seemed to have been a trifle ashamed of this frankness.

As time went on, even these means proved insufficient for the Jacobins, and their opponents were completely excluded from the electoral assemblies. Thus followed the phenomena, dwelt upon by Taine and other conservative historians, of almost unanimous elections by a very small number of voters. The records of the clubs perhaps add little to what we know of the results of Jacobin methods, but the following excerpts may help us to understand how the Jacobin mind brought itself to such methods. A member of the club at Vannes, in royalist Brittany, is urging the election of a *comité de surveillance* of twelve for the town:

> But the city government has recognized with us the impossibility of having the twelve members elected by a primary assembly as numerous as the law (of universal suffrage) requires, for that assembly would contain more than 800 persons. Certainly the greater part of these 800 would belong to those known as having little love for the Revolution, since those who ordinarily take part in these assemblies number hardly 300. But if the

absentees, full of evil intent, should turn up at such an assembly, no doubt but that they would choose men devoted to their cause. To avoid this serious inconvenience, I propose that the club ask the city government to call a primary assembly to which would be called only 1. those who voted at the assembly to decide whether or not to accept the Constitution of 1793 (you know it was unanimously accepted) 2. the civil servants called to this town by their functions 3, the grenadiers of our national guard now in service on the road to Sarzeau.[63]

Such an assembly was held with 169 voters. Similarly at Toulouse, the club petitioned the National Assembly as early as July 1793 to be allowed to exclude from the primary assemblies the 1,200 signers of a petition in favor of the Roman Catholic Church, unless they retracted their signatures. If this isn't done legally, continues the petition "good citizens would in all likelihood refuse to allow the signers of this anti-revolutionary document to enter the election hall, and since this exclusion might seem to certain timid souls to be illegal and unjust, and there might be trouble about it, you can avoid all this in advance by a wise decree." [64] Even in 1792 these tactics were proposed openly:

A deputation appeared before the Paris Jacobins to notify them of the decree passed by the Mirabeau section, not to admit to the elections any citizen who had been a member of a monarchical club— This section decreed to include in this *ostracism* the signers of the petition against M. Pétion, and against the camp of 20,000 men. It asks the Society to help it make a list of such persons, which will be posted in the meeting-place of the section.[65]

Should all these methods fail, and an anti-Jacobin administration be elected, there was always the network of friendly societies and sometimes friendly superior authorities to fall back upon. The local history of the Revolution is full of inglorious—since they are provincial— but none the less interesting political struggles. The

clubs rose to power in a hundred ways, overcoming the
opposition easily there, here overcome, carrying through
the same purpose in circumstances so different that any
general description of the process seems a falsification.
Perhaps the only way is to cite examples. At the little
town of Eymoutiers in November 1791, the club's candidate for mayor was beaten, 39 to 58. The club at once
protested to the departmental *directoire* at Limoges,
which, like good Friends of the Constitution, arbitrarily
dismissed the mayor and his council, and appointed three
club-members of Eymoutiers to run the town temporarily. A special commission of the department and district combined, however, reversed the decision and
restored the mayor. The club then pursued a steady
policy of nagging the town government, a policy, indeed,
of what amounted to sabotage. After the 10th of August,
they appealed to Limoges, and a patriotic force from
that city and St. Léonard marched on Eymoutiers, routed
out the mayor once more, and replaced him by a commission of five club-members. All this happened before
the Terror had begun.[66]

At Aix-en-Provence, the local club, known as the
antipolitiques, was in 1793 considerably more radical
than the city government or the sections (wards of the
city, in which the citizens met as a whole in little direct
democracies). The club won over the city government,
which agreed to disarm and exclude from the sections a
large number of "moderates." To the amazement of
everybody, the moderates, even though deprived of their
arms, turned up at the section meetings, voted, and won
back the city government. Only the intervention of three
special commissioners of the department prevented a
little civil war, and saved the day for the *antipolitiques*.
These commissioners put all the sections under perma-

nent cloture until all "suspects" were disarmed. This victory was very temporary, however, for on the news of the 2nd of June Marseilles and Aix rose up to defend the Gironde, the sections met in full force, and announced the dissolution of the club. Some three months later, the entry of the army of the Convention under Carteau allowed the reopening of the club, which continued to rule during the Terror.[67] But until the army turned the balance, the struggle had been reasonably even, and surprisingly clear-cut; the club on one hand, the anti-Jacobin sections on the other. The club was a voluntary organization; the sections were legal political assemblies, not unlike the New England town meeting. The Jacobins, knowing they would be outvoted, did not go to the section meetings. Yet the section meetings themselves contained merely a slightly larger minority of the citizens of Aix than the club. The struggle is at bottom a struggle between two groups, in which the smaller and better organized group, thanks to outside aid, finally won out.

The sections in cities all over France were indeed the last stand of respectable, liberal middle class gentlemen against the better disciplined, less gentlemanly and not at all liberal Jacobins who were creating the first French republic. At Strasbourg in 1793 the sections proved a rallying point for the moderates, and the Jacobins quite illegally broke up their sessions.[68] At Lille, in July 1793, the sections conceived the idea of forming *sociétés populaires* in each one of the six sections of the town, as centers from which to undermine the Jacobin club. After much debate, protesting, and petitioning, the Jacobins won, and five presidents of the sections were sent to Paris before the revolutionary tribunal, which actually acquitted them.[69]

Even before the time of their complete ascendancy, however, the Jacobins were sometimes obliged to use irregular methods to influence elections. A little incident at Angoulême illustrates not only the pertinacity of the Jacobins, but the weakness of the central government, and its failure to enforce its own laws. The club at Angoulême had issued an "Address to the country people on the elections" signed contrary to the law by the club in its collective name. The royal commissioner at the Angoulême tribunal therefore prosecuted the club. He wrote on January 28, 1792, to the Minister of Justice at Paris that his life had been endangered by this step, and that four Jacobins had assaulted him one night. The club at once issued another edition of the address, with a violent appendix attacking their "persecutor." The commissioner sent a desperate letter to the Minister of Justice asking to be allowed to use force, soldiers if necessary. The letter is annotated by the minister (Duport-Dutertre) "write to M. B.-C. Cahier (Minister of the Interior) to get in motion the public forces." Cahier, in turn, passed the whole affair on to the departmental administration of the Charente, with pious hopes that the club would behave itself and that the commissioner would be protected. But by this time the monarchy had fallen, and *M. le Commissaire du Roi* presumably had fled.[70] The Jacobins under the monarchy pursued much the same ends in much the same ways as the apparently more proletarian Jacobins of the republic. The Terror has respectable social origins.

The Jacobins occasionally, it appears, were sinned against. The "greater part of the active citizens of Angles, near St. Pons" complained to the Paris Jacobins that, "betraying them most atrociously" a *ci-devant* noble had actually got himself elected justice of the peace. Noblemen acted as election clerks, fooled the poor illiterate common people, cheated generally, so that at the second ballot there were more votes than voters.[71] A "society of free and patriotic citizens" of La Mothe-St.-Héraye complained in 1790 that a "cabale" headed by an aristocrat who dared imply "by his soft discourse that one ought to choose as justices of the peace only men learned in law, rich and satisfied people" had actually by drawing out interminably the length of the meeting sought to keep out the busy workingmen. Members of this same cabale had even employed to seduce a good patriot "the attractive women of their artificial society, so that by their soft words they could gain his vote." [72] But in general one is struck by the incompetence of the opposition to the Jacobins, an incompetence which need not be accepted offhand as a sign of superior morality. The opposition is divided, timid, inept. Even when it attempted to organize itself into clubs, as had the Jacobins, the result was rarely more successful. *Clubs des Amis de la Paix* sprang up all over France in 1790-1791, with the most laudable intentions and principles. The Friends of Peace of Limoges, for instance, announced their intention of "filling themselves with the true spirit of the Constitution of the kingdom and propagating it by all gentle and persuasive ways." [73] But this society soon drew upon itself the suspicion of the local Jacobin club, and after a short struggle, was obliged by pressure from the authorities and the Jacobins—not unaided by local hoodlums—to disband. The usual procedure of the Jacobins towards rival groups is illustrated at Poitiers, where street rows were provoked, stones thrown at windows, clubrooms raided, and the blame for disturbing the peace thrown on the rival club. The authorities, who were forced by law to permit freedom of association,

could thus be brought to close the rival club as a public
nuisance.[74] The *Club Monarchique* of Paris is another example of the ineptitude of the conservatives. It embarked
on an elaborate and undisguised system of charity, involving a free distribution of bread to the poor, which
offered the best possible handle for the Jacobins. The
aristocrats were clearly trying to corrupt the poor. A
whole series of indisputable historical analogies lay open
to the Jacobin orators and journalists: *panem et cir-
censes*, Sulla, Cæsar. The *Club Monarchique*, too, was
forced to close its doors.[75]

There can be no doubt as to the effectiveness of Jacobin
electioneering, even at the very beginning, when their
opponents were still free and articulate. In the departmental elections for the Vienne in 1790, there were only
twenty club-members out of 422 electors. Yet these
twenty got ten seats out of thirty-six in the council, and
six out of nine seats in the administration.[76] In 1791,
the society of Dijon could write to the mother-society,
"We number among us three members of the administration of the department, the president, the *procureur
général syndic* and three members of the district, all the
members of the city government, finally all the judges
in the tribunals." [77] The new bishop of the Cher himself
told the Paris club, "it is chiefly to the interest which the
Friends of the Constitution of Bourges were good enough
to take in me that I owe the votes of the electors of the
department." [78] The society of Cherbourg, not a very large
town, succeeded in getting three of its members elected
to the Convention.[79] In general, though statistics on such
a matter would be very difficult to draw up, it may be
said that there was a steady increase in the number of
Jacobins elected to national, departmental, district and
municipal offices from 1790 to 1793.[80] After that year,

elections became a mere formality, and the Jacobins no longer needed to practice the art of vote-getting.

IV

The president of the club of Toulouse, retiring in December 1790, summed up the activities of the club during his incumbency. What gave him most pride was that under his leadership the club had "established just recently a direct surveillance, an open inspection of the three administrative bodies (department, district, city) whose seat is in this city." [81] Ultimately, the problem of the place of the clubs in revolutionary politics comes down to this: how real was the control exercised by the clubs over government authorities? Propaganda, intrigue, electioneering all lead up to this final purpose of the clubs, to run things.

Common opinion, and especially the opinion of their enemies, has from the very first been willing to admit the complete success of the clubs. An early attack on the clubs may be found in the *Feuille Hebdomadaire* of Lorient, in Brittany, in October 1790. The author writes:

> A decree of a certain club is often more respected than one emanating from legal sources. . . . The club-members' daily occupation is to survey the executive body and to make a scrupulous revision of the decrees of the legislative body. . . . By what right do these men, to whom their fellow-citizens have by no means given suffrages, usurp the authority of functionaries? [82]

In April 1790, there was hawked about the streets of Paris an anti-Jacobin pamphlet with the title "Great decrees of the Club of the Jacobins, which will be converted into decrees of the National Assembly, as usual, in the course of the present week." [83] The newly elected president of the club of Trévoux, in 1791, began his inaugural speech with the warning: "This is not an inquisition, but a meeting of good citizens inspired with a desire to uphold a liberty limited to the good man in society." He continued by admonishing his brothers not to denounce other citizens too freely, not to be disorderly at meetings, not to try and cut a prominent figure before the public, not to interfere with government officials in the exercise of their duties—which is, even to a quite uncynical temperament, pretty clear proof that the Jacobins were doing just these things.[84] Historians have tended to accept all this at its face value, and most accounts of local clubs make them out to be complete masters of the territory from which they were recruited.[85]

This mastery was certainly not attained without a struggle. It is broadly speaking true that almost everywhere in France the first elections under the new constitution put into power in the numerous local administrative bodies for department, district and town men of political moderation—essentially conservative, orderly, respecting the monarchy, anxious to carry out from above the theories of the Enlightenment. With these administrations the clubs of the Friends of the Constitution came into conflict almost everywhere. No simple formula can describe even the final outcome of all these struggles. True, the downfall of the monarchy and subsequent events in Paris eventually turned all France over to the revolutionary government, which does not, however, by any means imply government by the clubs. Yet before August 10, 1792, the clubs had yielded to the government in certain towns, had maintained a fairly even contest in others, had triumphed in still more. The incidents of all these struggles, the methods, the political technique of both parties are equally varied, and we can but attempt to classify certain common features. It must be remembered that throughout the Jacobins had one immeasurable source of strength—their pyramidal organization in affiliated societies culminating in that of Paris, and bound together by constant correspondence.

As long as the administrations could meet in private they possessed a very obvious advantage. If, on the other hand, their meetings were public nothing could be easier for the clubs than to take advantage of the devotion of the club-members to politics, and attend sessions of the local magistracies, and shout down the moderates. It was still easier, of course, to pay a claque to do so. The clubs are, then, practically unanimous that the interests of democracy demand public sessions of governing bodies of all kinds. From Tulle, in January 1791 the national assembly was petitioned to decree "perpetual and constitutional publicity of the sessions of legislative, administrative and municipal bodies." [86] At Avallon, "a member read a speech in which he established the system of publicity in all our institutions as the only way to form men of virtue, to enlighten them and instruct them." [87] In the summer of 1792, the club of Amiens petitioned the National Assembly, complaining that the departmental administration had dared to blame the good city of Paris for the troubles of June 20, and adding that the administrators would never have dared to take such a step had the public been admitted to their place of meeting. The Assembly was therefore asked to decree that all officials conduct their business in public.[88] The Republic was soon to grant its citizens this boon: but all through this agitation, deputations had freely passed to and fro between the clubs and the administrations, and to all intents and purposes the Jacobins had long had their way. The authorities were too numerous, and too well watched, to concoct anything in secret.

The humblest and simplest relation between the clubs
and the authorities is that implied in the petition.
Throughout the Revolution, the clubs turned out petitions,
addresses, memorials on almost any subject brought before them. There was, as we have seen, a law against
petitioning in a club's name; and this law supposedly was
valid until the fall of the monarchy. But as we have seen,
it was pretty universally disobeyed.[89] The city government was constantly petitioned on all matters from that
of moving the post-office nearer the center of the town [90]
to that of arming the people with pikes.[91] The comman-
der of the royal troops at Besançon, Custine, was petitioned by the club to order his officers at once into the
new national uniform, and held the club in sufficient
respect to reply that he would do so within the three
months' delay accorded by law.[92] Districts, departments,
and national assembly were similarly petitioned at one
time or other by every self-respecting club. Frequently
deputations from the clubs carried the petitions directly
to the administration involved. Perhaps here a direct
citation from the documents can best show this activity
of the clubs. The following is not quite an example of an
average day in the life of a Jacobin club, but it is certainly typical. In one session of the club of Perpignan,
late in 1793, the records show:

> Deputation to Headquarters (of the army) to get it to give
> orders for the distribution of wood to the soldiers to be so made
> that they may use it without having to split it, for not every sol-
> dier has an axe.
> First deputation to the district to get it to order the commis-
> sioners around the Canigou to continue to burn charcoal and to
> come to Perpignan to sell it as they used to, inasmuch as the vil-
> lage governments seem to be coalized not to burn any or at least
> not to come to Perpignan to sell it.
> The members of the deputation reported that the *procureur*

syndic had already busied himself with the matter, and orders to bring in charcoal have been given.

Second deputation to the district to get it to order the communes to bury any corpses left on their territory. (This was on the Spanish frontier, where the Republican armies were engaged with the Spanish.)

First deputation to the city government to request it to make at once requisitional visits to all cobblers and shoemakers to see whether any have stocks of shoes they refuse to sell. This measure is essential, as some brothers in arms lack shoes.

The members of the deputation having returned said that they would report tomorrow.

Second deputation to the city government to get the pavements repaired and to keep the streets clean.

Third deputation to the city government to have the *fleur de lis* removed from the steeple of the church of St. John.

Fourth deputation to the city government to get it to search in private houses to find surplus candles.

Second deputation to Headquarters to get it to order the captains to inspect weekly the booty gathered by the soldiers. If any soldiers are discovered selling or possessing extra boots, they should be arrested.

The deputation, having returned, reported that there was no one at Headquarters.[93]

Petitioning, however, was but the first step. The club might well be met with a refusal. It could of course, repeat the petition, nag the administration into yielding.[94] But the best way was to find someone or something to denounce, and make the denunciation thoroughly public. The original petition, indeed, may well have taken the form of a denunciation. Aristocrats and non-juring priests were at first the customary subjects of these denunciations. The society at Libourne denounced before the local court the Sieur Beaumalle, who had announced that he would continue to have his coat-of-arms on his sedan chair in spite of the revolution, and that he would shoot anyone who tried to prevent him.[95]

The club at Blaye having heard that M. Lison, who as a private citizen had subscribed 150 livres to the patriotic fund, had on being elected city counsellor got hold of the fund register and changed the sum to 72 livres, denounced him to his fellows, and demanded his exclusion from the city council.[96] Paris was naturally a center for such denunciations. There "two deputies from the regiments of Chartres and the Dauphin denounced the criminal manoeuvres employed by the officers of these regiments, who to arouse their soldiers against the new régime alter for the worse the quality of the bread served out as rations and diminish its weight." The club listened to these soldiers in indignation, and advised them to go before the National Assembly with their complaint.[97] As early as March 1790, a Comte de St. Aldegonde had denounced certain abbeys for cutting down their forests in anticipation of their confiscation by the nation.[98] But it is useless to go into details when any history of the Revolution affords countless examples of this craze for denunciation, though it led into matters apparently of purely private concern. Some protests were indeed made in the Paris club against excessive concern with private matters, but Collot d'Herbois replied:

> When the Revolution shall have been completed, say in thirty or sixty years, then citizens will not need to assemble in clubs. The respectable majority of the nation will make and execute good laws; but until that time it is necessary to survey the administrative, judicial and other bodies, to prevent them from betraying the people. The duty of a society to Friends of the Constitution is to be official defender of any injured private citizen. I approve the proposition that the society should not cease to occupy itself with private affairs.[99]

If petition or denunciation failed before the first administrative body appealed to, the next step was naturally enough to appeal to another, and preferably higher, body. The Jacobins of the monarchy excelled at putting the various parts of the very new government of 1791 at loggerheads. Here again we can but cite.

The Jacobins at Sisteron established themselves after a long struggle with the hostility of their fellow-citizens, and after displaying the usual Jacobin virtues of pertinacity and willingness to adapt their methods, if not their ideas, to practical necessity. The city government consented to the founding of the club in 1791, though reluctantly, since it feared "that the purpose of the founders was to get hold of the city government, for it was said that they were saying openly that the Friends of the Constitution were established to survey the administrative bodies, and to force their hands if need be." There were anti-Jacobin riots, and the mayor was obliged to dissolve the club. The club-members appealed to the administration of the department, which supported them, and wrote to the mayor to protect these good citizens. Nevertheless the Jacobins thought still more tangible support was advisable. They warned the mayor that "if the peasants of this town permit themselves the slightest insurrection, five hundred men under arms are at our orders." Apparently the Jacobins went around and bought off the physically more dangerous among the rioters who had opposed them, and then reopened the club in triumph. Within a few months they had forced the resignation of the mayor who had obliged them to shut down.[100]

From active measures by the city government designed to prevent their meetings, the Jacobins were protected by the case of the club of Dax, a case which set a definite precedent valid for the whole period of the monarchy. The mayor and council of this little town in the Landes

were sound conservatives, and shocked by the novelty of
the local club's ideas on self-government, simply refused
to let it meet. The club at once appealed to the highest
authority possible, the National Assembly, and aired
its case freely in the Paris press. Other clubs, too protested at about this time to the Paris club against persecution by their city governments.[101] They were re-
warded by a decree, 13-19 November 1790, reasserting
the right of citizens to peaceful political meeting and
ordering city governments to cease their persecutions.[102]

From the Jacobin clubs, however, the authorities were
not similarly protected. The department of the Indre-et-
Loire refused a petition from the club of Tours on the
ground that the club had legally no right to petition in its
collective name. The club at once placarded the walls of
Tours with a radical address signed with its collective
name. The department haled the officers of the club before the ordinary criminal court. The president made an
eloquent and well-reported speech, threatening the
authorities for interfering with the club, citing the example of the mayor and council of Dax, and generalizing
beautifully on free speech. The court contented itself
with a nominal fine, and the club gained what is for some
reason called a moral victory.[103] The club at Gray kept
getting into trouble with the 12th regiment of horse quartered in the town, the royalist officers going so far as to
egg on their men to snowball the Abbé Lempereur, president of the club. The club petitioned the National Assembly to have the regiment removed; this petition, though
refused at first, was finally granted on the renewed insistence of the club.[104] The club of Saverne quarreled with
the national guard, whose officers it found too aristocratic.
It sent an address to the club of Strasbourg, detailing its
grievances against these officers. An officer of the guard

sued the president of the Saverne club for libel. The department of the Bas Rhin, appealed to by the club, suspended the whole staff of the Saverne guard before the case was brought to trial, and the victory went to the club.[105] A deputation of street-merchants, supported by Tallien, appeared before the Paris club, to complain that a recent ordinance of the city council had injured their trade; the club, most sympathetic, agreed that they had a good case, and advised them to appeal to the department —a step which would normally occur to a Jacobin.[106] Later, the representative on mission could be appealed to. The citizen Lacau of the club of Toulouse presented the society with an accusation in twelve heads against the *procureur géneral syndic,* which the club passed on to Mailhe, on mission at Toulouse. Mailhe said that an extract from the club's minutes would be quite enough, and that the official would be broken at once.[107]

A good example of the use the Jacobins made of higher authorities is afforded by the campaign of the club of Poitiers against non-juring priests—a campaign much like that waged by Jacobin clubs throughout France. Since the city government was not sufficiently active against the clericals, the club forced a meeting of the voters of the town, which declared for the banishment of the local *capucins,* and the closing of hospitals and other charitable institutions run by the regular clergy. The city government still refusing to go beyond the letter of the law, which allowed the regular clergy to continue in the town under certain conditions, the club appealed to the department, which ordered the city government to obey the will of the voters. The club then decided to petition the National Assembly to decree the closing of all convents and convent chapels. Meanwhile a hearing before the city government proved that non-juring priests were

holding Mass in convent chapels, and even celebrating
saints' days in their former parish churches, now occupied
by the legal but unpopular constitutional clergy. Six hundred anti-Jacobin citizens petitioned the department for
the continuance of these chapel services. The Jacobin
society got the list from the department, and published
it as a kind of list of proscription. These citizens then
petitioned the king, protesting against their betrayal by
the department. A Jacobin admitted this petition to have
had more signatures than the petition to close the chapels
made by the Jacobins, but added "cela ne doit pas être
d'aucune considération" an interpretation of democratic
rule in 1791 already perfectly in accord with the principles of 1794. The department soon decreed the shutting
of the chapels. It then accepted the Jacobins' suggestion
that *capucins* be forbidden on the streets in the costume
of their order, that individually obnoxious priests be kept
away from their former parishes. The club was discussing
a law of deportation on the very day the law was voted
in Paris.[108]

The Jacobins were able to manipulate different administrative bodies partly, no doubt, because the combination of inexperience and traditional French sense of
hierarchy made members of one body only too delighted
to exercise their authority over another body. But the
Jacobins also had at least a minority of their own members on almost every administrative board, and their discipline over these members was absolute. It is the old,
but in democracies never worn, story of the determined
minority. The club at Chablis, discontented with an act
of the *procureur* of the town, a member of the club, summoned him to account. He refused to appear before the
club as before a tribunal. The club, regretting his refusal
to come before them as before brothers, suspended him

provisionally, and within two months he had apologized and was back in the club again. The reconciliation was celebrated by a fête to Marat, where all swore to "abjure on the tomb of the immortal Marat all the hatreds which divide us"—Marat dead playing a rôle of peacemaker which he certainly never played alive.[109] The president of the directory of the Haute Vienne signed an address not approved by the club of which he was a member. Under the censure of the club, he backed down completely, and publicly regretted his signature.[110] The Paris club was always insistent that the tradition of the Club Breton be kept up, and its members in the national assemblies were held to voting as a unit. Furthermore, the club would allow no slackers, and if absentee Jacobins permitted a ministerial victory, took pains to post the list of the absentees.[111] The club at Le Havre similarly kept firm hold of the national guard, the last asset of the Jacobins throughout France. It insisted its members do their guard duty regularly, and turned them out of the club if they missed three times without excuse.[112] Of course, the Jacobins did not neglect to get as many members as possible among the routine civil servants, though at first political ideas were rather against the spoils system or anything like it. The society at Bergerac, for instance, was duly exercised in conscience over recommending one of its members for a job in the departmental offices, but decided to support his application since his chief competitor was obviously not a good citizen.[113]

All appeals to official bodies failing, the Jacobins could always turn to their network of affiliated societies and their agencies for propaganda, and work upon what is called public opinion. The society of the Norman village of Manneville-la-Goupil, at the moment bearing the revolutionary name of Zèle-de-la-Patrie, having failed to prevail with a neighboring town council, sent out a public letter which deserves quotation in the original:

> The town government of "La Récompence ci-devant Hoquetot" had committed a certain crime, "délis qui est certainement atentatoire aux voix des sociétés populere dans les mains des quelles est le gouvernement républicain son affermissement, c'est les sociétés populere qui ont sonné la larme sur tous les entregants et les enemis de la révolution: la convention sentant le bezoin de déposer dans leurs mains la surveillance des corps constituez et celle de tous les citoyens." [114]

The society of Bourbon-Lancy found out that the administration of the district could not be made to do anything about the non-juring priests, so it sent out in its own name a circular to all the towns and clubs of the district urging them to survey the doings of their priests. The club was deeply hurt to learn that the district administration regarded this as an usurpation of power, and wrote at once to the Paris club to secure protection. The current was against the non-jurors everywhere, and the society eventually won out.[115]

One of the chief uses of the affiliation system, of course, was to organize the clubs in favor of some particular measure, and to bring pressure to bear upon the National Assembly by repeated petitioning. The growth of agitation against the orthodox clergy, for instance, is a case in point; so too are the frequent protests against the high property qualification necessary for office, the decree of the *marc d'argent*.[116] Again, an ambitious man who had failed to get himself elected to office could, by nursing the clubs, make a name for himself. Robespierre is a classic example of a man who owed almost everything to a club. The career of Kersaint is an even better example. He was consulted as a naval expert by the naval committee of the National

Assembly, but his plans were turned down. He took them at once to the Jacobins, where he secured a great success. This ensured his election to the Legislative Assembly, and launched him on his political career.[117] Finally, if the club were definitely defeated and suppressed by a turn of local politics, it could always use the methods of political conspirators everywhere. The radical *Club National* at Bordeaux was closed during the Girondin reaction. But meetings were held in the homes of its leading members, who, after agreeing on plans "scattered about in all the sections of the city, to enlighten their brothers and to persuade them out of their errors." [118] The Jacobins of Paris, though certainly not persecuted, could hardly bring about the fall of the monarchy by decree. Their activities in the sections undoubtedly helped, however, to make both June 20 and August 10 possible.[119]

All these means to power were used by the Paris club, and we have cited frequent examples from its records. But the position of the Paris club, especially in the years 1789-1792, was a peculiar one, and needs a few additional words. In brief, the Paris club was for a while a rival of the National Assembly, and one of the three bodies (Assembly, Paris Commune, and Jacobin Club) whose complex interaction determined the political events of the Revolution. In January 1792, a speaker at the Jacobins refers to the "old custom" of the Jacobins by which on a given day the question to be treated next day at the Assembly would occupy the order of the day at the Jacobins.[120] According to Lasource, this was actually provided for in the regulations of the club.[121] Even the famous night of the 4th of August was preceded by a discussion of the question of feudalism at the Breton Club on August third.[122] Similarly petitions are read, or denunciations made one day at the Jacobins, and very soon after come up in the Assembly.[123] Official bodies—town councils, district councils, and so on—corresponded with the Paris club as with an official parliament.[124] Sillery, representing the naval committee of the National Assembly, read its report to the Jacobins before he read it to the Assembly.[125] *Le Lendemain,* a journal hostile to the Jacobins, has in 1791 many items like this: "The National Assembly opened its session with 50 members, the Jacobin opened its session with 300, continued it with 700, and closed it with 400." [126] The Jacobin Club was indeed a replica of the National Assembly in more ways than one, to judge by a report like this: "Jacobin Club. Session of Monday, 12 July 1790. The order of the day included the establishment of a Supreme Court and the organization of the army. The first subject was not touched, the second barely begun. These important discussions were continually interrupted by addresses, deputations, etc., etc." [127]

The provincial societies, however, were quite as eager for power as the mother society, and in attempting to describe the relation between the societies and the authorities it is very hard to say when the societies are merely influencing the authorities, and when they are supplanting them. Certainly many instances can be collected in which the societies definitely take upon themselves the direct business of government. Negative evidence is afforded by the papers of the club of Pellegrue: "Letter from the administration of the district of La Réole to know whether the society imposed any taxes on individuals arrested or suspect. The president is charged to reply in the negative to this administration; the society never permitted itself any operation not in accordance with the law." [128] Obviously not every society had so confined itself. The little society of Cézy in the Yonne,

having summoned the town authorities in vain to give a
M. Le Vert a certificate of *civisme* (a very necessary
document in those days) wrote out an official certificate
for him on its own authority, and announced it was just
as good as the town's would have been.[129] The club of
Chablis, after learning that church services were still held
in certain villages, sent for their mayors to appear before
it to answer for this unrevolutionary state of things.
They all came, and humbly excused themselves, as the
people was "beaucoup fanatisé" in their communes.[130]
Quite on its own initiative, the club of Avallon named
five of its members to coöperate with the city government
in regulating the market.[131] The club at Toulon asked
categorically for the retirement of a rear-admiral and a
harbor master it disliked, and was obeyed by the naval
authorities. It then proceeded to volunteer a list of sea-
men worthy of promotion, which the minister, Monge,
promised to consult attentively.[132] The club at Chateauroux conducted a long warfare with the town authorities,
similar to those already described. The mayor attempted
to get hold of the registers of the club, but failed entirely,
though the club was forced to refuse to recognize his right
to requisition the registers.[133] The society at Tulle expressed its amazement that the new constitutional bish-
ops had chosen a vicar who did not belong to the society; within twenty-four hours the vicar had applied
for membership.[134] The club of Villeneuve-sur-Yonne
quarreled with a Colonel Ségur over a matter of disci-
plining a private soldier. The Colonel refused to have
anything to do with the club, and drew this indignant
protest upon himself: "M. le colonel Ségur committed an
indiscretion when he said he wasn't responsible for his
acts to the Friends of the Constitution; he committed an
error in saying that the city government alone had the

right to question him on this affair." [135] One understands
the despairing question of an official in the Jura ("the
most inept and most brutal of men," according to the
minutes of the club) who asked a deputation of the club
of Lons-le-Saunier "Is this another law passed by the
clubs?" [136]

V

There is one phase of Jacobin political tactics which
may here be very briefly indicated—their use of violence,
not merely of physical violence, but even more of that
sort of moral, symbolic violence which groups like the
Pataria, the Jacobins and the Ku Klux Klan have exercised throughout the history of the West. Violence in
both senses, however, is so woven into Jacobin methods
that we have already, though attempting to analyze other
aspects of the subject, given many examples of the use
of compulsion by the Jacobins. Need we again insist that
what really matters is the act itself, unique and incredibly composite, produced by a hundred cross-purposes
which yet were one purpose at a certain moment in time?
Our method, which does not even attempt to recapture,
as would narrative history, the time-sequence, but sub-
stitutes logic for time and tries to find similarities
(classes) instead of describing uniquenesses (events),
must at best proceed somewhat apologetically.

A few examples will perhaps help to bring out still
more clearly this quality of violence so important to Jacobin tactics. The mustache, like trousers, had come to be a
republican symbol, the mark of true virility as against the
smooth face and knee-breeches of the aristocrat. The club
of Rodez drew up in 1793 a list of 72 of the "sacrée
noblesse de chien reconnue en 1789" together with others
unworthy of wearing mustaches, and then ordered its

committee of surveillance to get any such persons who dared to assume this mark of manly privilege shaved "taking good care to get the job done without soap, and with the worst razor available."[137] There is undeniably a streak of cruelty in many Jacobin actions, sometimes, as in the above instance, an ingenious and youthful sadism, sometimes the high-minded cruelty of the persecutor. This last may be illustrated by a proposition of a member of the club Provins, that in the future witnesses and seconds at duels be branded on the cheek with the letters T.D. (*témoin duel*).[138] Jacobin humor, too, is often enough a grotesque conjuring up of impossible punishment for their enemies. Varlet proposed to the Paris club to get rid of non-jurors by "an exchange with the Barbary pirates, where for one European captive we should give them in exchange two priests." [139] Brother Schwartz at Strasbourg "told the club that there was at the civilian hospital an *émigré* afflicted with scurvy and asked that without waiting any longer he be guillotined to make his cure more prompt." [140] One of the favorite tricks of the Jacobins was to parade non-juring priests about the streets on asses, their faces towards the animals' rumps.[141] Even here, provincial traits come out in the Jacobins, so often supposed victims and victimizers in the leveling process of democracy. Where else but in Normandy could the following incidents have taken place? At St. Romain, the Montagnards obliged the moderate town council to cut down and burn the tree of liberty, planted by the moderates, by getting some boys to "dishonor" it. Then they took the charred remains of the tree and used them to mark the doors of their enemies, so as to guide the mob against them. At St. Jean de la Neuville, the triumphant Montagnards themselves cut down the tree of libery planted by their opponents "taking good care to make it fall in the direction of the prison where these citizens were held." [142]

Violence was, of course, not always so subtly, so metaphysically, emphasized. We have seen how often the Jacobins succeeded in evoking riots to get rid of their enemies. How much lies behind this simple postscript to a letter from the society of Alais! "P.S. The club called club of true Frenchmen will no longer be a subject of scandal and anxiety for all our good citizens. It was dissolved in the course of certain disturbances, by our city government, which has thus given us unequivocal proof of its patriotism." [143] At Cosne, late in 1793, the real Jacobins, though in a minority, entered the hall of the society and "energy more than making up for their small number," drove out the moderate members and constituted themselves the club.[144]

Jacobin violence, however, was not limited to rioting and hazing. It frequently took the form of an extraordinary and sometimes brutal interference with what in normal times we have come to think of as private concerns. A speaker before the club of Montaigut-en-Combrailles "found aristocratic pride too high, especially among the women. He proposed therefore to name a committee which should go at once to ladies who hold themselves aloof from the wives of artisans, workmen, and peasants, the most honorable of classes, and invite them to an Equality Ball." [145] "Invite" in this sense is a common Jacobin expression. At Auch, brother Pourquier suggested that women who dressed up on Sundays (the revolutionary calendar, substituting *décadi* for Sunday, was then in force) should be put to cleaning the streets.[146] The neighboring society of Condom actually petitioned the Convention "on the subject of wives of émigrés who to protect their property from confiscation have limited

themselves to divorcing, without re-marrying friends of
equality." [147] At Ars-en-Ré, a member asked the club
why Pierre Favereau, who was exempted from military
service for bad eyesight, "never missed the smallest bird
when out hunting." [148] So obvious a measure as boycott
was bound to occur to the Jacobins, and numerous examples could be cited. The Vedette, a Besançon newspaper, appears with this item: "The Society of Friends
of the Constitution expelled on Monday M. Dumont,
manufacturer of umbrellas, convicted of having specu-
lated on the depreciation of the *assignats;* consequently,
we ask all good citizens not to honor him any longer
with their patronage." [149]

Another indirect use of violence is to be found in the
pressure put upon individuals to subscribe to patriotic
loans, subscriptions, or gifts. Memories of other democratic wars may be revived by items like these:

> Citizen Bron is charged to keep an exact list of the names of
> citizens who refuse to subscribe for ships to invade England with,
> and to draw up a succinct account of their replies to the commis-
> sioners raising the fund." [150] Langelin grows indignant over the
> indecently small subscriptions towards the war-ship made by the
> aristocrats: at Suippes very rich people actually presumed to give
> ten or fifteen livres. The names of subscribers will be posted. [151]
> Borie, on mission at Limoges, told the club that the city could not
> arbitrarily tax the rich, "but he invited the club to send com-
> missioners to the homes of people of easy circumstances who have
> made no sacrifices since the Revolution. He assures the club that
> he and his colleague will do all they can to get these citizens to
> subscribe to present expenses of the government." [152]

Nor was this sort of pressure limited to financial matters. The Duke of Béthune-Charost, naturally enough a
vile aristocrat, had protected himself by getting the peasants on his country estate in the Eure-et-Loir to swear
him a certificate of residence. The club of Dreux, hearing

this, sent out commissioners and got nine of the peasants to withdraw their signatures.[153]

Finally, this pressure extends itself to public opinion, and makes possible that suppression of free speech by fear so well brought out in Anatole France's *Les Dieux ont soif*. The club of Rouen decreed in 1793 that the *comité de surveillance* be charged to pick a sufficient number of *patriotes* "to watch over public opinion in coffee-houses and other public places, and especially the development of conversations tending to weaken the revolutionary spirit." [154] The club of Rodez decided to "survey with the greatest care all printing-presses in town," in order to prevent the clericalists from printing pamphlets—and this early in 1791.[155]

VI

Yet it must not be assumed that the clubs, as corporations, were omnipotent in revolutionary France. Even in the period before 1793, when the clubs were pretty generally an advanced minority seeking to oust elected officials, there are many examples of clubs at peace with the government, and still more of inactive and unambitious clubs. After 1793, when the Jacobins were everywhere victorious, though leaders in the clubs get control of the machinery of government, the clubs themselves, as corporations, become very generally mere passive cogs in that machinery.

Peace was often patched up fairly early between the club and the city government, and though this usually comes after the triumph of the club's principles—or desires—it none the less means a reduction in actual agressiveness on the part of the clubs. At Toulon, after 1791, conflict between the city government and the club ceases.[156] At Rodez the city government and the club were hand in hand from the early days.[157] At Besançon the *Vedette* tells us that "there was a time when the governing authorities of this town did all they could to stifle the club, still in its cradle. . . . Today the magistrates of the people feel the necessity of establishing an harmonious agreement between themselves and the people." [158] And, of course, incidents like the following, where the club discreetly backs down, are not uncommon:

> A member announces that the city government has ordered M. l'abbé Gastandias to leave the city for the sake of public tranquillity. Another member moves that, as the conduct of the said abbé seemed suspicious, there be sent a deputation to the city council to ask it to have his home searched, as incendiary writings against the Constitution might be found there. Adopted. Ten commissioners were sent to the city hall and the city councillors present requested the demand be made in writing, which was done. The petition presented, the council asked for an hour to consider it. Their reply is that they do not think it wise to take such a step as to search the abbé's home. The club renounces the project. The members present all agree to observe strict secrecy about the whole matter.[159]

Furthermore, the club of Paris was by no means the ultimate authority it sometimes appeared to opposing pamphleteers. The National Assembly very frequently failed to accept the Jacobin program. The club, still in its infancy, seems to have decided in favor of trial by jury in civil cases as well as criminal. The assembly decided to limit the jury to criminal cases.[160] The Jacobins wanted to abolish all testamentary freedom where direct heirs existed, but the Constituante contented itself with putting bounds to the distribution *ab intestate* of an estate.[161] The Jacobins on 25 April 1791 were enthusiastically for the annexation of the Comtat Venaissin, yet on 4 May of that year the assembly voted against it.[162]

Many of the Jacobins' most cherished projects were realized only under the Convention.

There was even within the club itself a certain element of moderation, a feeling that the club ought not to behave too much like a parliament. Mirabeau, as president, once dared to call Robespierre to order for talking against a decree already passed by the National Assembly.[163] Thuriot in October 1791 urged the society not to listen to a deputation come to complain about the city government "for, said he, the society ought not to listen to anything against the governing authorities, since there are superior authorities, such as the department, to which complaints can be made." [164] It is true that the club did not usually follow these counsels of moderation.

Finally, the Paris club was reduced to comparative powerlessness in the assembly itself for some time after the break with the Feuillants, when a majority of the deputies left the Jacobins. There was a time when the club discussed what had happened the day before, or the morning before, in the National Assembly, instead of virtually preparing the morrow's agenda for the assembly.[165] That is, the club served as a rallying point for the temporarily beaten left, a means of meeting and keeping up their spirits. But although the Jacobin club in 1792 was a focal point of agitation, and extremely important in the overthrow of the monarchy, the actual work and intrigue was done in the Commune and in the sections. A rival parliament in the full sense to the assembly the Jacobin club was not in 1792, nor at any other time. It was a party headquarters.

When, with the overthrow of the Gironde in June 1793, the Jacobin party (which was also a sect) had destroyed all opposition outside its own ranks, the position of the clubs was greatly altered. All government officials, both elective and appointive, were for the moment of the same party; all were Jacobins. The Jacobin clubs, then, could not set about ousting their own government; they could not oppose their own political principles merely because they were triumphant. The clubs, if they were to continue at all, had somehow to be fitted into the government of France. They might, of course, have continued as what we now know as a political party; their actual organization, as a matter of fact, would with very little change have become a nationally organized series of fractional steering-committees like the *cartels* of the Third Republic. But these latter groups can exist only in a parliamentary state, and their whole function is to out-manoeuvre opposing groups in elections. In the Jacobin state, however, there were no parliamentary elections, no articulate opposition. The clubs had to be given something to do in the revolutionary government or languish.

This revolutionary government was itself, of course, the outcome of three years of struggle between the Jacobins and their opponents—royalists, constitutionalists, Feuillants, Girondins—and had been devised and manned by leaders trained in the clubs. A detailed description of this government would be out of place here. Suffice it to recall that by the autumn of 1793 a firmly centralized administration had been imposed upon the decentralized state set up by the constitution of 1791. The two great committees at Paris formed the head and center of the system. The Convention served well as a republican gesture, and provided the chief agents whereby the committees ruled the provinces. These representatives on mission were sent out on various errands, military and civilian. The ones which interest us chiefly are the representatives sent out to organize the revolutionary government in accordance with the laws of frimaire an II. These "proconsuls," after consulting with recognized patriots of a given town and usually after a public meeting of the local club, turned out of the elected councils, municipal, district, and departmental, all who were not certified good Jacobins, and arbitrarily filled their places with good ones. Each of these administrative bodies, which under the constitution of 1791 were linked to the central administration only by an elected *procureur* or *procureur général syndic*, was now assigned an *agent national*, chosen by the central administration and responsible to it. The representatives on mission also purified the personnel of the revolutionary committees (*comités de surveillance*) which formed a kind of special and very active political police attached to the Jacobin cause. Finally, they purified existing Jacobin clubs, where it seemed necessary, and took steps to form clubs in communities where they did not yet exist. Thus the Jacobin state—which its enemies have always maintained coincided with the Jacobin government—was set up. The clubs (*sociétés populaires*), the revolutionary committees, the municipal, district, and departmental administrations, the Convention, the Committee of General Security, the Committee of Public Safety formed an administrative hierarchy, a pyramid of which the clubs were the base. Within this hierarchy, none but Jacobins sworn and true; outside this hierarchy, the great majority of Frenchmen and French women.

The exact function of the clubs within this government is not easy to describe. Here, too, complexity defies classification. In theory, the clubs were spontaneously representative of the sovereign people; they were to make articulate the demands of the people, and to watch over those in office lest they betray their trust. To the more theologically minded Jacobins—including many, like

Robespierre, in high position—the clubs were indeed the people, the right-minded people, the elect, the only ones who could be allowed to be free in a free government. To less exalted but uncritical Jacobins, the clubs must have served to quiet questionings of conscience, to satisfy the longing honest men have, even in politics, to live up to their ideals. In reality, the clubs had many functions under the Terror; they were subsidiary administrative bodies, they provided a reservoir from which the new officialdom could be drawn, they served, within the limits of Jacobin orthodoxy, as an outlet for the opinions of the average Jacobin, and as a more or less democratic restraint upon the bureaucracy, and they made a center for the ritual of the new Jacobin religion. What sort of work the clubs did in the administration, what ideas guided them, what this new religion was, are all matters we must consider later. For the present, we are interested only in determining how far the clubs maintained their independence in this hierarchy, how real their corporate power was.

Certainly by contrast with their self-assertiveness against governing bodies before 1793, the clubs now seem pretty tame. It will not do to maintain the clubs ceased to badger government officials, to denounce and seek to oust those who offended them, to set themselves up as sovereign assemblies. But over all of France, there are after 1793 more examples to be found of Jacobin submissiveness to higher authority than of Jacobin claims to direct rule on the part of the clubs as corporate bodies.

To begin with, all men in office were now club members, and the prestige and experience of these official members was usually sufficient to restrain the more irresponsible private members. Many clubs on the frontier and in newly occupied regions were almost wholly made up of officials, civilian and military, sent in from old France to govern the new. But even in the interior, the proportion of club-members who held some position or other under the government, from that of *agent-national* to that of *concierge,* was very high. At Moulins, when Boisset, representative on mission, purified the society late in 1794, out of 183 members 99 were functionaries or elected officials. This proportion is not extraordinary, as the following examples will show: Toulouse, 103 officials out of 731 members; Castres, 107 officials out of 480 members; Albi, 81 officials out of 361 members; Brive, 84 officials out of 295 members; Metz, 61 officials out of 148 members. St. Jean de Maurienne, a small town in newly occupied Savoy, actually had 36 officials out of a membership of 39.[166] That membership in the clubs was not always a voluntary step of the official is indicated by the following entry in the minutes of the club of Thonon: "It is found surprising that citizen Appy, member of the revolutionary committee is not registered as a member of the club, and it is decided to invite (that favorite Jacobin word again) him to resign if he does not put himself up for membership." Appy immediately took steps to join the club.[167]

In the construction of the new revolutionary government, the clubs seem at first sight to have played a decisive part. As a matter of fact, a close reading of the correspondence of the representatives on mission who were charged with making over local government makes it evident that almost everywhere the representative consulted a local ring—club-members, it is true—and that the official meeting before the "people" or the club was a mere matter of form.[168] Furthermore, the representative often purified [169] the club before he permitted it to pass on the continuation in office of the various administrative bodies. Merely from Aulard's great collection, it is clear that the representatives usually dominated the clubs. Garnier writes from Alençon that "the virtuous sansculottes who had been turned out of the society now have in it free scope for their energies. In the fear lest it become again what it was, I am going to take the vigorous but necessary resolution to exclude forever from this society those former members who are on my list of proscription." [170] Féraud writes from Mauléon how the society had taken up the defense of some suspects arrested at his order. "At once," he continues, "I went to the meeting of the society, which was very numerous; I spoke like a Republican, I enlightened it, and I told it that I knew my duty and the execution of the law, and that I should perish rather than compromise, and I refused the society's request. The people applauded, and asked of its own free will for the punishment of the guilty ones." [171] Laurent writes of the clubs of Douai and the Nord: "In general, the system of denunciations seems too established in these meetings, which are busied only with veiled recriminations and personal hatreds. I wrote you recently that they also want to see what's in our arsenals, and to talk about it in public. I have opposed this sort of thing in Douai with success. The club passed in these respects wise measures." [172] The representatives sometimes found the clubs acting independently, and lording it over the authorities, but they took good care to remedy matters, and restore discipline. Lefiot described his difficulties in the Morvan: "The *société populaire* of Clamecy was led to annul on its private authority a decree of the town council of Clamecy. . . . The society pronounced itself arrests which were made on its own premises. . . . I was obliged to take my position against such violations of principles." [173] Mallarmé found the society of Longwy extremely corrupt and threatened to dissolve it. "But the *patriotes*," he writes, "promised me to get adopted an austere method of purification and political vomiting—to expel heterogeneous elements and remake the society out of more homogeneous and more healthy elements." [174] Occasionally one finds from the milder representatives reports like this from Bentable: "I purified the governing authorities without making any great changes, but I followed here, as everywhere, the wishes of the *sociétés populaires* and their revolutionary committees." [175] Yet even in such circumstances, the real work was probably done in consultation with local leaders. Three representatives write from Bernay: "We called to us the citizens best known for their revolutionary energy to consult with them on the changes which are necessary in the governing authorities and *to give us information about the spirit which prevails in the société populaire*." [176] Ingrand writes the Committee: "I have just come from a meeting held with representatives of the society and the members of the revolutionary committee; this meeting lasted nine hours, and the results I obtained prove to me that the people of Niort have been influenced by intriguers and counter-revolutionaries." [177] After this meeting, the rest was no doubt a pretty easy matter.[178]

Nor do the societies commonly take such a high hand with local authorities as before the Terror. There is to be found in the city records of Amiens a curious passage between the society and the city council late in 1793, a passage symptomatic of the new courage of city councils in general. The society asked the council for a list of the intriguers who, in the council's opinion, were still to be found within the society; then the society would return the compliment, and tell the council just what councilors ought to be held to be intriguers. The council suggested the society begin denouncing first. But when the society denounced a councilor named Sellier, the city council stood behind him, and refused to let him resign at the behest of the society. The *procureur* is actually recorded as observing that "a private society had no right to pass decrees relative to public officials, especially decrees putting them under the necessity of ceasing their functions." [179] The *agent national* of Carcassonne seems to have had the society of that town pretty well under his control. He used the society to provide commissioners to carry out various duties—requisitions for the army, censuses of food supply, inspection of special government services—but he very carefully prevented these commissioners from going beyond routine work.[180] And yet, when the society timidly petitioned Chaudron-Rousseau, representative on mission, in favor of a prisoner, he dissolved it and presided at its regeneration. The *agent national* calmly reports the incident "A fault committed by the *société populaire* of Carcassonne against the revolutionary government—in receiving evidence in favor of a citizen arrested by order of the representative of the people, has provoked from this representative a vigorous measure; the society is dissolved." [181] Carrier closed the society of Nantes for three days simply because one of its members had ventured to reply to a bitter attack of Carrier's against the city.[182]

Sometimes local bodies, even when unaided by the august power of representatives of the people, deal severely with the pretensions of the societies. The district of Auxerre in the spring of 1794 maintained a requisition of thirty *bichets* of grain against a member of the club of Mailly-le-Vieux, even though that club had issued an "edict" to the contrary. The district invited the club "to abstain from passing decrees on purely administrative matters." [183] The society at Dreux got into a long quarrel with the local authorities over the appointment of members of the revolutionary committee. According to the society, which apparently had no illusions about universal suffrage, it possessed "the exclusive and irrevocable right of choosing one of its own members directly as member of the revolutionary committee." [184] It chose a member, but the committee refused to receive him, and after many appeals, and threats to go to Paris about the matter, the society apparently let the thing drop. Public authorities even before the Terror had known how to stave off importunate societies, and they did not hesitate to do so now. The society of Le Havre asked Siblot, representative on mission, to order citizens who had gone into the country to come back to the city. Siblot replied that the step would be a trifle unusual, and asked time to consult with the Committee of Public Safety about it. He thus gained time to postpone and eventually to refuse the request.[185] The club of Noyers had to put up with the presence at each session of two delegates from the town council and two from the revolutionary committee sent to "keep account of what may be said and done in these sessions, and the various opinions there delivered." [186] The club of Montbard, reorganizing itself in the spring of 1794, meekly submitted its new rules to the town council, which objected to several articles. These the club at once removed. (They were provisions that the club exercise a general supervision over schools, that it criticize freely public authorities, that members of the departmental or district councils be ineligible for membership in the club.)[187]

But there is worse than this. Sometimes a club seems positively supine under the Terror; sometimes a club is attacked by a strange inertia, as if its general will had tired itself by over-exertion. Often enough, of course, the failure of a club to get its way is perhaps not wholly its fault. But the ideal Jacobin club—the Jacobin club of most local historians—would have hounded on the laziest of local authorities to action. The club at Lille was much concerned over the necessity for an improved public slaughter-house, and petitioned the city government several times on the subject. The slaughter-house was built in 1826.[188] The club of Castelnau-Rivière-Basse had petitioned the town council about the water supply, but nothing had been done for months when the matter was brought up again in June 1794, apparently without better success.[189] Clubs all over France kept insisting on the destruction of churches, or at least of the more idolatrous parts of churches, and though they unfortunately succeeded often enough, they still more often failed, as, for instance, at St. Jean de Maurienne, where the *clocher* survived innumerable petitions for its destruction.[190] So too at Le Havre the society reiterated to the city council a request that *Temple de la Raison* be inscribed over Notre Dame du Havre-de-Grace, that the goddess of Reason be placed in the interior, and the hideous forms of fanaticism be removed from the church and destroyed. The city council seems to have won out by doing nothing.[191]

Even towards their own members, and in their own internal policies, the clubs sometimes failed to display that heroic firmness usually attributed to them. They were always threatening, and not always carrying out their threats. This is particularly true of measures against members who failed to attend regularly. The minutes of almost every club are filled with proposals to expel those guilty of three successive absences; but these proposals are so often repeated that it is clear that their adoption was rarely followed by action. One club, after voting to exclude absentees, continued by voting to exclude all those who should leave a given session before its close. For the same session, the secretary notes, after the public reading of newspapers: "Claude est sorti; Charles est sorti." [192] The registers of another club contain this illuminating entry:

> A member asked that citizen François Horeau be required to go and join the army as subject to the draft.
>
> Another asked that citizen Horeau be excluded from the society.
>
> A third, that the municipality be invited to make him depart at once for the army.
>
> From these different propositions, there was no result. [193]

At least one society was so apathetic that it allowed itself to be purified by the local town government. This was too much for the *agent national* of the district, who referred the whole matter to the society of the important neighboring town of Colmar. [194]

To the list of societies which, as groups, showed during the Terror little genuine initiative or independence must be added almost all the rural societies. For the study of the political consciousness of the French peasantry, as well as of the beginnings of the characteristically modern aspects of sectionalism in France, the papers of these village societies, and even the mere established fact of their existence, are of great importance. But to the development of Jacobinism itself they seem to have made no contribution. Certainly they added nothing to Jacobin tactics. Their members were so ill-educated, so unused to abstract words, to political intrigue, to group action that these clubs never really had a corporate life, for they never committed any act of corporate aggression. Again, we can but choose from numbers of clubs examples which seem typical.

At Fleury-lès-Faverney, a purely agricultural village in the Haute Saône, with a population of 354, a society was founded on 1 November 1793. Its total membership was 53, rather over half the adult male population. Its proceedings cover a period of 18 months, and are contained in a sort of schoolboy's note-book of which twenty-seven pages are written on. The whole municipality—mayor and town council—were members of the club, and the few decrees of the club (mostly concerning price fixing) are countersigned "Nous maire et officiers municipaux de la commune de Fleury-lès-Faverney approuvons le présent arrêté." [195] At Vaulry in the Haute Vienne, a little town of eight hundred or so, the register of the society was kept by its president, Imbert, *agent national* for the place, and one of its few intellectuals. On one side of each sheet of the book are to be found the proceedings of the club, on the other the deliberations of the municipality, both in the same hand. Here too there are no signs that the club asserted itself.[196] The society of Arre, a village in the Gard, when required during the Thermidorian reaction to turn over its papers to the government drew up a paper wherein it said: "We, the members of the *société populaire* of the commune of Arre—certify and attest that our society has existed for 17 months, and still exists. We have no registers it is true, but at the time of formation a list was drawn up for members to sign. Not having had to deal with any matters of consequence, we have not kept a register." [197] For eighteen months in 1793 and 1794, this society dealt with nothing of consequence! [198]

VII

The Jacobin clubs, then, when they cease to be in opposition to a government and a bureaucracy wholly manned by their own members, cease to practice the tactics associated with their name. With regard simply to political practice, and omitting that aspect of Jacobinism which makes it a religion, one may say that in general the final rôle of the clubs as such is that of auxiliary administrative bodies. Such bodies have their uses, especially in time of war, and the clubs in this rôle did work not unlike that of the Red Cross, the Y. M. C. A., and various volunteer citizen committees in the late war. Much of the less responsible work of raising supplies for the armies, requisitioning food stuffs, policing markets to insure the observation of the *maximum*, and other economic activities were entrusted by public authorities to the clubs, and carried out by delegates or committees of these latter.[199] Many of the clubs did the sort of thing we are familiar with as the work of civic improvement associations; that is, they pressed upon the authorities, and sometimes got carried out, various projects of purely local interest. Most of the clubs, at least in the larger cities, were active in the distribution of charity.

An analysis of all these activities, a list of all the things the clubs did or tried to do, would fill several books. We can but run hastily over some of the records. All the clubs were set by the Committee of Public Safety to work gathering saltpetre for ammunition making. Possibly the Committee wanted to give the clubs something to do to take their minds off more controversial matters. At any rate, clubs all over France were soon engaged under the leadership of those of their members most versed in chemistry, in getting saltpetre by wash-

ing out "stables, sheep-cotes, wine-presses, wine-cellars,
sheds, etc., etc." [200] Just how much saltpetre was produced it is unfortunately impossible to estimate. The club
of Chablis purchased and distributed grain for sowing in
vineyards spoiled by a severe and unseasonable frost; [201]
the same club sent out a member into an adjoining department to buy potatoes during the food scarcity of
1794, and distributed them at cost price to the "peuple
des tribunes." [202] The club at Le Havre appointed commissioners to aid General Beaulieu, at his own request,
in plans for coast defense; [203] that of Toulouse on the
invitation of the municipality named six of its members
to guard the local artillery park. [204] As early as 21 March
1793, the society of Gray, with the consent of the municipality, divided the city into sixteen quarters, named a
commissioner for poor relief in each quarter, and provided for a distribution of grains at a reduced price. [205]
The club of Millau undertook to teach the peasantry
scientific farming, and its members reported at length on
such subjects as the improvement of cattle raising and
the use of artificial fertilizers. [206] Even the rural societies
were given some administrative work. The club of Fleuryles-Faverney in Franche-Comté appointed, after receiving a circular from the minister of the interior, three
commissioners to aid the municipality in checking up on
pensions "deûs aux veuves, pères et mères des deffen-
ceurs de la patrie." [207]

The club of Montbard appointed a special committee
to go about the near-by villages and find out directly
what effects the speculative operations of a certain Hugot,
who had attempted a local corner on wool, had really had
on prices. The committee were honest enough to report
that evidence was extremely conflicting, and suspended
judgment—surely not the way Taine's Jacobins would

have acted.[208] One club appointed a committee which examined carefully the town fire apparatus, and reported that only trifling repairs were necessary.[209] The club at Blaye appointed a committee to study what we should now call the problem of civic improvement. It reported in favor of moving the post-office to a site nearer the center of the town, establishing a weather-bureau at Blaye, repairing roads, and cleaning up the fair grounds.[210] The club at Le Havre took upon itself the rewarding of heroism, and at one of its sessions publicly recognized the courage of some sailors who had saved fifteen lives when a ferry overturned; this same club carried its solicitude for the humble so far that it occupied itself with securing better accommodations for transient seafaring men.[211] Public hygiene frequently occupied these clubs, even in the villages, and is one of the very definitely modern things about them. At Aiguesmortes, for instance, the society invited the municipality "to have all citizens remove waste and dung-heaps in their yards, in order to make the air more salubrious, and also to have those citizens whose wells have filled up re-dig them again, in order that there may be plenty of good water." [212] The club at Toulouse was very exercised over poor sanitation and careless nursing in local hospitals, especially in those taken over for the army, and urged the abandonment of one as "infect et malsain." [213]

Education too gave the Jacobins as much concern as it gives public-spirited citizens to-day. The rules of the society of Pont-à-Mousson provide for a committee on instruction "which shall have general supervision of public education, which shall give an account to the society of abuses or faults which it shall discover, and which shall propose means of remedying these faults." [214] The clubs fairly commonly took upon themselves the examination and certification of candidates for teaching positions under the new system of education decreed in principle by the National Assembly, but never really put into practice.[215] Discussion of candidates, where, as in large towns, they were numerous, was often warm and not impersonal. At Le Havre, each candidate was obliged to appear in person before the club, and answer any questions as to his morals, civic virtue and talents. A member suggested, indeed, that the club limit itself to discussing the virtues, public and private, of candidates, but the general opinion prevailed that the club "ought not to pass lightly over the question of talents." [216] The club of Moulins took upon itself to recommend the establishment of a museum from the spoils of near-by châteaux.[217]

Charity, too, was usually a concern of the clubs, and with the breakdown of the customary distribution of charity by religious groups, this function became very important. No doubt political expediency as well as eighteenth century benevolence went into Jacobin charity, but without affecting its reality. Hardly a register fails to mention some charitable activity. The club of Toulouse, while perhaps rather more than usually busy in this way, is not untypical. We find from the books of its *comité de bienfaisance* that it distributed bread twice a *décade* according to a list of needy persons, gave a suite of furniture to the widowed mother of a soldier, experimented with a machine to chop horse fodder finer, and with a machine to dry linen at the military hospitals, provided for daily registration of deaths at these hospitals, and the proper notification of relatives, got an honest job for an ex-priest, supported a nine-year old orphan who had somehow got lost in Toulouse. Nor is all this merely charity on paper. From the books of the club itself, it is clear that in one month, for instance (from

17 pluviôse an II to 16 ventôse) ninety-six people received free bread from the club. Furthermore, the club gave fifteen virtuous young women of republican inclinations a dowry of 1000 livres apiece to enable them to marry and produce "little republicans for the Fatherland." [218]

All sorts of private business finds its way into the club, some of it hardly of historical importance. For the clubs, which were in a way clearing houses for almost everything, actually are at times bureaux of information. Citizen Année of the Harfleur club asked the club of Le Havre for information about his son, who had enrolled in the Havre volunteers, and had not written to his father since. The same society was asked by J. J. Lapalme to get him the means of traveling back to North America; and the soldiers quartered at Le Havre complained to the society that they have actually to be in barracks at 6 P. M., though the law gives them till 9.[219] Another society was requested to get the local ferryman to be more attentive to travelers, who often called him in vain from the farther shore.[220] The papers of another show this entry: "A letter from the society of Vesoul invites that of Moulins to look for a lost package belonging to citizeness— which she thinks she left at the inn of citizen Roux before she took the coach." [221] The club of Toulouse, at the request of some busybody, appointed a special committee to see that a certain citizen Chanzolles did justice to his illegitimate daughter.[222]

Something, indeed, of the curious complexity of modern group life, a collectivism of fact which has for well over a century underlain modern theoretical individualism comes out from a study of these Jacobin papers. Sanitation, bread lines, public schools and school teachers are surely modern enough. One is tempted to distinguish, in the Jacobin clubs of the brief period of their triumph, a sort of undifferentiated nucleus in which it is possible to see in embryo those quasi-public groups which do so much to make modern life unbearable for more robust spirits—Parent Teacher's Associations, Societies for the Prevention of Cruelty to Animals, Salvation Armies, Chambers of Commerce, Rotary Clubs, and so on indefinitely, even in non-Anglo-Saxon countries. The marginal résumés which guide the reader through the very neat books of the Toulouse club produce in themselves an astonishing impression of this all-pervading activity. Here they are for a single session, that of 11 ventôse an II:

> Motion on the subject of fowl for the hospitals—offering from the commune of Paullac—commissioners to the municipality on the subject of prostitutes—reading of addresses to the Convention by the society of Villemur—address concerning old age pensions referred to a committee—motion of order—diploma—notice instructing the public to take their certificates of *civisme* to the *comité de surveillance*—reading of a letter from Montsarrasin (Castelsarrasin)—commissioners to request changing names of squares and *faubourgs*—affiliation requested—reading of an address from the society of St. Omer—news—letter from Langantier on the suppression of revolutionary committees in rural communes—diploma—Reynier dead at Perpignan—*civisme* of his nephew, citizen Reynier, attested to—nomination of commissioners for distribution of corn—decree on the subject of fowl repealed—deliberation of the commune on objects of first necessity—entry to sessions for young citizens.[223]

Yet it is not by insisting on either the omnipotence or on the efficiency of these clubs, considered as active instruments of political action, that we shall close this chapter. Jacobin political strength has perhaps been sufficiently described; Jacobin weakness in practical politics is not merely a result of the impracticality of their aims;

it is, more fundamentally, a result of the inadequacies of their methods. Successful as agents for propaganda and for electoral intrigue, the clubs were failures as administrative bodies. Even before thermidor, many clubs suffered serious drops in attendance. In the drama of the struggle for the great Revolution, there had been interest enough to hold the spectator—that is, the average club-member. In the details of administration, there was no obvious drama, and a very obvious responsibility.

"For a long time the meetings of our society have been cursed with a kind of sterility which alarms good citizens." Thus begins an editorial in the Besançon *Vedette* in the summer of 1794, and continues to reproach the society with having done nothing to teach patriotism in the countryside, nothing to carry out laws and decrees of the revolutionary government, nothing to ruin fanaticism, nothing even to keep up correspondence with Paris.[224] But for similar criticisms one need not go beyond club records. "Our registers, remarks a member, are full of the best decrees, the execution of which would no doubt contribute to the public good, but I see with regret that they are not followed up, and that almost all of them remain buried in neglect." [225] Even at Paris, Terrasson "complains that the measures adopted by the society are not put into execution," a complaint repeated next day by another member.[226]

Jacobin activity, indeed, does not measure up to Jacobin ambitions, or even to Jacobin curiosity. The various committees set up to help the revolutionary government did not always work well. The municipality of Carcassonne wrote twice to the society of that town, complaining of the inactivity of the society's *comité des subsistances,* and reproaching it with a lack of warmth.[227] This same club, like many others, was intrusted with the task of giving visas to *certificats de civisme*. The municipality writes it late in 1793: "The citizens hereafter listed have been inscribed at the city hall and their names posted on the door, both here and at the *société populaire*, for from 15 to 20 days, without your having given us any information whatever about their *civisme*—You will oblige us, citizens, if you will busy yourselves at once with these visas, in order not to delay longer citizens who are urgently requesting these certificates." [228] The club at Le Havre, indeed, was reluctant to appoint commissioners from its ranks to help draw up a departmental grain census, and refused to do anything until it learned that the representative on mission, Siblot, had ordered it to do the work.[229] Here again there is no use piling up instances. Time and again the reader will find in the records of these clubs passages like the following, perhaps a bit extreme in its spelling, but not in its very human and very democratic irresponsibility.

> On a ensuitte passé à la discussion de la petition qui devai être présentée à la munisipalité tandente à faire disparaitre tout les signes de féodalite qui etait encore dans le Scimtière et dans l'église aussy que pour les invité à continué à faire dépose les grains dans la alle au couvent des cidevant Hurselines, et que la Société les proposait de les assisté dans leurs operations, un des commissaires a dit qu'il ne s'était pas encore acquitté de leur mission mais qu'il san acquiterait le plus prontement posible.

This step had been decided on a week before, and it was to be another week before the commissioners "acquitted themselves of the matter with the greatest possible promptness." [230]

CHAPTER V

PLATFORM

I

Towards what purposes were Jacobin tactics directed?
The answer might well be that each Jacobin had his own
purposes, his own desires. Such an answer, however,
would have the serious difficulty of making the new history wholly impossible, not merely as a science, but as an
art. We must make some effort to draw up a kind of platform acceptable to the Jacobins who have left these records behind them. At one time, it might have been possible to call this chapter, "The Political Ideas of the Jacobins." But, quite apart from the fact that one does not
dare nowadays attribute a capacity for entertaining abstract thought to the man in the street, such a title would
hardly answer our purpose. For it is pretty clear to us
nowadays that political ideas and party platforms are
not identical. The school of Taine is amply justified in
attributing to the formal political philosophy of the
eighteenth century an important part in Jacobinism. But
if we start with a study of these philosophical elements in
Jacobinism we run the risk of falling into the error of
Taine, that of attributing to the Jacobins as an actual
living political group a rigidity which they may not always, in the face of the event, have possessed. Under the
headings of ritual and faith, then, we may study those
elements of Jacobinism Napoleon liked to damn under
the name of ideology. In the present chapter we must

simply ask ourselves what did the Jacobins, as far as we can learn from their own words, seek in the way of concrete and personal satisfaction from their party? We shall for the moment forget eighteenth century philosophy, and consult the records of the clubs.

Now the terms, platform, ritual, faith which we have used to express different aspects of Jacobinism as a living abstraction, as an object of human loyalty, have all three this in common, that they are concerned with the indirect, or corporate, satisfaction of men's desires. Examples are perhaps necessary to make this clear. X has an empty belly and a shabby wardrobe. He joins a Jacobin club with a clear, self-acknowledged desire to profit by his membership. He gets a good fat government position. Now this is a fairly simple case where a man directly satisfies a personal physical want by entering politics. Y, who also has an empty belly and a shabby wardrobe, joins a Jacobin club with a vague hope of getting a better lot. He gets no direct satisfactions. But he can vote for his deputy (platform), he can kiss the bust of the martyred Marat (ritual), and he can rejoice in his "purity" as a Jacobin (faith). Whether or not these two kinds of satisfactions, which we shall call the concrete and the abstract, correspond to two different kinds of desires is a matter we can hardly debate here. Nor does it matter very much to our argument. For assuming that certain simple wants of the sort we have called concrete (any sociologist will list them for you) do rule ordinary men, it is clear that they cannot get concrete satisfaction for themselves in this world. X has a good job out of politics, but even in democracies there are many more men than jobs. Y, not X, is the Jacobin we must study.

This whole point about the vicarious satisfaction afforded by politics, the place of slogans, patriotism, stereotypes, is important here. For although political philosophers and sociologists have long considered the subject, and have now arrived at a very encouraging state of skepticism about it, historians, and in particular historians of the French Revolution, have unduly neglected it. Of late years, the doctrine of the economic interpretation of history has been very ably applied to the French Revolution. Now, if a certain crudeness of statement can be pardoned, it is clear that the doctrine of economic interpretation says virtually that ordinary men are ruled by wants of the sort we have just called concrete, and that they seek in politics as in other activities for concrete (i.e. "economic") satisfactions. The less able of the school of economic interpretation seem to go on the assumption that everything human beings have done has had an economic motive, and that once that motive has been discovered one can forget all about the thing done. The abler members of the school will grant that men have as individuals certain ideas, moral codes, idealisms not too obviously dependent on economic motives; so too men in groups find these ideas, laws, morals, idealisms existing in the group. But these abstractions are quite unimportant. They are drawn up to salve men's consciences. They are unconscious bits of hypocrisy. Men are really moved to act only by economic motives. One can, with Pareto, assume an individual, a, and draw one line, a-b, to indicate his "ideals" and another, a-c, *at right angles* to indicate his real desires. The two lines have no point save "a" in common.

All this is not unreasonable, particularly as a generalization that does not exclude the freak, the sincere idealist. That men often act according to interest and believe according to conscience was a truth known to many

Christians before Pareto. The error of the orthodox followers of economic interpretation is to assume that only
the economic motives actively influence men and their
history. Pareto himself was wiser. He knew that the
whole abstract, ideal, fictitious portion of human desires
and achievements had an influence on the concrete desires and passions of men, and on their *actions*. Para-
doxically, it may even be true that our modern times,
when the doctrine of economic interpretation was discovered, lend themselves least to its use in its too simple
form. For, if economic motives are concrete, personal
motives, motives that must work themselves out in direct, immediate conflict, motives that demand realiza-
tion in sensation, then the modern state is much less
suited to their free and natural play than the ancient
or feudal state. For politics and political life are now
abstractions to most citizens. The personal economic
benefit to be obtained from any political action is by
no means always clear to the citizen called upon to
judge it. Local politics may continue to allow the inter-
play of economic motives. In the modern nation-state,
economic motives work chiefly through parliamentary
intrigue and in administrative boards—that is, in the
old way, among people who know each other. Great questions of national policy, however, war, education, religion, seem curiously dependent on the pooled emotions of the ordinary man, and but little on his economic
interests.

The student of the Jacobin clubs cannot, then, content himself with the formula that the Jacobins were
above all engaged in the class-struggle. Let us assume
that by class-struggle is meant the process of lifting the
physical standards of life of a given group, against the
opposition of another group, or other groups. Then,

failing to achieve this end, the Jacobins could yet give
some satisfaction to their members in their platform,
their ritual, and their faith. Moreover, it is worth considering whether this abstract side of Jacobinism did not
itself effect changes in the concrete side of Jacobinism.
In other words, we must try and decide whether, his-
torically, Jacobinism is finally best described as a phase
of the class-struggle or not. We shall, then, be constantly preoccupied, in our study of the Jacobin platform, Jacobin ritual and faith, with the problem of
relating these abstractions to the living, tangible, Jacobin
and his concrete "economic" motives.

II

Before we attempt to see what, if anything, the
Jacobins promised their members in that other, and
perhaps better, world where common sense and the senses
are properly subordinated, let us see what they promised them in the world empiricists and idealists alike
seem willing to call "this" world. For a platform, though
it is not in itself a personal, concrete satisfaction, is at
least the promise of such a satisfaction. It is one degree
nearer to what we may call individual *interests* than a
ritual or a faith. There is no single authoritative Jacobin
platform, and we can but group under certain headings
—political, social, economic—the kind of demand most
frequently on the lips of our Jacobins.

The first thing the Jacobin asked of his state was that
it be under a republican form of government. The phrase
is American, but it applies perfectly to French history.
Its negative content was more important than its posi-
tive content. The Jacobin wanted no hereditary ruler,
no hereditary nobility. Mere birth must give no position

whatever in the government. Circumstances soon obliged
the Jacobin to define the government of the republic
more positively. But on one important point the Jacobin
was as clear as any modern republican. "Let us not con-
found" wrote a member of the society of Clermont-Ferrand, "the *republic,* or *common thing,* with *democracy*
or *popular government.*" [1] Jacobins might differ very
much as to the proper degree of democracy desirable,
particularly in economic life, but all were republicans.

At the basis of the republican state is the sovereign
people. "There is only one legitimate authority, that of
the people in its simplicity; it alone is good because the
people, who exert it, is both active and passive, can
strike only the people itself, and therefore is sure of
falling, if it goes wrong." [2] As political theory, this is
perhaps a bit naïve, but it is clear. Now, though certain
societies accepted the imposition of property qualifications for voting under the first constitution, the clubs
as a whole protested, and Jacobinism very soon identified
itself with *political* democracy to the extent of championing universal manhood suffrage. [3]

As to the government elected by universal suffrage,
the Jacobin had definite ideas. In spite of the centralization of the Terror, there remained in Jacobin politics a
certain strain of Montesquieu—or at least, a certain distrust of a strong executive power. It is too easy to say
that the Jacobin trusted a Jacobin executive and distrusted all others; moreover, the Jacobins were longer
out of power than in it, so that their normal attitude is
perhaps one of distrust. The strong executive is a part
of Jacobin tactics, and a main feature of the Jacobin
legend; it is not a part of the Jacobin platform.

The doctrine of the separation of powers appears in a
hundred forms. It may be true that the doctrine is

merely a mask for Jacobin hatred of the actual executive. But it was a mask that helped to mold the features
underneath it. Power in 1790-91 was so subject to checks
and balances that it disappeared. Barnave told the Paris
club in 1791 that local authorities should not be allowed
to call out the militia of neighboring districts in times
of crisis without consulting the department, which in
turn must consult the legislature at Paris.[4] Another
member was so obsessed by the theory of the separation
of powers that he was forced to provide for cases of
impeachment by erecting a special committee of legislators, who, once the trial was over, should satisfy the
dogma of separation of powers by dropping out of the
legislature for the rest of the session.[5]

Not only are the different branches of the government
to check each other. Private citizens, especially when
organized as friends of the constitution, or of liberty
and equality, must keep an eye on the branches of government. "Unity of power is in the nation; the emana-
tions of this unique power are the different powers which
make up the different kinds of administration. The more
you multiply these powers, the more you restrain them,
and they will be the more easy to watch over and control, the less extensive they are." [6] The club of Beauvais
asked for public sessions of all governing bodies as early
as the spring of 1791, and quoted Rousseau in support:
"Tout corps dépositaire de la puissance exécutive tend
fortement and continuellement à subjuguer la puissance
législative, et y parvient tôt ou tard." [7] Ministries were
especially loathed for their associations with the past.
The club of Tulle was asked to back up that of Angers
in requesting the National Assembly "to take in its wis-
dom measures to preserve us from ministerial corruption." [8] The famous petition of the Cordeliers in June

1791 contains good republican theory: no one ought to be powerful enough to corrupt; no position in the government should be inaccessible to any citizen; the more a position in the government is important, the shorter should be its tenure. From this, of course, it follows that royalty is impossible.[9]

As for the legislative, and indeed all other elected servants of the people, they are to be kept closely to account. Bicameral government, tainted with English moderantism, is rejected. Jacobinism everywhere is associated with the single chamber.[10] The Jacobin definitely holds that his representative must fulfill the wishes of his electors, and not set himself up as an independent judge. "The society, penetrated with these natural and undeniable principles, that all men are free and equal, that political associations are the sole judges of the laws which should rule them, that the rulers are but their mandatories, on such conditions and for such a period as pleases them——." [11] Thus begins an indignant protest of the club of Lons-le-Saunier against executive tyranny in 1790. From this, the recall is an easy assumption, and one made by certain Jacobins, though it was never formally worked into an organized scheme of government. The club at Limoges, after long discussion, decided to support the suggestion of the Paris club that deputies who voted for an appeal to the people in the trial of Louis XVI be recalled. A member "expressed his astonishment that one should find it dangerous for the people to withdraw from its unworthy mandatories the powers it had given them" and added "let us not wait before recalling them, until certain of our deputies have caused further evils." [12] The club of Arnay-sur-Arroux proposed "a law which would require the representatives of the people, at the end of each session, to give a strict account of their actions to their constituents, to receive rewards if they have served well the commonweal, or death if they have conspired against liberty, sacrificed the interests of the nation and attacked the rights of the people." A national jury, composed of members chosen one in each department by universal suffrage, should try the deputies in this fashion.[13]

Under such a government, the obvious duty of good Jacobins was obedience. The Jacobins would afford to the common people an exemplary spectacle of republican devotion to law and order. "Order was the first need of men in their primitive societies, order alone sustains them, and the friends of liberty and equality ought in their assembly to give the salutary example of order to their fellows."[14]

The Jacobin republic then, will be based on popular sovereignty expressing itself through universal suffrage. Legislative, executive, and judicial powers will be duly separated. The executive will be properly subordinate to the legislative, will be chosen for short terms, and will preferably be in commission. Save for clerks and other subordinates, all government officials will be elected, and subject to recall in some way or other. The legislative body will be unicameral, and the deputies merely servants chosen to carry out the desires of their constituents. Even the judiciary will limit itself to deciding with perfect objectivity what the law is; the judge will put nothing of himself into his decisions.[15]

Such was a republican form of government to the Jacobin. But there is one master characteristic of the Jacobin republic which no commentator has left untouched—centralization. The republic, one and indivisible, was to be ruled from Paris. Local liberties, local initiatives, if they differed from the purposes of Jacobin

Paris were wrongly directed, and if they did not differ,
were superfluous. Expressions of this desire for centralization are common enough. It appears as a theory of
sovereignty: "What really makes the sovereign is the
union of all members of the state acting and deliberating
together. To divide this sovereign is to destroy it. It can
only produce a legal and legitimate opinion when it is
formed into a single assembly. Diverse wills, manifested
in partial assemblies, are often very different from what
they would be in a general assembly." Therefore if
France is to be a direct democracy, she must be divided
into dozens of little republics. But this is absurd and
undesirable, and we must consider the national assembly
truly sovereign.[16] It appears as a very practical assertion
of Jacobins in office: "We shall not leave a single heterogeneous body in France." [17] It appears mixed up with
the semi-religious desire of extreme Jacobins to leave
none but the elect in political life. "Is there a (conservative) Right in the Jacobins and in other *sociétés populaires?* No, of course. Why then should there be one in
the Convention?" [18] It appears in Robespierre's famous
maxim that the revolutionary government was the
despotism of liberty against tyranny, and in Chabot's:
"In England, liberty of the press is necessary against a
despotic government, but in France, the press is not
free to curse liberty—i.e. democratic government." [19]

But this aspect of Jacobinism is so obvious that it has
perhaps attracted too much attention. Jacobinism after
all is not wholly summed up in Robespierre, St. Just and
the Paris society. If one goes over the papers of the
provincial societies centralization seems less a rigid
scheme of political orthodoxy, and more a normal form
of nineteenth century political organization. With the
Gironde went the federal republic, whatever that may

have been. But the Gironde was as often as not assimilated in the provinces, rather than guillotined or proscribed. In many a quiet country town, like Vesoul, the social and political ideals of Robespierre were never really accepted by the local club. The republic to the Jacobins was always one and indivisible. Such a concept, however, is not exclusively Latin, Roman, or French. The theory of sovereignty which best embodies this desire for unity in the state is known as Austinian; and Webster, and other Anglo-Saxons, have had much to say on the inseparability of Liberty and Union. In major political questions, these provincial societies did usually follow the lead of Paris. In matters of fashion, the Jacobins were as imitative as the royalists had been. But there remains a residual of local pride, of local freedom of action.[20] The representatives on mission, those agents of a centralizing power in Paris at least as old as Philip Augustus, had no easy time of it in the provinces, and their reports of their dealings with the local *sociétés populaires* bear abundant witness to the existence of provincial independence during the Terror.[21] Yet centralization remains an important plank in the Jacobin platform—centralization less for greater governmental efficiency than for social uniformity, for practical equality. The provincial Jacobin was torn between local pride, which would preserve differences, and revolutionary ambition, which would destroy them. Yet he was more intolerant of class, than of geographical, inequalities, and was perhaps aiming at that sort of centralization whereby variety, initiative, eccentricity are all planed down to respectability, at that sort of middle class society so thoroughly damned by European writers in the nineteenth century, and by American writers in the twentieth.

The Jacobin state must also be a nation; indeed, its

unity was to be based on common ethnological unity, real or supposed, on a common language, on a common feeling. The Jacobin started as a *patriote* in the eighteenth century French sense; he ended as a patriot in plain nineteenth century English. Few subjects in the history of thought are so subtly illuminating as the process whereby the French revolutionist changed, within a few years, from a cosmopolitan to a nationalist. We can here but suggest one or two of the links in this transition.

The theory of 1789 is pretty completely cosmopolitan —all men are equal, there is one right way of life, therefore all men in the new world of the Revolution will live the same way—Englishman, Frenchman, Chinaman and negro. No doubt there was in practice—that is, in the consciousness of ordinary Frenchmen—much national feeling, much dislike of the foreigner in the flesh. But officially the Jacobins were cosmopolitans. All freemen—Frenchmen, Englishmen, Poles and Americans— were brothers, and the rest of the world, once freed from kingly tyranny, would also become brothers.[22] This pleasing illusion was, of course, destroyed almost immediately by the failure of the other peoples to accept the French gospel. But the war, long foreshadowed, at first meant for the Frenchman merely an opportunity to aid other peoples to free themselves. The society of Cognac as early as December 1791 was regaled with patriotic verse, wherein, after much about flying to defend the fatherland, there was the passage

> Jusques à Vienne et dans Rome
> Faites des Droits de l'homme
> Connaître la majesté.[23]

The outbreak of war was greeted by an orator in the same club not with regret, as under the old régime, but

joyfully, for such a war was not destructive, but crea-
tive.[24] When the war went wrong, and peoples refused
to rise, Frenchmen were almost obliged to consider themselves the only virtuous people. The society of Guéret
waited nobly until January 1794, and then removed the
American and the English flags from the tree of liberty.
The tricolor flew alone.[25]

But the *patriote* might have been transformed from
a lover of mankind to a lover of France even without a
foreign war. For Equality, like all other political abstractions, must touch reality at some point within the
common man's emotional capacity. If men were obviously unequal in strength, in intelligence, in beauty
and in virtue, they were at least equal as Frenchmen.
Other qualities are accidental; Frenchness is fundamental. Frenchmen are equal in the eyes of the nation.
"Is it not true that all Frenchmen are born and are
citizens before being Christians, before being Protestants,
before being Jews?" [26] If the Jacobins had got that far
in 1791, is it surprising that in 1794 the unitary Republic
was a nation in the full modern sense? "Republicans are
neither from Lyons nor from Paris, nor from any city,
nor from any department; they are Frenchmen, they
are all brothers." [27]

Nationalism with the Jacobins early took on its characteristic form of suppressing cultural and linguistic
minorities within the state. In their early zeal for propaganda, the clubs had not hesitated to win over the common people by translating pamphlets into their language,
by holding sessions partly in French, partly in the local
tongue. The club of Vannes addressed the peasants in
Breton; that of St. Jean de Luz translated the decrees
of the National Assembly into Basque; that of Nice
posted the Rights of Man in Italian.[28] The Alsatian so-

cieties commonly had certain sessions in German; that at Colmar translated the Marseillaise.

Auf, Bürger, auf zu Wehr! Erlegt die Höllenbrut!
Glück zu, Glück zu. Es dünge bald das Feld ihr schwarzes Blut![29]

But these minorities soon came into distrust, even when they repeated in their own tongue the best Jacobin orthodoxies. As a little Provençal society said, "there should be no tongue in the Republic other than French, which would have the effect of bringing Equality nearer."[30] The society tried heroically, but not very successfully, to speak French. The club of Strasbourg wrote to surrounding clubs and asked for teachers of French: "As long as diversity of tongues is not proscribed in the Republic, as long as the language of freemen is not the sole one used in France, we shall have amongst us men who are not Frenchmen."[31] This club, largely composed of outsiders, was particularly bitter towards those who spoke only German. Discussing the matter in 1793 "some suggested that the German speaking Alsatians who refuse to learn French be deported and that a column of sans-culottes be brought in from France; others, that they be given a trip to the guillotine, to effect their conversion."[32] So many religious, as well as national, prejudices embittered the Alsatian question even in 1793 that few heeded the protest of a member against the decree forbidding the use of German: "How is it possible to instruct, enlighten, and persuade a people, in a language which it cannot understand?"[33] Even where German continued to be used, the secretaries felt it needed apologies: "Kriegelstein gets the floor and delivers a speech in German, subsequently translated *en langue républicaine* by Teste."[34]

The war brought out other familiar aspects of patri-

otism. England became the great enemy, a nation to be
hated with satisfying vehemence. There is some trace
of the old missionary idea. The English government is
bad; the people, if it can only be appealed to, is
sound. Let the Convention tell the English nation, writes
a little club in Périgord "that if it does not cut off the
heads of two monsters (Pitt, George III) whose presence
on the earth is an outrage to humanity, two hundred
thousand Frenchmen have decided to bring the fraternal embrace to Fox and all friends of liberty, and
death to the two tyrants and their infamous band." [35]
But there are still more indications of that curious pas-
sion of hatred for other nations in the abstract. A
Lillois "who had travelled" told the club that there were
no wolves in England, and "suggested that a shipload
be sent over the Channel." [36] The president of the Rouen
club, embracing the English-born Wild told him, "I am
sure that in embracing you I embrace only a Frenchman." [37]

Civilian courage was not lacking among the Jacobins.
Citizen Germain of Le Havre would not have peace
"until the children of the Mountain have flown the flag
of liberty on the walls of London, Madrid and Berlin." [38]
A young citizeness of Toulouse, at a commemoration
service in honor of Lepelletier, delivered a patriotic
speech urging young men to go to the front and earn
the love of young ladies like herself.[39]

This patriotism may be, as superior persons like to
assume, an indulgence of unrefined and uncriticized passions; but the important thing to notice is that the
passions were aroused. Much of Jacobin ritual was directed towards making la patrie a reality to the senses.
One club even preserved order by having the president
wave the tricolor, instead of by the traditional French

method of having him put on his hat.[40] Current diction
may have exaggerated the importance of the emotions
it attempted to describe. But there is something behind
such phraseology as this: "The cry, the Constitution or
death, was repeated for several minutes, and patriotic
intoxication, as well as holy enthusiasm for liberty, were
carried to their maximum." [41] "O holy love of country!
What delights, hitherto unknown to Frenchmen, dost
thou not bring to their noble souls!" [42] Possibly the club
of Versailles was right when it declared "these words,
patrie and *nation* are no longer abstractions." [43]

The Jacobin made one more demand upon his state, a
demand which in spite of its complications, is best treated
as purely political. The state must be secular. Probably
most Jacobins really went further, and desired the proscription of the Roman Catholic Church. But the whole
subject is full of difficulties, and we shall do better to
rest on the assertion that the Jacobin state recognizes
none but laymen. We have seen how the constitutional
priests played perhaps the chief rôle in the formation of
the first societies; [44] and there is at first no obvious break
between the societies and the Roman Church, at least
as far as that church is embodied in the Civil Constitution of the Clergy. Clubs commonly mourned Mirabeau's
death with a mass, or celebrated the king's recovery from
illness with a Te Deum. Yet the rise of anti-clericalism
was too sudden not to have been prepared. Anti-clericalism flourished beneath the surface of these societies of
friends of the monarchical constitution. Whether or not
the quarrel between Jacobinism and Roman Catholicism
was inevitable or not need not here be considered. Once
the Civil Constitution of the clergy was promulgated,
the break with Rome could not have been avoided; and
once Roman Catholic Christianity became the enemy of

the new state, it was easy for radicals to point out that constitutional priests held the same unreasonable dogmas as non-juring priests. Finally, as we shall see, Jacobinism itself became a religion, and like all new religions, intolerant of old ones.

Again, the extent to which Jacobinism is to be identified with the rabid dechristianization of the year II—Fouché at Nevers, for instance—need not be answered too precisely. Few provincial Jacobins talked open atheism. Even the worship of reason took on curiously theistic forms, and Robespierre's Supreme Being was welcomed by most of the clubs. There is plenty of evidence of a certain degree of toleration of Christianity, or at least of the Constitutional Church. The club of Chablis, as late as the spring of 1794, notified the mayor "that it intended to exercise the cult of Reason every *décadi* in the Church, and that in case *décadi* should fall on a *ci-devant* Sunday, he (the mayor) should notify the citizen curé to hold all his services in the morning, so that the cult of Reason might be celebrated in the afternoon." [45] When the little village club of Fleuryles-Faverney had to name a committee to verify pensions to widows and dependents of soldiers, in the midst of the Terror, it appointed the curé, still exercising his functions.[46]

Yet the bulk of the evidence is overwhelming. Orthodox Jacobinism, even in the provinces was at open war with the Catholic Church, both Roman and constitutional. With protestantism it seems to have had little quarrel. Indeed, the society of Bergerac refers to "its good friends, the protestants" [47] even in the year II. But in a hundred ways the Jacobins attacked the catholics. The club of Le Mans asked the National Assembly in January 1792 to forbid legacies to priests or to the church: "Where priests, pretending commiseration and charity, succeed in making rich and credulous women believe that they will please God by disinheriting in his favor their legitimate heirs, and thus . . . they extort considerable legacies by means of a bill of exchange drawn on heaven and payable at sight." [48] A provincial Voltaire, indeed; here is a Rousseau: "The society requests the district to close all churches and chapels within its jurisdiction, on the ground that freedom of religious belief does not imply ownership of the churches, that they should be considered as national property, and that therefore they cannot be opened without reviving an exclusive cult, which is contrary to liberty." [49]

Sometimes there is a trait of that sophomoric humor not uncommon among the Jacobins, as when the club at Lille renamed the Porte St. Maurice the Porte de l'Egalité, because it led to the cemetery; [50] or when the society of St. Arnould requested the municipality to help tide over hard times by selling the hay to be got from the cemetery.[51] Again there is good plain hatred for one's enemies: "It is proposed to send commissioners into the country to convert churches into temples of Reason, and to arrest all priests, priestesses and silly believers as suspects." [52] The club of Auxerre issued a particularly violent circular against priests, urging that all ex-priests not working at some useful occupation be deported unless they had given evidence of repentance by getting married.[53] Sometimes the new faith appears stronger even than dislike for the old. "Mirabeau used to say: 'Kings will pass, nobles will pass, privileges will pass, and the People will remain'; and I say, 'priests will pass, persecutors will pass, fanatics will pass, and Reason will remain.' " [54]

III

In the narrow field of politics, the Jacobins then demanded a unified nation-state under a republican form of government, efficiently centralized and wholly lay. But the Jacobin had social, economic and moral aims quite as definite as his political aims. Socially, his aims are summed up in that protean word, equality. No doubt to most Jacobins the word had a metaphysical, almost a mystical, connotation. But consideration of equality in this sense—a sense much like that in which Christians are equal before God—we shall reserve for a later chapter. How far equality meant economic equality to the Jacobin we shall consider in a moment. But there are still plenty of meanings for the word. The most obvious one is that of equality of opportunity, that of the career open to talents. The club of Mainz was told that among the advantages of the new French gospel was the "freie Wahl der Obrigkeit, die der Geschicklichkeit und Tugend die Wege öffne." [55] A traveling orator in the south was moved to eloquence over this aspect of equality:

> It is thou, O holy Revolution, who hast brought us happiness; it is thou whom I should love with all my strength, whom I should defend with my life-blood, that thou mayest triumph over the tyrants banded against thee! Thou, O holy liberty, O holy equality, who makest it possible for me boldly to say: I am but a poor peasant, I am but a simple workman, and my son may become a magistrate, a legislator, a ship's master, a general.[56]

Yet, at least in its purely social sense, equality did not for the Jacobin mean the kind of free competition it meant for what are called classical economics. There is more talk of virtue than of talents, even where equality means equality of opportunity. The president of the club of Rouen, addressing an actor in 1790 assured him

prejudices no longer existed, and continued, "all men
are equal by nature, they are now equal even by law
. . . today the applause of the society proved to you that
talents, honesty, and *above all patriotism* are the only
titles of consideration for free men." [57] Much later, at
the Paris club, "Tollède presents himself (as candidate
for a military commission) to the sound of applause; he
admits that he is not a soldier, that another would fill
the place better, seeing that he has nothing but courage
and patriotism. 'That's enough,' cry all voices, 'so many
others have neither of these qualities. Let him have
it.' " [58]

The truth is that the Jacobin was more of a leveler
than the Nature he talked so much about.[59] His society
would correct tendencies towards selfish aggression perhaps natural to uncontrolled man. His society would be
as far as possible a comfortable place for the middling
man, a comfortable place for his vanity even more than
for his physical needs. The mere abolition of nobility
seemed to have achieved equality

> "Parfaite égalité, tu n'es plus un mensonge.
> Des nobles et des rois il ne reste plus qu'un songe." [60]

The clubs were always hounding on municipalities to
remove all coats of arms from public view, to change the
names of streets, to forbid private pews in churches. The
club of Nice ordered the manager of the theatre to
forbid people "to enter the theatre before the regular
opening of the doors, for that is contrary to equality." [61]
Dufourny at Paris observed that equality is the basis of
education and proposes that in the new system of schools
"the children of the rich shall be essentially the equals
of poor children." [62] He objects to riches, not in themselves, but in their effects on human vanity. One aspect

of equality, then, and for the Jacobin of 1794 perhaps the
main one, is simply the familiar democratic insistence
that men should be externally, in their manners, morals,
dress, language, roughly alike. We shall later be able to
give a more specific meaning to what the Jacobin meant
by morals, for instance. But one small item will perhaps
give some meaning to this external sort of equality, to
this Jacobin desire to make the average man a real man.
The Jacobins distrusted bachelors. "A time will come,
perhaps, when the Convention will declare unmarried
men ineligible to places in the government." [63] The club
of Gray requested the representative on mission that
"bachelor clerks employed in government positions be
replaced by married men." [64] This distrust of democracies
for bachelors, not unknown in American history, might,
if properly sounded, go very deep into man as a political animal. Superficially, the average man may be
said to find the bachelor objectionable because he enjoys
an economic advantage, because he sometimes appears
to eat his cake and have it, a highly immoral offense,
because he does not pull his share of the load, or simply
because his status is different, because he does not conform to the average. Perhaps a sound superficial explanation is worth more than a strained profundity; yet
the common man's dislike for bachelors would seem to be
an instinct worthy of a higher dignity than music hall
jokes can give it, an instinct closely related to the fundamental collectivism of modern societies.

Jacobin equality meant also the abolition of customs
and traditions not obviously common property, customs
that brought back a romantic but unjust past. The
club of Strasbourg, after a year's agitation, forced the
municipality to abolish the *Kraüselhorn,* a trumpet
sounded certain nights in memory of "a reputed treason

of the Jews." [65] The same club later suggested that "in these times, when crowns are put into the national crucible, those which our women carry under the name of *Schneppenhauben* should be put aside, affording as they do the spectacle of slavish, harsh manners." [66] This quaint and elaborate headdress soon disappeared entirely. Costume in general, particularly for men, was leveled down in ways with which we are all familiar. The Jacobin hated the past for the same reason Burke and Scott loved it, because it was full of external variety. "Thanks to a republican education, we shall have men above prejudices; they will not share the opinions of their fathers." [67]

Nor could equality brook group-differences within the state. Politically, this dislike of group-heterogeneity took the form of hostility to federalism. Socially, however, the same dislike appears. Clubs, other than Jacobin clubs, are to be discouraged. Priesthood makes a man a member of a caste. Therefore the Jacobin insisted on the marriage of abjuring priests. Even in 1790, we find a club attacking the chapter of the cathedral of Sens because it was a *confraternité,* a body apart.[68] At Strasbourg, a member "proposes that Jews be obliged to marry Christians," with the obvious hope of breeding out Jewishness.[69]

It is but fair to add that education appears as prominently as equality among the social aims of the Jacobins. And education was to be universal, open to the poorest child. Yet education is a word that has come to have the same sort of abstract logical structure and concrete emotional value possessed by words like progress, liberty, science. In a sense, any child who survives receives an education. The important thing is what he learns. Jacobins would have their children learn Jacobinism—

the whole complex way of life we have been trying to describe. Jacobin education, then, must be judged on the basis of what we can make out of Jacobinism itself.

IV

The economic aims of the Jacobins afford an excellent example of how difficult it is to draw up a Jacobin platform. For what Varlet, Jacques Roux and the other *Enragés* wanted was very different from what the Jacobins of a quiet provincial town wanted, and even different from what Robespierre wanted. Similarly, there is usually a great difference between the social and economic program of a club in 1791 and that of the same club in 1794—it is in economics, indeed, that there is to be found the best argument for the thesis that the clubs altered their identity completely in this period. We shall none the less attempt to separate the universal from the particular, taking as a guide in a degree even greater than previously, what seems to have entered most deeply into the Jacobin legend of the next century.

It is perhaps inevitable that this enquiry into Jacobin economic aims should be largely concerned with answering the question, how much socialism is there in Jacobinism? Yet in just that form we cannot attempt to answer the question. For socialism itself is an abstract noun, and its definition would involve us much too deeply. Is socialism essentially economic egalitarianism, or group ownership of capital, or state operation of industry, or what? We shall do better to try to answer the question, what did the Jacobins of hundreds of clubs throughout France conceive to be a Jacobin economic order?

One thing is certain. The Jacobin believed in private

property. He did not always respect all forms of it, particularly when it was in the hands of his political enemies. But with the commoner forms of ownership in modern society, including ownership of land, he was quite satisfied. It is perhaps to be expected that the earlier clubs should insist on property as one of the Rights of Man, and on law and order as its guarantee.[70] One club had difficulties of conscience: "Yes, we swear to respect property as one of the Rights of Man and the citizen; pretended nobles, your nobility was not a property, it was a prejudice contrary to nature, contrary to Reason." [71] This sort of logical difficulty, that of reconciling absolute private ownership of property as a right with various measures expropriating property owners pursued the Jacobins to the end.

Even during the Terror the Jacobins professed their respect for private property. The action of the Convention in swearing never to pass a *loi agraire* is of course well known. But the provinces were quite as emphatic. "Eternal War against tyrants! Peace to the cottages! Respect for property!" was the mild slogan of one club in the winter of 1794.[72] The club of Ars-en-Ré decided in October 1793 to have an auto-da-fe of feudal titles, but it took good care to save "those which justify real property." [73] At Limoges, in the same month, the municipality inserted the phrase "respect due to property" in the oath required for a certificate of *civisme*. A certain Imbert, at the club, proposed to suppress this phrase. He was "emphatically censored" and called to order.[74] "Be silent, corrupt rich," ran an address to the people of the Gers in the autumn of 1793, "do not spread it about that the Mountain wants a partition of lands, a seizure of your property. . . . The Convention, on the contrary, assures you your property." [75]

With this respect for property went a regard for the traditional virtues associated with small property in Europe, for thrift, for commercial uprightness, for solvency. "The society was moved to see a child bring his savings as an offering to the fatherland: five livres. The club will give him a badge to wear on his little breast inscribed: 'Grow and multiply.'" [76] The club of Blaye decided unanimously "that there should be drawn up an address to the citizens of the countryside to exhort them to obey the law and to pay or buy up the feudal dues which they refuse to pay under different pretexts." [77] Several societies, among them that of Nantes, had clauses in their rules forbidding membership to bankrupts. This again is true of clubs even in 1794.[78] Robespierre himself "complained of the abuses of principle the societies indulge in. 'Observe the direction which the zeal of the society of Bayonne takes. It busies itself with excluding —whom? Conspirators? Nobles? Hébertistes? No! Those who, in a time of revolution, were not rich enough to pay their debts!'" [79]

The clubs, as befitted gatherings of respectable men, did much, as we have seen, for charity.[80] Yet though they were fashionably sorry for the unfortunate,[81] the Jacobins had no use for the idle, and no sympathy for beggars. "A citizen makes a motion concerning the poor who assail our windows, which is contrary to principles. He asks that the society busy itself with finding some means of getting rid of this mendicity, odious as it is to all lovers of equality and fraternity." [82] This motion has not, somehow, the fraternal tone one would expect from a reader of Rousseau. The club of Le Havre asked to have beggars expelled, on the ground that too many rascals were masquerading in the "respectable rags of indigence." [83] Another club got the municipality to eject

three persons "without domicile or calling." [84] Somewhat
later, the club of Le Havre refused to do anything in
favor of some poor squatters near the Porte d' Igouville
who had been evicted by the city, and this in spite of a
very touching appeal to revolutionary principles by their
spokesman.[85] The *sans-culottes* of Havre-Marat had all
the trappings of proletarian revolutionists, but their acts
are the acts of respectable middle class people.

Naturally enough the early clubs believed in *laissez-
faire*. "A minister who should interfere directly or indi-
rectly with the getting of a nation's food-supply should,
because of this infraction of free circulation of goods,
be punished as severely as possible." [86] This the Paris
club was willing to accept in 1790. One of the first acts
of the Strasbourg club in the same year was to petition
the National Assembly to permit absolute freedom of
tobacco culture.[87] Practical necessity later dulled the
dogmatic sharpness of this Physiocratic doctrine of freedom, and the Terror saw much regulation. Yet even in
this period the Jacobins seem to have clung fairly solidly
to the basic principle of *laissez-faire*, as they did to that
of private property. The society at Moulins, in the spring
of 1794, replied to a request that it investigate the affairs
of a wine merchant accused of selling for more than the
legal maximum: "The society, recalling article 17 of the
Declaration of the Rights of Man which says that no
kind of labor, cultivation, or commerce can be forbidden
to the industry of citizens, passes to the order of the
day." [88] Nor was the normal accompaniment of this
theoretical freedom lacking. The society of Rouen forbade its members to wear any cloth not made in France.[89]
Free trade within the nation-state, barriers against other
states; the nineteenth century formula had already
appeared.

The clubs naturally enough show no signs of recognizing the dangers of the industrial revolution. This entry from the registers of the club at Toulouse, in the midst of the Terror, would not be out of place in the minutes of an American chamber of commerce. "Citizens Gau, Fournier and Laurier made their report on the factory of citizen Fonfrède (a Bordelais, related to Boyer-Fonfrède) and the discussions on wages between workmen and the said Fonfrède. The commissioners have got the parties to come to an agreement. Their report was very satisfactory, both by the details which it gave of the beauties of this establishment and by the great necessity of maintaining it in Toulouse by favoring it in every possible way." [90] Another extract from the minutes of the club of Crest is equally pertinent:

> Vernet, foreman in the factory of citizen Daly, said he came to offer children a means of escaping that state of idleness and unprofitable play which harms them so. He offered to receive in the shop which he directs young boys aged from 10 to 12, to teach them to card wool, and then the trade of weaver, and to pay them from the start, without apprenticeship costing them anything. The club applauded this generous and truly civic offer, and invited fathers of families to have their children profit by it.[91]

The attitude of the clubs in industrial disputes is almost always that of the employer class. The club of Aiguesmortes, accepting the law establishing maximum prices, took occasion to insist on the observation of maximum wages for workmen.[92] At Toulouse, in a dispute between a factory owner and his female workers, the club definitely sided with the owner, and reproached the workers with carelessness and irresponsibility.[93] Nor were the clubs less exacting towards their own employees. Citizen Glavet, *concierge* of the club of Le Havre asked for a raise "for the third time." The register notes laconically, "It was decided that Glavet was no longer *concierge* of the society." [94] Workmen building the galleries in the new club of Vire—galleries intended for the "people"—threatened to strike unless they received an extra bread ration. The club decided that if the workmen "refuse to work tomorrow, they will be pursued according to the laws." [95] The workmen yielded; but the *sans-culottes* of Vire would apparently have welcomed so useful a legal weapon as the American injunction. Citizen Ithier of Vienne, absentee owner of a spinning factory at Romans, actually wrote the society of that town, complaining of the idleness of the youth of Romans, and asking the society to urge them to industry—in Ithier's factory.[96]

The societies were then usually on the side of the masters against the workmen—naturally enough, for as we have seen, the societies even in the year II were not composed of men of the lower classes. When, as at Chablis, we find a club asking for a higher maximum wage for day laborers, the reason is obvious. The club of Chablis was composed of wine growers, employers, who had pressing need of seasonal labor; and the laborers—many of whom had small plots of land of their own—simply refused to work at the legal wage.[97] The following incidents, confirming the patronal character of the societies, throw also no little light on the question as to how far Jacobinism was a real faith among the masses in whose name it strove for power:

Azéma and Verdagues, master masons, were asked to explain why their workmen refused to work on a *ci-devant* Sunday; they replied that it was probably because of a trace of fanaticism still surviving, but that they hoped it wouldn't occur again.[98] The society decrees that members of the society owning factories shall be invited to conform to the law concerning the opening of workshops on Sundays; that consequently, they shall dismiss employees who persist in not working Sundays; and that those who do not dismiss such workmen shall be excluded from the society.[69]

Note here that the masters are members of the club, but not the men; and that the men seem to prefer the old-fashioned Sunday to the new *décadi*—either out of genuine faith, or because one day's rest in seven is better than one in ten.

Now, if the foregoing evidence be accepted, it is clear that the Jacobin normally desires an economic society substantially like that described by nineteenth century classical economists. Yet the Revolution did two things directly opposed to the structure of such a society: It expropriated property-owners without compensating them, and it regulated prices, retail and wholesale, as well as wages. The contradiction is not, however, real, and the Revolution did nothing to disturb the fundamental economic individualism of the Jacobin clubs. For those whose property was seized—*émigrés* and priests—were not within the society where individual property was protected. They were quite definitely outlaws, in the Jacobin mind, and the Jacobin state could proceed against them as it would against foreign subjects in war time. The right to property, like the other Rights of Man, could apply only to the full-fledged human being, to the Jacobin. Nor is this sophistry or hypocrisy, but the normal functioning of the human mind in social matters.

The matter of price-fixing demands somewhat more attention. Yet, with certain qualifications, it is not untrue to say that the famous *maximum* was a war measure for food control, that its real analogies are with the rationing, the bread cards, the saccharine pellets and other restrictions familiar even to Americans who remember the war of 1914-1918. At a certain point, the food supply in a besieged city or in a country at war becomes so short that to permit the free play of demand and supply means that the poorer citizens will get nothing to eat; therefore societies much less open to the reproach of socialism have taken action similar to that of the French government in 1793. The minutes of most of the clubs are full of demands for the *maximum* before it was passed, and its enforcement was one of the main concerns of the clubs. Yet it was pretty generally regarded as a form of rationing. The club of Fleury, for instance, decreed "that no innkeeper can give to citizens drinking at his inn more than one *chopine* of wine, on the pain of being declared suspect." [100] The club at Montbard drew up an elaborate plan to regulate the cattle trade at the source. Only those with adequate pastures may buy cattle. They in turn may sell only to army furnishers and to licensed butchers. The desire here is obviously not regulation for regulation's sake, but regulation to prevent speculation and to insure supplies to the army.[101] In the city clubs, there is often evident an irritation against the farmer, the old hostility of the city for the country. When the club at Dijon demands control of the grain trade in language like the following, it is obviously not thinking in terms as general as its phraseology implies: "Grain is the food of the people, and ought to be at its disposition and at that of the government. . . . The farmer is master of the grain he raises only to receive its market value." [102] Yet even here a regard for property underlies the desire to take the farmer's crop by force. Certain clubs even repented of their use of the maximum to further economic egalitarianism. That of Chablis decreed on 24 germinal an II that all grains should be brought to a common stock, bread baked and distributed equally. On 26 germinal it took back this decree as too radical.[103] Other clubs refused to worry over abuses of the *maximum*. In reply to a letter from the society of La Ciotat, suggesting severe measures against "discrediters of *assignats* and monopolists of all sorts" the society of Moulins decided: "The society, while approving the patriotic zeal of their brothers of La Ciotat, considering that on one hand there is no longer any way of discrediting the *assignats* in this region since there is no longer any gold or silver, and on the other that all good citizens are on the alert for infractions of the beneficent law of the *maximum,* passes to the order of the day." [104]

No doubt many of the clubs welcomed the *maximum* as a measure defending the poor against the rich, as a step towards a more complete Equality.[105] But it must be remembered that the Jacobins were leading a revolution and fighting a war, and that the support of the common people, of the poor, was absolutely essential to them. That in this emergency they sided with the poor is far from proving them socialists. Here, as in other places, when Jacobin clubs rail at "les riches" it is usually at "les riches corrompus," that is, the non-Jacobin rich. The *maximum* promised not only to solve the problem of feeding the poor, but also to foil the crooked stock-market operations of anti-revolutionaries. Again, the Jacobin, if not an economic collectivist in the Marxian sense, was what we may call an emotional collectivist. The maximum seemed to him to make the general will more real, to help separate the elect and the damned. "Report on infractions of the maximum; it is decided to draw up a list of bad citizens." [106] This state of mind, too, should be familiar to those who recall the late war; it is in no sense a purely socialistic state of

mind. Furthermore, the maximum, properly adminis-
tered, seemed to guarantee the food supply, and in many
towns not merely the poor, but also the middling people
and the rich were threatened by an absolute lack of food.
Finally, the Jacobins, as we have seen, though prosperous
people, were not often of classes dominant before 1789,
and were not therefore in the average community of the
very highest economic stratum, particularly as regards
landed wealth. There was enough hostility to ex-nobles,
to tax-farmers and bankers among the Jacobins so that
their language is occasionally that of a social revolutionary. The *maximum* prevented members of the old
nobility against whom no accusations could be invented
from using their wealth or their position to lay in large
stocks of food. Once in operation, of course, the *maximum* became part of the Jacobin system. It was merely
as an article of faith that the pathetic remnants of the
clubs defended it after thermidor; and even then they did
not adhere to it with socialist fervor.

It should be evident that the Jacobins were not of
the breed of such revolutionists as Spartacus, John Ball,
or even Karl Marx. Yet it will not do to leave the impression that Jacobinism was a purely political or religious movement, that the Jacobins were socially and
economically entirely the same kind of people as their
opponents, in the sense, for instance, that both parties
to the Wars of the Roses were much the same kind of
people. To a nobleman of the old stock, the Jacobins
were disreputable innovators, inferior people aiming at
the wealth and station of their deserving betters. To the
rich merchant who had failed to join the club, they
were quite as definitely rebellious inferiors. And even to
us, who for the purposes of the social sciences must be
presumed to be of no class, they seem to have had

certain economic aims that put them on the side of the
under dog.

For, if Jacobinism, in spite of the *maximum* and the
confiscation of enemy property, is quite firmly in favor
of private property and *laissez-faire,* it has rather more
than a touch of economic egalitarianism. As early as
1790, an Auvergnat society, attacking the Assembly's
decree on feudal dues, quotes Rousseau with approval:
"Bring together extremes as far as possible; do not
permit either opulence or rags." [107] This principle
translates itself into a preference for small property. The clubs were pretty generally in favor of an
agrarian society of small proprietors. This was of course
the opinion of rural clubs. One of them petitioned the
Convention on favor of small farms: "There are farmers
who exploit farms capable of supporting four farmers;
moreover, farmers with too much tillage to attend to too
often neglect to raise cattle proportionately to their crops,
which deprives the Republic of an essential part of its
food." [108] The petition continues as a detailed defense
of small farmers—but insisting as much on efficiency as
on the small farmer's right to life. "There followed a letter from the society of Gonneville which communicates
a decree passed by that society suggesting that each
father of a family should own an *arpent* of land." [109]
The clubs were anxious to see the confiscated lands of
the *émigrés* (the best of church lands had already been
sold) disposed of so as to encourage the small pro-
prietor. That of Ligny-sur-Serain as late as September 1794 asked the Convention "that in the future national property derived from the *émigrés* be divided into
small lots so that the rich and the powerful shall not be
the only ones to acquire it." [110] As a matter of fact, very
little was actually done directly for the deserving land-

less peasants, and if the Revolution did result in a wider distribution of land, it was rather as a result of resales than of governmental encouragement to small buyers at the first sale.

There is less evidence of Jacobin championing of the petty tradesman. The historian of the club of Dijon writes: "Rich shoemakers, who perhaps do not hesitate to charge more than the *maximum,* obtained at wholesale the best leather for shoes. The society, 'remarking in this fact an infamous coalition of tanners and the richer shoemakers,' took up the defense of the poor shoemakers. On a complaint of the club, the city council order the tanners to sell to shoemakers without distinction and by small lots the hides they tan." [111]

In general terms, there is to be found in the records of the clubs in 1793-4 much vilifying the rich and praising the poor. Even in 1792, Simond at Strasbourg "moved that in the next city elections neither the educated nor the rich be chosen, but the poorest citizens, who certainly can fulfill these functions." [112] Earlier, the club at Nantes had told the city government to quarter soldiers only with the rich.[113] With the Terror, the attack on the rich becomes a chorus.

Yet, just as with the *maximum,* we admit so many qualifications and alternatives that the revolutionary roughness even of this hostility to wealth is quite worn down. The club of Montbard in its new rules of 1794 provided "There will not be admitted into the society citizens who possess an annual revenue of more than 3000 livres unless they have constantly given since 1789, proof of a pure *civisme,* an ardent love of liberty and equality, a probity safe from all attack, an attachment to the democratic constitution of 1793, and *unless* they have shown an aversion for places and lucrative employments." [114] This already provides for the rich Jacobin; but the municipality, judging it too revolutionary, requested the club to omit the clause entirely. The club conformed meekly enough to this request. Much of this hostility to the prosperous is also merely a form of city hatred for a countryside extremely unwilling to sell its produce at the legal maximum. Brichet at Paris suggested as a guiding principle for revolutionary armies "the wealth of farmers. The army should, on arriving in a village, ask 'is the farmer rich?' If the answer is yes, he can be guillotined, he is sure to be an *accapareur*." [115]

Even though the rich—the non-Jacobin rich—were to be made to pay all sorts of irregular levies, there were very few who would take away their property altogether. The famous scheme of Robespierre and St. Just for effecting a distribution of the lands of the suspects was limited to lands of anti-Jacobins.[116] And Robespierre and St. Just were far more radical in such ways than the average Jacobin. Maure, on mission in the Yonne, told the club of Chablis "that the greatest possessions would be nothing, without the arms of the people, and that a day would come when each individual would possess a certain amount of property, and would live in comfort from the labor of his hands; *but while awaiting that happy epoch, the poor man should respect the heritage of the rich.*" [117] The words of Hébert "The people, who made the Revolution, must enjoy the fruits of that Revolution" [118] could not honestly have been spoken by many Jacobins of the year II.

There remains the task, if we are to determine the economic program of the Jacobins, of deciding in what sense those favorite phrases "class-struggle" and "class-consciousness" can be applied to Jacobin activities in this field. Now the Jacobins can in no sense be described as a class-conscious proletariat. Nor of course were they nobles, nor even predominately an "upper-class" faction. They were middle-class people. Our real task at the moment is the difficult one of deciding whether, having said they were middle class people, we have said anything of importance, anything that helps to define Jacobinism.

From their social origins and their income it is clear that the Jacobins were middle class people. From their own words and deeds, it is clear that they were conscious, not only of being as a fraternity a group apart, but also of being part of a wider group distinguishable from nobles on one hand, and the "peuple" on the other. Class-consciousness over against the nobles goes back well before the revolution, and is too much a commonplace of Jacobin records to be worth insisting upon.[119] Class-consciousness over against the people is almost equally obvious if one reads between the lines, though it could not assume a hostile form. That the clubs distinguished between themselves and the people is evidenced by the universal separation of the club and the "peuple des tribunes." Many clubs did in the year II seek to do away with that difference, and make entrance for the "vrais sans culottes" easy. Yet there is little evidence that laboringmen accepted the invitation in large numbers.[120] In most clubs, the distinction remains; and it is a distinction not only between club-members and non-members, but between a prosperous and educated middle class and an uneducated and hardly class-conscious proletariat.[121] Even when workingmen joined the clubs, they were made to respect the alliance between the middle class Jacobins and the people. In one club a member complained that another member had "held forth indecently, going so far as to say that they ought to cut off the heads of *ci-devant bourgeois* and master-tradesmen." The offending Jacobin apologized, and said he was drunk, but was none the less expelled.[122] At Bénévent, Sarazine ainé was chosen president when a voice called out "Those who name *bourgeois* are—scoundrels, we don't want those—for presidents." But the *bourgeois* remained president, and the interrupter was reprimanded.[123] In many clubs, workingmen were only admitted during a brief period at the height of the Terror, and that often only under pressure from representatives on mission, or from traveling radicals like Philip at Nancy. The latter reports the club of Nancy in the autumn of 1793 as composed of "lawyers, rich merchants, and priests who do not bother about the interests of the people, whom they call *canaille*." [124] Philip remedied that, though many rich men remained even in his club; and many towns never had a Philip. Again, in some communities, a more radical and presumably more proletarian group organized itself outside the Jacobin club, and ruled as *société populaire* for the briefest of periods in 1794.[125]

The term "middle class" is not, even in the usage of the social sciences, of an altogether scientific precision; yet, especially as regards what a middle class person desires the economic order to be, there does adhere to it enough definiteness to enable us to make use of it here. Now, emphasize though we may the Jacobin's respect for private property, his fundamental attachment to the competitive economic order,—the small farmer, the small artisan, a free market, his suppression of the guilds, his aversion to communism and the "loi agraire"—when we have emphasized all this, it is none the less true that the Jacobin aimed at, and often put into execution, economic measures not commonly associated with the term "middle class." He confiscated property without compensation, he regulated prices and production by law, he encouraged an equal distribution of landed property and aimed at a general equality of fortunes not wholly consistent with the "career open to talents." Furthermore, qualify as we will the extent to which the clubs in the year II talked and acted like genuine social revolutionaries, like underdogs determined to have their day, like the poor in rebellion against the rich, we cannot honestly deny that the records of many of the clubs do evidence precisely that kind of talk, *and less often that kind of action.* The club at Castres would not pardon great wealth even to true believers. It voted "not to accept an individual possessing a monstrous fortune, unless, recognized as a pure and ardent *patriote,* he has caused by every means within his power, that inequality to disappear." [126] The very rich were pretty universally condemned. The club of Beauvais accepted the proposition "We must all be comfortably off, but there must be no more millionaires." [127] That of Loches very early asked the department to control funerals, for "we have daily beneath our eyes, the revolting contrast between the simple burial of the poor and the funeral pomp of the rich." [128] Yet this sentiment goes further. The *aristocratie marchande* is denounced.[129] Jullien on mission told a club to maintain "the most active watch on all merchants, on all rich men, who have taken the place of the aristocrats and the nobles." [130] At Paris a speaker in June, 1793 urged the *maximum* "to restrain the cupidity of the merchants, those true aristocrats." [131]

We are faced, then, with a paradox. The Jacobins, good middle class people, yet behave, where economics are concerned, in a way not wholly like the way good middle class people have usually behaved, where eco-

nomics are concerned, in the last two centuries. We
need not anticipate a concluding chapter which promises
to be complicated enough. But the simple way out of the
paradox is to assume that the Jacobins, although middle
class people, were also much else, that they had many
interests other than economic interests, and that these
interests modified their economic interests. We shall
doubtless find that these other interests now coincide,
now differ from the interests we have come to associate
with the middle class (for the word is protean enough,
and middle class morals are even more real and even
more difficult to define than middle class economic
views). Jacobinism will then appear to be much more
than a class movement, and the Terror much more than
an aspect of the class struggle.

V

The Jacobins were Puritans in morals. So persuaded
are foreign critics of the French, and Frenchmen themselves, that the French people are at all times and places
thoroughly Rabelaisian that this simple truth may appear a trifle startling. Yet only if Puritanism be defined
far more rigorously than anyone has yet succeeded in
doing is the above statement even slightly hazardous.
Here again we must first go to the records of the Jacobins
themselves, and find out how they wished themselves—
and still more others—to behave in a Jacobin world.

Against the more normal vices the Jacobins were always firm. It is too much to expect any movement for
prohibition of alcoholic drinks in the 18th century—not
even in America had morality at that time made such
progress. But the Jacobins held drunkenness to be a sin.
Most clubs made some provision in the rules for the

expulsion of drunkards. The club of Treignac generously provided exclusion for drunkenness only "if a member appears six times in the room in a state of drunkenness judged such by the society." [132] Cognac was much stricter, and declared that "a drunken man, being without morality, could not be admitted, and that whoever contravened this rule would be excluded from the society for good." [133] Perhaps, at Cognac, this was mere commercial prudence. Another familiar form of hostility to alcohol crops up occasionally. Wines and beers are to be permitted, but not strong drink. The club at Lille was horrified with conditions at Dunkirk "absolutely soaked in brandy and gin." [134]

Gambling was hardly approved even by the earlier clubs, where rooms were sometimes set aside for games. The club of Perpignan, for instance, prohibited bets of more than one sol a round at lotto.[135] The club of Toulouse, as early as November 1790, declared open war on gambling, edited a pamphlet against it, and petitioned the municipality to fine all persons playing for money in public places.[136] As the Jacobin republic became more and more a republic of virtue, agitation against gambling increased. Thonon went so far as to attack the evils of lotteries, including government lotteries, and to suggest their abolition.[137] Following what is perhaps the inevitable course of reform, another club, after condemning the vice of gambling, asked "for efficacious measures against those who nourish it by playing *in their own homes.*" [138] Still another explained at length why gambling could not go on in a true republic; "Always urged on by ambition, the gambler is pursued by regret for his money, which makes him brutal, insatiable, vicious even. Desirous of extirpating this moral evil, the society invites all citizens to play only social games, for purely recreational purposes; and wishing to give the example, it decrees that any member convicted of having lost in one evening more than 5 livres shall be expelled." [139] The fanatic, always a useful gauge of the movement he carries to excess, has his say here, too. At Limoges, the club was discussing the substitution of republican cards for the kings, queens and knaves (*valets*) of the old pack. A member arose, and said that cards caused more harm than good, and asked therefore that the club recommend complete prohibition of their manufacture and use. The club passed to the order of the day.[140]

Prostitution naturally offended the clubs quite as much as drinking and gambling. Mildly, the club of Lorient in 1791 listened to a motion "to relegate *filles publiques* to the most disagreeable part of the hall." [141] By 1793, the club of Toul would ask the municipality to incarcerate "women of evil life, and prevent the consequences of a dangerous promiscuity." [142] At Besançon, the club set up a committee to investigate the possibility of diminishing the number of prostitutes.[143] The club of Blois invited the municipality "de surveillé très escrupuleusement les feme du monde." [144] At Toulouse, the club sent commissioners to the municipality requesting a regulation of prostitution.[145] Nor was all this caused merely by a political distrust of the prostitutes, who were notoriously royalist. The club at Le Havre sought to suppress fornication as far as possible, and asked to have certain temporary wooden buildings removed, as "pouvant servir de retraite au libertinage." [146] The club at Gray had a record worthy of a modern vice crusade. It prevented the holding of dances, even interfering with a *noce*, (18 frimaire an II.). It succeeded in getting cafés and billiard rooms shut, and asked the municipality to turn some women of evil life out of their lodgings. It is true that the motive of all this was ostensibly a patriotic elimination of waste in a war crisis; but surely there were more effective and less dramatic ways of effecting economies? [147]

All this, however, may be dismissed as evidence merely that the Jacobins had a sound middle class attitude towards vice and its suppression. But the Jacobins went further, and showed unmistakable signs of a censorious, even prudish, morality of their own. The club of Provins listened with approval to an ode to **La Pudeur**:

> Les bonnes moeurs des Républiques
> Sont le soutien, font le bonheur.
> Parmi nos vertus domestiques,
> O Français, comptons la Pudeur.
>
> Que dans le sein de nos ménages
> Soit un autel en son honneur.
> Tous les sexes et tous les âges
> Doivent un culte à la Pudeur.[148]

One club actually established a committee of six "to examine plays given at the theater so that they may not offend the moral purity of true republicans." [149] The reign of virtue in the spring of 1794 merely heightened this Puritanism. Collot d'Herbois at Paris could remind the club of the excesses of the Hébertistes, and of "those mortal and complaisant goddesses of Reason who, beneath a gauze robe, appeared with rouge and patches on the boards of almost any theater"—a reminder which must have heightened his hearers' sense of virtue.[150]

There are even signs of a curious kind of Puritan reaction to the sensuousness of Roman Catholic civilization. At Thonon, "a member protests against the indecency of a picture of the Virgin giving the child Jesus to suck, with the inscription: *Meliora sunt ubera tua vino.*" [151] At another club "a member explained that it would suffice to tell the citizenesses of this commune not to wear about their necks gold or silver crosses, or any kind of necklace, as well as ear-rings and other little effects in jewelry invented by pride, and proved that they needed no adornment beyond their virtues." [152] Manuel at Paris in 1792 made a curious speech to the assembled *fédérés,* warning them against the dangers of the city, urging them to imitate the Americans in their struggle for freedom and abstain from *filles,* and including this lovely sentiment, which is eighteenth century, but which is also Puritanical: "if I were a *fédéré,* I should spend my time among the poor, for a glass of water offered by Liberty is better than the best wine offered by the hands of slaves." [153]

Unquestionably what the Jacobin meant by virtue was largely a collection of eighteenth century stereotypes, in which sentimentality and humanitarianism have a large part. This is especially true of the culmination of the Terror during Robespierre's brief apotheosis. Robespierre and the Paris Jacobins, having put virtue and the Supreme Being as the order of the day, the perfection of Jacobin organization spread the movement all over France. Yet this phase of Jacobinism was not an unnatural development, and deserves to be included in any synthesis. There are abundant signs in the early days of the societies that Rousseau and Shaftesbury and the other sentimentalists have left their mark. The club of Troyes seeking affiliation from Paris writes: "You will not find in us citizens recommendable for our erudition. We are neither men of letters, nor scholars, nor nobles; our merit is in the simplicity, in the purity of our morals, and in our ardent love for the new constitution." [154] The republic was of course to be a republic of virtue. "We consecrate thee, sacred enclosure, to the principles of pure Republicanism, that is, to that Republicanism which cannot exist without virtue." [155] At Tours, the ladies of that city presented the club with a banner inscribed: "One must have morals to belong to us." [156] Coutances decreed that "all the virtues shall always be the order of the day." [157]

These virtues, if one attempts to find what they specifically were, are mostly the traditional Christian, and especially Protestant Christian, virtues—modesty, industry, temperance, the family virtues, honesty, and so on. "A gambler, a drunkard, a bad father cannot be a republican" said the good Philip to his club of Nancy.[158] Occasionally there is a trace of heroic and Roman virtue. "An anonymous letter is placed on the desk. Following its decree the Society burns the letter without reading it." [159] At Limoges, a member "persuaded the club to vote its meeting-place the Temple of Truth; any member convicted of a lie was to be expelled." [160] Still more numerous are the traces of the old religion. The minutes of the club of Ars-en-Ré beg Frenchmen to "oublier tous les préjugés, en y suppléant la Ste. Morale." [161] Abbreviation and capitalization remind us that habit is stronger even than the great Encyclopædia. At Lons-le-Saunier "a priest made an interesting motion wherein he proved according to his system that the Revolution is entirely in the Gospels." [162]

To disentangle eighteenth century philosophical elements from other elements in Jacobin ethical aims is difficult, and not very useful. For what chiefly differentiates the ethics we loosely call Puritan from those of the philosophic century is less the moral code itself than the method of its enforcement. The *philosophe* trusted the individual to guide himself to virtue through reason; the Christian, and still more the Puritan, enforces obedi-

ence to the moral code upon the individual by the use
of authority—governmental, church, or communal according to need. Now the Jacobins here are definitely
on the authoritarian side. They did not even trust the
faithful to remain virtuous unenforced by frequent examples of the power of the community. At their height,
the clubs exercised over the morals of their members,
over their private concerns, the same sort of inquisitorial
power exercised by the church of Calvin at Geneva or
at Boston. Examples crowd upon the investigator.

From the rules governing admission of a club in 1793:
"Article 4. A register will be provided for the names
of candidates, their profession, residence, their political
conduct since 1789, their ways of life, and their
morals." [163] The club at Nancy very nearly endowed itself, after serious discussion, with a "censeur des
moeurs." [164] With domestic affairs both of members and
non-members the clubs interfered freely. "A member dis-
plays his indignation at the conduct of citizen Pergoz,
who beat his wife, and asks that he be censured, which
is done." Pergoz was not a member of the society.[165] The
club of Boulogne turned down a candidate with the satisfying name of Décadi for, as a member said "we do not
want merely men who love the Revolution. All members
of our Society must be moral. Décadi has not treated his
wife decently, has abandoned her without motive to
carry on with another woman." [166] The club of Montignac
expelled a priest even though he had very completely
unfrocked himself, because he admitted having taken
money for masses which he never said, and because he
seduced a young girl and then fobbed her off on another
man.[167] Another club pursued a citizen who, though
he was rich and prosperous, did not support his niece.
The niece turned out to be only a distant cousin but

the society was still convinced of the citizen's immorality, and denounced him to the revolutionary committee.[168] Still another haled before itself a rich father who refused to let his daughter marry a poor but deserving suitor. All parties appeared at the bar of the society, and a temporary reconciliation took place.[169]

There is a petition from the society of Auxerre to the Convention late in 1793 which affords an astonishing example of how far a club considered the private morals of citizens its concern. The society recites at length how citizen Le Comte married a poor girl, settled his fortune of 200,000 livres on her, and then committed suicide because of her unfaithfulness. The widow none the less inherited the 200,000 livres. The society asks a retroactive law to make such injustice impossible.

> You will remark, Legislators, in the conduct of this woman an immorality shocking to that virtue which is the basis of republican government. The story of her scorn, her indifference, her aversion, put beside the solicitude, the care, finally the despair of her husband revolted all true Republicans, and the first cry of the Society, always animated by the principle that he who does not love his fellows is a blind person . . . that he who could hate them is a monster, was to ask the Convention for a repressive law which could prevent this sort of thing from happening.[170]

It is not to be wondered that citizen Dubois of Bénévent consulted the club before he married a young lady whose relations were not good Jacobins.[171]

Prohibition of, or at least regulation to prevent any excess in, the commoner vices, drinking, gambling and prostitution, more than a trace of prudery, a distrust of great wealth, much insistence on purity and virtue, acceptance of traditional Christian ethics, and finally a well-developed system of interference by the group in the lives of individuals, a kind of interference not unfairly described at times as censorious and inquisitorial —all these characteristics of Jacobin morals are shared by what now passes as Puritanism. Real Puritanism, ideal Puritanism, or Puritanism in Milton's time, may all be very different from this. But such words seem subject to a kind of Gresham's law, whereby the worse meaning drives the better out of common circulation. We can hardly do otherwise than accept the word at its face value, however much we may regret that through much tempering by Lewises and Menckens it no longer rings quite true. Not only Robespierre, then, but the Jacobins in general, must be labeled Puritans in morals.

VI

To summarize, we may say that our mythical "average" Jacobin would have accepted as a statement of his aims something like this: An independent nation-state, a republican form of government, universal manhood suffrage, separation of church and state; equal civil rights for all, and the abolition of hereditary distinctions and social privileges; a competitive industrial and agricultural society, with private ownership of property, but without great fortunes and without dire poverty; a virtuous, hard-working society, without luxuries and without vices, where the individual freely conforms to standards of middle-class decency.

CHAPTER VI

RITUAL

I

There is little in the aims, or even in the combination of aims, outlined in the previous chapter as the Jacobin platform that is uniquely Jacobin. The most that can be said is that the warmth with which the Jacobins hated priests and the devotion with which they followed Christian ethics combine rather distinctively. But for the rest, what the Jacobins wanted to make of this world was not very different from what similar middle-class people in Europe and America wanted to make of it. Jacobin practical aims in social, political and economic life hardly went beyond what the nineteenth century was to achieve, and the twentieth century to call Victorian; there was little in the Jacobin program that should have shocked the Second Empire.

If, then, the Jacobins were socially too disparate to have been held together by genuine class-feeling, and if their actual program was too much like that of ordinary men of their time to be distinctive, Jacobinism must have embraced some other common thing, or common things, or else have been a mere name. Now, men who do things together often form a genuine group, a corporation, even though as men they are quite unlike, and even though their ultimate aims are like those of many others. Jacobin tactics, their technique of political action, certainly helped to keep the clubs together. But sufficient oppor-

tunity for action hardly lay open to the clubs; and at
best group action must be dramatized, extended by ritualistic devices to members too timid or too lazy to take
part in direct action. A study of Jacobin ritual cannot
fail further to define Jacobinism, to show just how a
true Jacobin differed from other Frenchmen of his time.

II

Ritual is a commoner form of human activity than is
always realized, and certainly is not limited to what is
usually meant by a religious usage. Hardly a group—
family, school, club, nation—but observes a certain ritual,
a ritual sometimes merely a matter of words but more
usually embodied in symbolic objects, in music or in other
forms of art. The French Revolution was peculiarly rich
in ritualistic devices, and it is difficult to say with cer-
tainty of a given device that it was peculiar to the Jacobin clubs, that it originated in the clubs, that it helped
to make them aware of their corporate existence. Here,
again, the best way is to consult the records of the clubs,
and find what went on during Jacobin meetings. But first
it may be well to sketch briefly the chief revolutionary
cults, cults which arose no doubt largely through Jacobin
patronage, but which are not exclusively attached to the
clubs as such.

The first of these cults [1] in time as in importance may
be called simply that of *la patrie*. With the fall of the
Bastille it found its first symbol in the tricolor cockade.
Then *autels de la patrie,* simple stone blocks, suitably inscribed with moral aphorisms of the Enlightenment, were
erected on village greens and in front of city halls. Trees
of liberty—and here the revolutionists adopted for themselves the immemorial custom of the maypole—were

planted by municipalities and patriotic societies. As the Revolution developed, party symbols like the Mountain, symbols of emergency like the *oeil de surveillance,* and symbols more directly borrowed from Christianity, like the martyred trinity, Marat, Lepelletier, and Chalier, were introduced. People were gathered together for ceremonies built up around these symbols. The "federations" of July 14, 1790, at Paris and in the provinces were probably the most sincere and the most universally shared of such moments of collective emotion. But there were also fraternal meals held in the open air, where the youths served simple dishes to their elders, assembled with no distinction of rank or wealth. More obvious imitations of Christian practice began to appear. There were civic marriages, civic baptisms, civic burials. Revolutionary songs were written, and the songs became hymns. The Declaration of the Rights of Man took on the authority of scripture.

In this general cult of *la patrie,* there grew up special cults, much of a piece with the parent cult, and only to be distinguished from it by some dramatic quality, by a personality or a patriotic creed. The cult of Reason, culminating in the ceremony at Notre Dame that forms one of the picturesque commonplaces of the Revolution, has a completeness of its own. So too has that of the Supreme Being, in whose honor Robespierre led the famous procession of 20 prairial. After the Terror the cult of *la patrie* was in part continued in what came to be known from its calendar as the *culte décadaire.* Still other odds and ends of eighteenth-century thought were fused into the "theophilanthropy" associated with the name of La Révellière-Lépeaux.

The Friends of the Constitution early adopted a kindred ritual for use in their ordinary meetings. Their

masonic origins may in part explain their liking for ritual, and their early use of it, but masonry will hardy explain all the forms Jacobin ritual was to take. As time
went on, the sessions of the clubs grew more and more
ritualistic, until under the Terror they are more like
religious services than club-meetings, or parliamentary
proceedings.

A complete catalogue of all Jacobin activities to which
the word ritual might not unfairly be applied would take
volumes. We must limit ourselves to examples first, of the
actual decorations of Jacobin meeting-places, then of
ritualistic elements in their procedure, and finally, of the
various fêtes and holidays of the new religion sponsored
by the clubs.

Even the simplest of Jacobin halls had its appropriate
pantheon of busts. At first the great thinkers of the century and the traditional heroes of ancient and modern
struggles for liberty made up the pantheon—Rousseau,
Voltaire, Mably, Franklin, Solon, Brutus, Sidney, Wash-
ington.[2]

During the Terror, busts of the "martyred trinity,"
Marat, Lepelletier, and Chalier, were to be found
in almost every club; and these busts were, at least to
many Jacobins, not merely ornaments, but the successors
to the saints. The club of Chablis requested "citizen
Thomassin to put the bust of Marat in the place of the
ci-devant St. James now in a niche on his house."[3] At
Limoges, the club had the bust of Marat carried in procession through the streets, and ordered the shops to be
closed during the ceremony.[4] To make its busts show up
properly against the wall, the club of Chablis had tricolor patches painted behind them; and having paint to
spare, inscribed one end of the hall with Indivisibilité
de la Republique, the other with Liberté, Egalité, Fra-

ternité, ou la Mort.[5] The *tribune* they had painted with the tricolor as early as September 1793.

Busts in suitable niches, republican inscriptions on the walls, red white and blue paint for important objects—such was the general setting of the Jacobin *salle,* even when it was a made-over church. The *tribune* and the president's chair were the centers of ornamentation, in some sense the altars of the new religion. At first all the flags of freedom—the French, the English, the American and the Polish—would often be draped behind the president's chair. But as their brothers in freedom failed them, and as they themselves became more nationalistic, the Jacobins abandoned other flags, and contented themselves with the tricolor.[6] A framed copy of the Declaration of the Rights of Man was sure to hang near the *tribune.* As the monarchy visibly declined, the Phrygian bonnet gained in popularity. As early as June 1791, the club of Sauveterre decided "to place some attributes of liberty in the hall. It was decreed that in the most prominent place should be put the Greek bonnet which is the sign of liberty, with this inscription—." There follows a large blank, never filled in by a lazy secretary.[7] Doppet, addressing the Paris Jacobins in March, 1792, contrived, while fumbling in his pocket for his notes, to fish out a liberty cap. The cheers of the club forced him to put it on, and even Robespierre could only postpone its formal adoption. Under the republic the president of almost every club was required to wear the cap as a symbol of his office.[8] Citizen Carréfour, of Beaufort-en-Vellée, dying, expressed his desire to be buried in his cap of liberty.[9]

To a hall thus filled with visible reminders of what was expected of him, the Jacobin came less for deliberation than for edification. At Aix-en-Provence, each mem-

ber as he entered the hall cried out: "Vive la République!
Vive la Montagne! Vivent les sans-culottes!" [10] Usually,
however, the meeting was begun by the presiding officer
according to a formula that varied somewhat from place
to place. The president at Thonon began solemnly: Egalité, Liberté. Au nom de la République une, indivisible, et
démocratique. La séance est ouverte." The society, as an
amen, repeated in chorus: "Vive la République." [11] As
early as 1791, the society of Monpazier began its sessions
by reading the Rights of Man; [12] in 1793, the society of
Largentière decided "that at every session at least one
article of the Declaration must be read." [13] The club of
Manneville in Normandy, now Zèle-de-la Patrie, closes
a circular letter on horse-breeding with "Vive la République une et indivisible. Vive la Montagne. Vive les
Sans-culottes qui l'ont preservée du Naufrage." [14] At Aix,
the club concluded a festival with the cry: "Vive la Montagne, Vivent les sans-culottes, Vivent les martyrs de la
Liberté et de l'Egalité. Vive la sainte Révolution." [15]
Oaths taken very ceremoniously in common and on all
occasions were probably of masonic origin, but they soon
became typically Jacobin in their religiosity. The much
adopted oath of the club of Moulins will do as a type: "I
swear to maintain with all my might the unity and in-
divisibility of the republic; I swear moreover to recognise
as my brother any just man, any true friend of humanity,
whatever his color, his height, and his land; I swear moreover that I shall never have any other temple than that
of Reason, other altars than those of the Fatherland,
other priests than our legislators, nor other cult than that
of liberty, equality, fraternity. Long live the Republic,
Long live the Mountain." [16]
Hymns were sung at other times in the course of the
session, sometimes by the club, sometimes by patriotic

ladies who volunteered their services. Hymns to Nature,
to the Mountain, to Liberty, and to Reason abound,
often the work of local Jacobins. But the Marseillaise
was from the first the favorite tune, though only later
were its words not to be tampered with. The society at
Rodez, for instance, listened to a poem on the marriage
of priests, set to the tune of the Marseillaise, with the
refrain:

> La nature et l'hymen sont les premières lois,
> Le coeur, le coeur nous dit assez nos devoirs et nos droits.[17]

At Limoges, the president first sang a couplet of the Marseillaise, and then was joined by the club in unison.[18] At
another club "the president sang the *Hymn to Nature,*
the refrain of which was sung in chorus by everyone
present." [19] The club of Chateau-Thierry sang its republican hymns to an organ accompaniment.[20]

The hymns and responsive reading were followed, ap-
propriately enough, by sermons. Sometimes, speeches of
the leading moralist-orators of the national assemblies
would be read—Vergniaud or Robespierre delivered sec-
ond-hand. Members of the club of Lunéville were obliged
to deliver moral discourses on *décadis,* and took such
subjects—one almost wrote texts—as "Let us be docile
to the lessons of Nature and we shall be virtuous" or "The
Golden Age." [21] To judge from most of the proceedings
of the clubs, these sermons must have been as dull as sermons should be.

Still other curious examples can be cited of the way
Jacobin meetings follow the precedents of Christian
services. One club had at its door a box labeled deliberately *Tronc pour les pauvres,* and inscribed "Remember
you have unfortunate brothers." [22] Another took up a
collection after the *morale* (sermon) of *décadi.*[23] At Cha-

teau-Thierry, "a republican catechism was read and afterwards a member sang." [24] "Patriotic ten commandments" were common, and show considerable variation under the inspiration of local patriots, a fact which perhaps lessened a bit their authority as rivals to the oldfashioned decalogue.[25] Republican marriages, christenings, funerals were encouraged by the clubs, and these ceremonies—lay only in narrowest meaning of the word, for they were completely religious in spirit—often took place in the club itself. "Bézu announces that he is father of a new republican, and asks that the christening take place in the club, and that the president and the *citoyenne* Andrieu be witnesses. At once the infant is brought in to reiterated applause, and the president delivers from the tribune a sermon on the errors of prejudice." [26] At Tonneins, the records describe a marriage at the club, and add "the nuptial benediction was given in the name of the God of the Revolution." [27]

The society at Thonon provided an adjoining room "for the instruction of young people during the meetings of the society." The Jacobins had discovered the uses of the Sunday School before that institution became common in organized churches.[28] From Avallon, we hear something of what the pupils in these Sunday Schools were doing. "The club began by hearing the pupils of the fatherland (*élèves de la patrie*) the pupils of Garnier and Millié, men-teachers, Virally and Chatelain, women-teachers. They gave an account of their studies for the *décadi*, recited the Republican Commandments, the Declaration of Rights, the speech of the president of the department, and the heroic and civic actions of republicans." [29] Young people of all ages frequently appeared at the clubs to show how well they had been brought up as Jacobins. At Le Havre "a little citizen of 8 years, named

Marguerite Campagny recites aloud the Rights of Man. The society applauds the excellent and well-employed memory of this child, and the patriotic care of her parents for her education; She receives the fraternal embrace from the president, and civic mention in the minutes." [30]

As early as 1790 the Jacobins of Paris were told that they had achieved the "apostolate of liberty." [31] The word apostle subsequently was on everyone's lips. The town clubs sent "apostles" or "missionaries" out into the country districts, still mostly in unphilosophic darkness. Ordinary propaganda is not sufficient to spread the "évangile révolutionnaire" in such places, says the organ of the club of Besançon. "The publications of the societies are not sufficient, few people read them; but everyone likes to listen to a man who has come especially to warm his compatriots' zeal by his discourse, and to raise their souls to the enthusiasm of liberty." [32] In many clubs, the number of these apostles was deliberately set at twelve.[33] The mission undertaken was no light one, for in many parts of France the hostility of the peasants subjected these apostles to serious bodily harm. Many an apostle became in some degree a martyr, a word also much in favor among the Jacobins. Even in 1790, when the president of the club of Brive was found dead from drowning in a weir, the club of Tulle referred to him as "that veritable martyr of the constitution." [34]

Sometimes Jacobin borrowings from earlier religious practices are so obvious that one seems to detect the instincts of the showman at play. When citizen Foucaud of Limoges advertised in the club organ his "Pater, Ave, Credo, acts of faith, hope, love, contrition, confiteor, decalogue, and revolutionary commandments of the Mountain," he may have been sincere; [35] but how the inventor of the "revolutionary sign of the cross" in the name of

"Marat, Lepelletier, Liberty or Death" can have been other than a mountebank is hard to conceive.[36] In the records of the club of Limoges we read how at the end of a celebration in honor of the new constitution the Jacobins filed in front of the tree of liberty, and "each one prostrated himself before this sign of union." [37] At the same club, the president kissed the bust of Marat before putting it in its place.[38] Suspects had for lack of space to be confined in the church at Auch where the society met. The society decided nevertheless to continue meeting there, and added "that the suspects should be shut up in the apse, where they could hear the patriots thrill with the cult of liberty, and that rosemary should be burned to purify the air infected by the suspects." [39] One club, moving its properties—Brutus, Marat, Rousseau and the rest—to its new hall, speaks of the "fête de la translation" of these relics.[40] At Meyrueis "a member moved that children born in the last two décades be carried, on the next décadi, to the tree of liberty, there to breathe in the first principles of liberty." [41] The club of Coutances celebrated July 14th by carrying about the city, as the monstrance used to be carried at the feast of Corpus Christi, a model of the Bastille, held on the shoulders of four veterans, and busts of Marat and Lepelletier. The latter bust fell to the ground, and lost its nose, much to the delight of the enemies of the Republic.[42] A bust of Rousseau was carried by the society of Louhans through the streets on décadi. The Marseillaise was sung by the marchers, "and after each couplet, each member drank from the sacred cup of Union and Fraternity, Rousseau had his part of the wine and seemed to smile on his work. . . . Back in the hall, Rousseau was replaced, the society applauded, the president embraced his neighbor, and each one followed this example." [43] Members of the club of Libourne all signed six "articles of faith." [44] At the news of the arrival of the American wheat ships at Brest, after the first of June, one club "to thank the Supreme Being for having protected in so visible a fashion the armies of the Republic, has sung to him an action of grace by the teacher and the mayor's secretary." [45] The worthy Avallonais decided "to assemble every *décadi* to sing hymns in honor of the Supreme Being of Reason and of the Fatherland (sic), to combat superstitions and destroy them by wise and civic discourses by philosophic reading from our philosophers." [46] Such a hodgepodge of objects of belief is witness to more mystic fervor, or more sheer stupidity, than usually accompanies the religion of humanity. We shall probably have to accept as fair the judgment of the secretary at Toulouse: "The cult of Liberty propagates itself and grows stronger every day. Already this august religion, emanating from the divinity who created all men free and equal has among us its temples, its festivals and its martyrs." [47]

Odd phrases of purely religious connotation keep recurring, and Jacobin language, in its higher flights, is extremely theological. At Lunéville, separate benches were preserved for proselytes; the poet laureate of this same club refers to the Marseillaise as a *cantique*.[48] The second register of the club of Bergerac is inscribed *registre sacré*.[49] At Aix, only "pure, true, and just men" will be admitted to the *Sanctuary of the Revolution*.[50] The hall of the club of Montauban is the *sanctuary of the temple of liberty*.[51] The adjective *holy* was used freely, *notre sainte constitution*, for example.[52] Sometimes there are phrases of an unction no doubt unjustly associated with certain aspects of religious belief. A constitutional priest addressing the society of Bordeaux saw fit to phrase his adhesion to revolutionary cause thus: "I believe in the all-powerful National Assembly, creator of good and of liberty." [53] And the president of the society at Bergerac hailed "the election of our new (constitutional) bishop, which will cause to flow through our souls the precious balm of a Constitution founded on the unshakeable base of a holy faith." [54] A Jacobin lady addressed the club at Le Havre: "Children of a constitution marked with the sign of Divinity, by the miraculous protection which that Divinity accords it, regenerated for Liberty, we wish to render ourselves worthy of its advantages." [55] The club of Beaufort signified its acceptance of the constitution of 1793 in the following language: "The holy charter which contains the constitutional act, where Reason herself traced the civil and unprescribable Rights of Man—the charter contains within itself all the elements of our political faith." [56]

There is to be found a tendency to allegory which has obvious analogies with European traditions of religious instruction. *"O People!* You saw in time the snare set for you; and from the lofty summit you were occupying you did but descend, your mass filled all the irregularities, and there appeared an enormous *Mountain,* at the very spot where once had been a *plain,* at first fertile, then dry and arid, and finally swampy." [57] Sometimes the training of the clerical members comes out in references to the Bible. The right club of Ollioules asked the Paris club to be sure and distinguish it from the wrong club, "the true worshippers of Israel from those of Magog." [58] Citizen David Morel, of Largentière, displayed much ingenuity with his Old Testament. "In psalm 109, David says *'Judicabit in nationibus'*—'I shall establish a revolutionary tribunal in all the nations"; *'et implevit ruinas'* —'I shall ruin all powers opposed to the principles of

common sense'; 'et conquassabit capita in terra mul-
torum'—'and the guillotine shall hurl to the ground the
heads of all madmen'." [59] The society of Vesoul consecrated a monument to Liberty in the language of the
pulpit.

> Beneath the rule of despotism, flattery raised statues to tyrants,
> fear raised altars to monsters; but tyrants pass, monsters pass,
> and the people remains; posterity rises, and the breath of truth
> overturns in a moment the statues, the altars, and their idols. Be-
> neath the rule of law, liberty alone has a right to the homage of a
> free people, and the monuments raised by gratefulness to virtue
> are immortal. [60]

Finally the clubs, not content with filling their own sessions with ritual, took a leading part in all public festivals in honor of the Revolution. The same elements we
found in club ritual enters into these festivals; but the
mixture is if possible still more capricious, the result still
less in conformity with good taste. Perhaps the best way
to classify some of these elements is to describe, from
club records, a few of these popular festivals.

The underlying purpose of most of these festivals was
to imbed revolutionary abstractions as firmly as possible
in the popular mind. Modern advertising technique
might have helped the organizers of these festivals, for it
would have taught them that mere repetition of abstract
phrases is in itself the best way of impressing them on the
popular mind. But to these reasonable eighteenth century men, it seemed that Truth must somehow be made
to appear to the senses. So we find that at Lyons, in the
long procession of officials, national guardsmen, and members of patriotic societies there were carried a carpenter's level in the name of equality, busts of the great
Frenchmen, Marat, Lepelletier, and Chalier, busts of
Brutus, William Tell, and Rousseau, "foreigners worthy

of being Frenchmen," a statue of liberty, tables inscribed
with the laws, jars and baskets of food for the communal
feast which was to mark the height of the celebration,
and "other emblems of the present cult of Frenchmen." [61]
At Le Havre, at the planting of the tree of liberty, equality was made real to the people by the skillful work of
the club "for everything was most excellently mixed,
the general grasped the horny hand of the brave common
sailor, the magistrate grasped in his that of the poor
beggar." [62]

Reason was a more difficult problem. No carpenter's
tool would do here. The task was pretty well given up,
and all over France young and if possible lovely women
became for the moment goddesses of Reason. Ceremonies
in which these young women figured are usually derived
from Christian usage. At Vaulry, for instance, after a
procession through the town, the goddess seated herself
before the altar (of the Fatherland). On one side of the
goddess, and a little in front of her was placed the oldest
man, and on the other the oldest woman, and between
them, on a table, the burning Torch of Reason. Four
young women, who had carried the torch in the procession, stood at the far corners of the platform. When the
people had solemnly entered, and got seated, the orators
of the day addressed them; each, while he was speaking,
wore the Liberty cap.[63] At Vire, just as the orator of the
day began his sermon, the veil which had shrouded Reason fell away and the goddess appeared in her glory surrounded by her priestesses, and facing a sacred fire. The
president of the club, after breaking two crosses over his
knees, received the oath of the club to recognize no cult
but that of Reason. Then the priestesses of Reason
placed a wreath on the president's head, and offered him
a cup in which he drank of the water of regeneration. Ex-

catholic priests brought up books full of the errors they had once taught. The priestesses of Reason destroyed the books, and offered the cup "to the former apostles of superstition, who are regenerated as they drink from the fountain of expiation." [64]

Sometimes these festivals appear to have been almost convivial. The society of Creyssac entertained its sister society of Bourdeille to celebrate republican victories in the Vendée. Each member of the club of Creyssac took a branch of green oak leaves, marched out of the hall and gave it to a member from Bourdeille, and accompanied him back to the hall to the sound of fife and drum. There was a joint session, followed by a civic feast.

> A thousand healths were drunk to our representatives, good Montagnards of the Convention, to our brave and generous soldiers, to all the clubs, to our brave brothers of Bourdeille; many patriotic songs were sung, now in chorus; and now confusedly. The feast ended, all the guests, marching in two columns, went to the foot of the tree of liberty. There was sung the hymn of the Marseillaise, and there was dancing about this beloved tree. Then the clubs proceeded in the same order to a meadow, where country dances were held around the red cap of liberty, placed on a little mound, and which each person kissed in turn. This ceremony ended, a return was made to the tree of liberty, which all embraced. Songs and dances terminated this act, so worthy of true *sans-culottes*. There followed another joint session, another civic feast, at the height of which the society of Lisle arrived in a body, and was duly embraced singly "Toute cette journée à jamais mémorable s'est passée dans les plus doux épanchements." [65]

At other times there is a bit of the Punch and Judy show, with none of the melodrama left out. The club of Lullier celebrated the taking of Toulon. "Arrived at the foot of the tree of liberty," the Jacobins chosen to carry out the ceremony "began to shoot at an effigy of the infamous Pitt, corrupter of Toulon, which was hung from a lofty gallows. As the shots rang out the head burst in the air, and his white cravat was stained with blood, which most agreeably surprised spectators unacquainted with the artifice. What was left of the effigy was then consumed on a funeral pyre—Afterwards two choruses sang hymns to victory and to equality." [66] At Chateauroux, the club decided that "each *décadi* there shall be burned at the base of the monument to Marat an effigy of a crowned tyrant until all kings shall have been thus burned in effigy." [67]

One final example, a long and arduous celebration at Guéret, held in honor of the Mountain. In a procession of all good Jacobins of the town, "Ingrand, representative on mission gave his arm on one side to the poorest woman in the city, on the other to the oldest; the children of these mothers surrounded them." A symbolical Mountain had been erected opposite the tree of liberty. "In its cavernous flanks were to be seen the graves of despotism, of feudalism, of all those filthy animals that for centuries made the misfortunes of the French people. Crowns half buried in the mud, and serving as refuges for toads and snakes was the allegory used to perpetuate the memory of the glorious epochs of the Revolution since the 10th of August." On one side of the Mountain were stacks of wheat, with the inscription *Law of 11 September 1793 concerning the food-supply. Public felicity assured.* A bundle of pikes, equal in number to the departments, and tied with a tricolor ribbon, surmounted the Mountain and bore the inscription *Our strength is in the union of all.* All sorts of revolutionary slogans were stuck over the surface of this Mountain: *Useful arts, you need no longer sigh beneath the chains of slavery* and *Mothers, see that your children suckle the milk of love of country.* The president of the society next addressed

the gathering. At the end of his speech, clouds were seen
to be gathering about the Mountain. But the sun soon
rose above these clouds bearing in its wake a streamer inscribed *Republican constitution freely accepted by the
people, 10 August 1793.* Then there were songs and
dances, and "at the cross-roads members of the society
distributed bread free to their unfortunate brothers at
the expense of the society." [68]

Occasionally the Jacobins seem to have had doubts
about their ritual. The president at Lille, describing the
festival in honor of the Supreme Being, made especially
emphatic "the great difference that exists between these
republican festivals and the foolish and ridiculous processions of fanaticism." [69] A brother at Nice "demanded
the suppression of songs, poems, et cetera during sessions
of the club, maintaining that they weren't there to amuse
themselves; but another defended them, saying that they
made the principles of Liberty better known, and more
beloved." [70] Yet many must have accepted this ritual,
even though they had not the simple faith of the Jacobins of Limoges who "merely by dancing the Carmagnole
and singing the Marseillaise would paralyse forever all
their enemies, internal and external, present and to
come." [71] And there was so much of it that, no matter
how absurd in matter and in structure, it produced some
effect. At least, France was never wholly to escape a
republican cult. When the Thermidorean Boisset was at
Moulins, releasing suspects, a festival was organized "in
which a goddess presented the representative with a cage
full of little birds, to which he gave liberty." [72] At Beauvais, after Thermidor, it was decided to paint with the
three colors of the Republic the Liberty cap suspended
over the city hall, since red "recalls rather the reign of
blood than that of liberty." [73]

III

It is clear that this Jacobin ritual was an incredible hodgepodge. Much of it, like the revolutionary credo and the pater, the revolutionary martyrs, the revolutionary sign of the cross, is crudely borrowed from Roman Catholicism. But the public celebration of the new cults, the processions, the altars, the cups of salvation, the prostration before the tree of liberty are more reminiscent of Roman Catholic ways than are the actual sessions of the clubs. Here the responsive recitations, the hymn singing, the long sermons, the Sunday Schools, are much more in the Protestant tradition. Some of the older folk-habits may have entered into Jacobin ritual. The tree of liberty may be distantly related to the maypole, and Jacobin dancers, to say nothing of the drinking of Jacobin healths, must have been quite in accordance with tradition. Classical heroes—especially the heroes of Plutarch —have their part in these ceremonies. Personifications like the goddess of Reason, abstractions like the civic and private virtues, though clear enough to middle class lawyers and doctors, thoroughly trained in the classics and familiar with current moralistic philosophy, must have meant very little to workingmen and peasants.

Because all these elements are distinguishable in Jacobin ritual, one need not go on to assume that the Jacobins achieved a synthesis of paganism, catholicism and protestantism. Ritual after all is but the costume in which men clothe the group; and very different men can wear the same clothes. Some sort of ritual is apparently necessary, as clothes are necessary, to man in society. It is sufficient for our purposes to make sure that the Jacobins had a ritual peculiar to themselves. Of this there can be no doubt. We must next try to see whether this ritual really held them together as a group; or rather, we must try to see whether the Jacobins who went through these rites had also a faith. To return, at the risk of being shockingly unscientific, to our metaphor; if there is a faith as well as a ritual, then there is a body beneath the clothes; if there is no faith, then Jacobinism is a humbug, a scarecrow, or something still more fitted to Carlylean rhetoric.

CHAPTER VII

FAITH

We have not, then, gone far enough into Jacobinism if we stop with its ritual. There is that trite phrase about "empty ritual" which should give us a clew. At the very lowest, a human being who makes certain gestures or recites certain words of a ritual hopes thereby to gain something. Scoundrels may go through a ritual better to disguise their real aims; but to assume all or most of the Jacobins to have been scoundrels is to overestimate human enterprise. Cowards may go through with a ritual to conform to what the majority does; but we still have the majority left. Men may go through with a ritual out of mere habit, at least for a time; but the Jacobins were innovators, and their ritual had no chance to harden into habit. Now, no ritual can be in itself empty; if neither hypocrisy, nor cowardice, nor habit make of a given ritual a mechanical gesture, then this ritual must have meaning to the believer. This meaning will be his faith, his theology, his political ideas. Put in the form of a code, this faith will discipline its holder as a member of the group; put as a description of reality above ordinary experience, and endowed with a ritual, this faith will satisfy the emotional longings of its holder.

I

Signs are not lacking in the records of the clubs that Jacobin ritual was accompanied by precisely that emotional expansion that marks a faith. Eighteenth century diction is no doubt even more susceptible to all the sensibilities than eighteenth century men. Nevertheless, even when we subtract a good deal for fashionable phraseology, the Jacobin records give many instances of what seems to be genuine emotion, of transport and of rapture. An exalted, and clearly religious state of mind is evident in the inaugural address of a president at Thann. His election raises him as it were above himself but makes him feel all the more his own insufficiency; he is aware that only the *lumières* of his fellows can make clear to him the narrow path where he burns to walk.[1] Such too are the feelings of a member of the society of female friends of the constitution at Besançon: "O precious effects of *patriotisme!* I feel that it raises me, that it expands my soul; I feel that I am more than myself." [2] Occasionally there is proof that this exaltation could be shared. The club of Eymoutiers took, amid an "indescribable delirium," an oath prescribed by the department of Haute-Vienne: "I call down anathema upon kings and tyrants, anathema upon dictators, upon triumvirs, upon false defenders, upon false protectors of the people; anathema upon any who under the title of chief, general, stadholder, prince or any other name whatsoever would usurp a superiority, a pre-eminence over his fellow-citizens; and I swear to pursue him to the death." [3]

Another curious example of group-emotion is found in the records of the club of Pau. A delegate brought back to the president a fraternal embrace from Monestier, representative on mission. The president embraced in turn the person next to him, and the embrace "was consequently carried, given and received from neighbor to neighbor, even in the galleries, a spectacle which brought joy and tenderness to all."[4] This is no doubt the sensi-

bility in fashion at the time; yet the historian, more than
most men, should be aware that fashion is usually sincere.

Even more feeling is apparent in the minutes of a
Bordelais *club de quartier*. So incredible would the mild-
est English translation now appear that it would better
be left in French and with the original spelling and punc-
tuation:

> "Je vous rapellerai d'abord ce jour si cher à ma mémoire,
> où nos yeux humides encore des pleurs données aux mannes du
> celebre auteur du Contract Social, errant dans cette vaste enceinte,
> cherchoient, comme au hazard, des hommes régénérés qui ayant
> senti le prix de notre nouvelle Constitution, se réunissent autour
> d'elle pour servir de remparts invincibles à ses Ennemis, ce grand
> but vous fait trouver des frères." The brothers found, and as-
> sembled, the orator continues "J'ai joui donc, dans cette première
> séance du saint entousiasme de l'épanchement de vos coeurs, et
> mutuellement avec vous j'ai juré avec fraternité inviolable une
> amitié éternelle, en outre le secours de toutes mes forces phisique
> et moralle, et dans ce moment que nos mains l'une dans l'autre
> recevaient les dernières expressions de nos âmes, vos yeux et la
> voix ellevée vers le Ciel vous vous êtes ecriés, voilà, voilà les vrais
> Enfans de la patrie, une Colonne de plus a la nouvelle constitution.
> Le fondement de notre Société, ah, ce jour est le plus beau de notre
> vie." [5]

There are abundant signs that the Jacobins did not by
mere accident employ a ritual and a vocabulary so reminiscent of Christianity. Their emotions must be accepted
as a variety of religious experience. For these emotions
appear not merely generalized as in the preceding examples, but attached to certain religious practices. Of these
the simplest is prayer. Jacobin minutes not infrequently
mention "philanthropic prayers," a form of devotion too
absurd not to have been sincere. For who but the very
devout by nature would ever have prayed to the god of
the deists? Such a prayer was composed by the commit-

tee of correspondence of the Lunéville society and given by the president during the regular meeting. After addressing the Eternal Being, who showed his existence so visibly in the harmony of the material universe, who had made for each need a corresponding satisfaction, the prayer suddenly cries, "Que ta foudre fasse justice de tous nos ennemis connus et cachés! Ils sont les tiens, Dieu vengeur!" [6] The transition from the clock-maker God to the avenging God is surprising enough; but it is quite of a piece with other Jacobin borrowings from religious tradition. Citizen Feuillebois of Chablis achieved a prayer which even the new biographers of Marat will hardly claim to be in accord with the character of their hero. "O thou, Marat, whose memory shall always be dear to us, watch from Heaven over that Liberty which thou defendedst so courageously, watch over that tutelary Mountain which thou lightedst with thy fires!" [7]

Prayer may be partly hypocritical. But the *épuration* is indubitable evidence of the working of the religious temperament. These *épurations*—the word is not quite translatable—were of two kinds. Politically at least the more important *épuration* was merely a device for getting rid of undesirable elected members of the municipal and district administrations. A list of all the members would be read from the platform, and the "people" assembled in the rooms of the society would decide what ones should be retained. In practice the meeting was of course packed, and the whole operation carried out at the dictation of the representative on mission sent out from Paris, who usually presided at the meeting. Psychologically, however, the other sort of *épuration* is more interesting. Sessions were held to determine the orthodoxy of the whole membership of a society, a process which often meant the stringing out of meetings for days. Only the private concerns of comparatively unimportant men were at stake, and the representatives on mission rarely bothered to attend these meetings. The usual procedure was for each member to take the platform in turn and justify his orthodoxy before a single judge chosen for his purity, or a small core of members admittedly irreproachable. Frequently a list of questions formed the test. What were you in 1789? What have you done up to the present for the Revolution? Have you been in any monarchical club or counter-revolutionary military organization, or signed unpatriotic petitions? [8] The result was something strikingly similar to "experience meetings" of certain Protestant sects. Indeed, the members of the society of Thann were called upon to "make a clean breast of it all at the bar of the assembly.[9] At Limoges, the secretary writes of the *confession générale*.[10]

These confessions are unfortunately not often recorded. But even from these bare records, it is easy to imagine the tautness of nerves, the contagion of excitement, which wait upon the dramatic possibility that under pressure something secret and damning will emerge. A provincial journalist protests against the *épuration* at Besançon:

> For more than a *décade* the meetings of the society have been consecrated to the *scrutin épuratoire*. It would seem that for the past few days the temple of liberty has been converted into a gladiatorial arena, into which each patriot has been obliged to descend in succession to make with his bloody wounds a spectacle for the public. . . . While reproaching one another for what are after all peccadillos, we have given and taken wounds whose scars we shall always bear.[11]

A member of the Lyons society writes of these *épurations* in terms that make equally clear how far they were tests of conscience and of ability to withstand a common inquisition: "This tribunal of the conscience of man and the justice of the people is terrible indeed, but it is also just. The most practised audacity, the most refined hypocrisy disappeared before the watchful and penetrating eyes of the sound members of the society and of the numerous citizens who filled the galleries." [12]

Most of the accepted confessions must have been dull enough, as that of Citizen Rebours of Fontainebleau. "I have scrutinized myself and found myself perfectly pure. I imbibed my revolutionary principles in England, and I have retained them. They caused me under the old régime to be distrusted by my superiors . . . I took part in the events at Paris from July 12, 1789, for two days and two nights etc." [13] The rejections are rather more interesting. At Beauvais, men were excluded from the society for having "abased the holy Mountain by calling it a handful of Maratistes," for calumniating another patriot, for intriguing to get public office, and for remaining a bachelor at forty. The rejection of one poor man, because he "lacked the degree of warmth necessary for a real republican," prompted another to defend himself by claiming that "if his physique was cold, his morals were warm." [14] At Bacqueville, Citizen Prouin was rejected "because he eats habitually with the servants of a *cidevant*." Poor Prouin, who was a gardener, resigned his job to preserve his orthodoxy. Citizen Masse was expelled because he delayed in bringing his produce to market; another farmer, because he refused to sell his produce to a fellow-member. Sellier, surgeon, was rejected because he consorted with priests, and the rejection was maintained in spite of Sellier's defense "that he was trying to convert them." Le Pley, another surgeon, was maintained after he had promised to make brief and purely professional calls on "aristocrats." [15]

The *épuration*, with its carping orthodoxy and its dis-

play of public confession—confession in the Roman
Catholic Church is not public—was constantly occupying
the clubs.[16] It goes back surprisingly early in the history
of the clubs, to a time when their membership was limited to the *haute bourgeoisie*. The society of Villeneuve
sur Yonne, at its foundation in 1790, provided for an
annual *scrutin d' épreuve;* or such an *épuration* might be
held any time at the request of two-thirds the membership.[17] A pamphleteer says in 1791 that the Paris Jacobins "have invented examinations where the acts of those
examined are scrutinized with extreme care. Slander and
calumny spread themselves without fear; there reputa-
tions are made and unmade; consciences, so to speak,
are put up to be riddled." [18] During the Terror, *épurations*
were the order of the day. The club of Pont-à-Mousson,
in providing for annual trials, was very old-fashioned; [19]
that at Châlons, which tried its membership every three
months, is more typical.[20]

A final proof that the Jacobins took their religious
practices in earnest is afforded by their sensitiveness to
persecution, a sensitiveness readily turning into a kind of
mania. There was, especially in certain parts of the country, reason enough for the Jacobins to be aware that they
were in a minority; sometimes, even, the majority turned
and did them harm. The women of Vouneuil-sur-Vienne
invaded the premises of the club in a body, demanded
that mass be held, broke up all the furniture and trappings of the club, and sounded the tocsin.[21] But chiefly
one hears of the petty complaints of the patriots; the
world is against them because of their known virtue. At
Le Havre, stones, hot water, and things unmentionable
are hurled at Jacobins from a window near the club.[22]
At Chablis, citizen Hélie had his vines mutilated by
malevolent enemies of his country; and wicked royalist

fathers sent their children to play on the symbolic Mountain, and gradually wear it away.[23] At Fleury-les-Faver-
ney, as at many other places, the tree of liberty had to be
protected by an iron grating from careless animals and
vicious men.[24] A Jacobin of Troyes writes indignantly,
"I must tell you the name these fanatics have dared give
the *Société populaire;* they call it the Sabbat." [25]

II

For many men, emotional fulfillment of a ritual is perhaps enough; they participate in certain common acts,
and thereby make themselves part of the commonwealth.
But most men go farther; and certainly the Jacobins did.
We have described as "The Jacobin platform" in chapter
V certain tangible measures they hoped to secure; we
have now to examine the state of mind that lay behind
these demands, and of which these demands were, so to
speak, a translation into the world of the senses. We have
to examine Jacobin political philosophy, or, if the
term is found more expressive, Jacobin political meta-
physics.

Of the very general truth that the Jacobins were thoroughly steeped in the writings of the eighteenth century
philosophers there can be no doubt. At Lyons, in the
Year III, a procession in honor of the transferring of
Rousseau's ashes to the Pantheon was composed, among
others, "of young men worthy of Emile, of young girls
worthy of Sophie, of mothers from among those who had
not neglected their duty by giving their children to wet-
nurses." There was also a copy of the *Contrat social*
borne by a group of officials, and a banner inscribed with
"these sacred words extracted from that work; *L' homme
est né libre—Renoncer à sa liberté, c' est renoncer à sa*

*qualité d' homme, aux droits de l' humanité, même à
ses devoirs."* [26] The club of Montauban insisted that the
first books in its new library must be the works of Rousseau, Voltaire and Mirabeau, since these writers "have
risen to principles, have found the source of governments
in the very nature of man, and, unwilling to stop at mere
ill-digested compilations of absurd and incoherent laws,
have made it their duty to follow the divine torch of a
wise and beneficent philosophy." [27] A Jacobin of Bergerac proposed to appoint four commissioners to "extract
all the passages of J.-J. Rousseau bearing on the French
Revolution, and make a table from which each member
might draw examples and lessons." [28] At Nay, in the
Pyrenees, the club decided to read every evening from
the speeches of Robespierre, preferring, apparently, the
text-book to the text.[29] The club of Vesoul staged a philosophical festival. Just before dawn, a member of the
society dressed to represent Descartes fired a cannon. As
the sun rose, "Voltaire, Rousseau, and Mably saluted
with a triple discharge of cannon the father of light, symbol of eternal truth." The members who represented these
philosophers, the minutes tell us, were themselves philosophers.[30]

Such instances could be multiplied indefinitely. A mere
general devotion to the memory of the philosophers may,
however, be no more than lip-service. We must seek for
more specifically philosophical tenets. They are not hard
to find.

The fundamental assumption of Rousseau's philosophy, the natural goodness of man, occurs in a thousand
forms in these records. The newly elected bishop of the
Haute-Vienne told a club that "the ethics of Nature has
so great an empire over the human heart that one need
but explain its principles and they will be adopted with

transports and cherished." [31] Paris had so little sophisti-
cated one Jacobin that he could declare, "I do not think
any man destined by Nature to be a monster. Men are
born good and become evil." [32] Camille Desmoulins,
praising the very democratic *Cercle social* to the Paris
Jacobins, said:

> I shall observe that the *Cercle social* is composed of 3000 mem-
> bers, and, in so numerous a club, it is impossible that reason
> should not dominate; for today, with this progress of philosophy
> and enlightenment, it would seem that reason makes to men the
> same promise that Christ made in the Bible, "For where two or
> three are gathered together in my name, there am I in the midst
> of them." [33]

"Reason" here is used instead of "goodness" but the
meaning is obviously the same. A Jacobin of Moulins,
starting from this same assumption of a benevolent Nature, arrived at a very modern condemnation of the
science of medicine. He lists these "eternal truths": "The
first is that Nature only makes sane and healthy beings.
The second, that this ruler of the universe needs only
its own energy to combat evil, which is foreign to it. The
third, that there is no incurable disease for Nature, but
that for our doctors, even for the most skillful, diseases
are all, or practically all, incurable; the fourth, that the
medical art is a thousand times more pernicious to men,
than the ills it pretends to cure." [34]

Now it follows very simply from this that, if all men
are naturally good, all men are naturally equal; that is,
equality is really a matter of goodness. Inequalities in
wealth, rank, bodily strength, intelligence cannot prevail
over this fundamental fact of moral equality. Nay, in so
far as such inequalities can be eliminated by legislation,
they must be eliminated in the Jacobin state. Since men
are also endowed with reason (this is the contribution of

the *philosophes,* not of Rousseau) they will, if given the vote—that is, political equality—soon see that this fundamental moral equality triumphs over the vicious inequalities of the present régime. Any temporary difficulties will be solved by universal education, for Descartes and Locke combined to teach the world that man is wholly the product of his environment. Then the Jacobin republic will be truly founded; the individual will then enjoy all his "natural rights"—that is, he will be free to be good in accordance with his nature, instead of being forced to be wicked in accordance with old laws, old conventions, old religions.

The genealogy of this political philosophy—a philosophy which must seem nonsense to the twentieth century social scientist—would go far to explain why so many intelligent men held it. But interesting though it might be to trace the origins of these ideas, our concern lies elsewhere. The point is that, granting the natural goodness and the natural reasonableness of man, and granting universal education, civil government is not necessary. Godwin was perfectly justified in pursuing eighteenth century political philosophy to its logical conclusion in anarchy. But the Jacobins were no anarchists—not even philosophical anarchists. And they avoided the anarchical implications of their theories by the famous doctrine of their master Rousseau—the doctrine of the General Will.

Much has been written about the General Will. We shall avoid certain metaphysical pitfalls if we begin by asking what the doctrine of the general will could have meant to the ordinary Jacobin. The words of a member of the club of Clermont-Ferrand will give us a clew. "For this revolting idea, *I have a master,* substitute this sublime thought *I do but obey the general will;* then what a vast career of virtues and enjoyments opens out!" [35]

The point is this: How can the individual who naturally (and rightly) acts according to his own will, be brought to accept the restraints upon his will which any society only too obviously imposes? Rousseau's answer is that the individual in a true society is joined to that society in no merely external way, but by a spiritual bond (the social compact) which is of the very stuff of his own will, and that therefore his real will and the will of society are one, and there is no problem. The individual is not linked to society as he is linked to his fellows, in relations which are subject to time and accident, *and which involve dependence and command,* but in a relation imposed equally on all his fellows, and expressed, not in terms of human will, but of divine law. M. Loyseau told the Paris club, in words we have cited in another connection:

> The judge is but the organ of the law, and he cannot apply to it more of his intellectual faculties than the attention which apprehends without deciding anything itself. In this point of view, man is given back to his own real nature, as soon as it is to the law which he himself has made that he is obliged to conform.[36]

This is the magic of the social compact; in the perfect commonwealth, the man who obeys his rulers obeys himself.

It does not much matter that to tough-minded persons this is mere metaphysical quibbling. Rousseau's idea of the social compact is not necessarily the devilish engine of destruction it appeared to many a conservative to be. Many men of what may be called strong and upright spiritual natures do really *feel* things this way. They accept and obey laws personally inconvenient to themselves because they feel themselves part of an organic society; for them, laws are dictated by a mysterious but real power embodied in the state. Other, and perhaps more numerous men, content themselves with obedience to inconvenient laws because of a vague feeling that it is all for the general good. Still others, happily perhaps for society, obey such laws out of mere habit.

But to the realist it must be obvious that there comes a time to most men when, faced with a course of action prescribed for them by law (that is, by society) they quite consciously say to themselves, I don't want to do that, and it's all nonsense to say that if I do it I'm doing what I want to. Here the realist would admit that if at such a moment the man obeys the law he is obeying out of fear, habit, inertia, out of any motive but free consent. Rousseau and his Jacobins would not have it so. Such an admission would have wrecked the ideal basis of their state; and since they were theologically minded people, since they were aiming at inhuman consistency, they were obliged to have recourse to a theological expedient. Then, with upright hearts and clear consciences, they could proceed to the Terror.

For at this point there enters the famous distinction between the general will and the will of all. If the individual does not share in the mystic loyalty of the general will, if he sets his will against that of a society, it is a proof that he is not in a state of grace. His is a will to evil. But no man is free in doing evil. To prevent him is to free him, and release his free will, which is that of the society. The Jacobins of Limoges have put it clearly: "Is it not to be in reality the friend of one's brothers to force them, in a manner of speaking, to accept the cup of salvation which is offered them in the name of reason and humanity?" [37] Robespierre said more neatly: "The revolutionary government is the despotism of liberty against tyranny."

In this way the element of consent was eliminated and
Jacobins could continue to develop all the authoritarian
and collectivist elements implicit in Rousseau's ideas.
The president at Sauveterre said in his inaugural speech:
"Members of the social body, we cannot be happy as individuals except as society shall be in the state of prosperity which the Constitution is preparing—Citizens, it
is not permitted to the individual to prefer, *even in
secret,* his private interests to those of society." [38] From
the very first, the pronouncements of the Friends of the
Constitution insist that they are not rebels, that they
recommend obedience to the law, and that they hold
anarchy to be the worst of crimes. An orator asked the
club of Toulon:

> We have respected, for centuries, the will of one man; shall we
> not learn to respect our own? Without virtue, you will make revo-
> lutions in vain—now slaves, now subjects, now royalists, now re-
> publicans, but never free—for why make of public officials reposi-
> tories of the fixed law which is your will, if each one of you does
> but wish to follow his own caprices, his own passions? [39]

But if one society is to decide what is caprice, there is
obviously an end to what common sense believes to be
liberty. To several Jews admitted to the society at Thann
the presiding officer "said that they should make themselves like other republicans by renouncing the usury
and rascality common to their race, and advised them to
get their beards shaved off." [40] After this, it is not surprising to find Lameth justifying a law against the
émigrés with the remark that "a nation can attach to its
benefits whatever conditions it pleases." [41] The benefit
in this instance seems to be the involuntary membership that comes from birth within its borders.

The modern nation-state was the inevitable end
achieved by the outburst of energy common to the west-

ern world at the end of the eighteenth century. The doc-
trines of Rousseau—social contract, general will, popular
virtue and popular sovereignty—fit themselves well into
the complex machinery of the modern state. A curiously
naïve statement from a Parisian Jacobin will show how
political abstractions can be merged with human emotions, how patriotism can make the general will only too
easily understood. The speaker was complaining of in-
sults to Frenchmen in Spain. "I shall observe," he continued, "that the French nation is sovereign; that each
Frenchman being an individual portion of this sovereignty, it is a question of the honor of the nation that
each of its members should be protected and honored
abroad." [42] This seems as absurd in content as in phraseology. Does being a Frenchman make a rascal honorable?
Perhaps *qua* Frenchman he is a being quite other than
himself *qua* rascal? Then we have a pluralistic universe,
and the rascal is as real as the Frenchman, and not to
be banished by political theology as unreal.

Jacobins, old and new, will not have it so. They will
have one society, one sovereignty, one will. The general
will, however, as we have seen, is no abstraction, but the
product of living relations. As such, it does not incor-
porate abstractions, like virtue, or even, alas, France, but
concrete realities, human beings. Since the concept
"Frenchman" comes nearer to the complex living human
being than the eighteenth century "Man of Virtue," the
modern nation-state is less an abstraction than the purely
theological state of the brief Jacobin triumph. But even
the nation-state incorporates only part of the wills of its
members. To just the degree that it fails to recognize this,
it is an abstraction, and must live on faith alone. Since
the nation-state has survived so well, faith is perhaps
commoner in the western world than skeptics will allow.

III

The Jacobins unquestionably held their political philosophy as a matter of faith. It is possible to sketch from the proceedings of the clubs the outlines of a polity held together by concepts primarily theological. Grace, sin, heresy, repentance, regeneration have their place in these records. Of course, no one individual is assumed to go through this cycle. The theological parallel is not a literal one; but it is not a forced nor an imaginary one.

That Robespierre and his more sincere followers conceived themselves to be the small band of the elect is of course a truism. The conception of election, however, like so much else in the Terror, goes back surprisingly far in the Revolution. Desmoulins speaks at the Jacobin club in Paris in 1791 of "the very small number of those *to whom only the witness of their conscience is necessary,* the small number of men of character, incorruptible citizens." [43] This insistence on an inner, emotional conviction or righteousness rather than on external rules—the very old opposition of faith and works—comes out again in the proceedings of the Paris club. "One must distrust," says the speaker, "liberty unaccompanied by virtue"; and by virtue he understands "not the mere practice of moral duties, but also an exclusive attachment to the unalterable principles of our constitution." [44] The club at Limoges was told: "It is not enough, in order to belong to a truly republican society, to call oneself republican, to have done guard duty, to have paid one's taxes; one must have given sure indications of hatred for kings and nobles, for fanaticism; one must have passed through the crucible of perilous circumstance." The idea of grace is actually complemented, in this same club, by the addition of a new Jerusalem, the city of the elect. Paris, for its work in the revolution, is to be "that holy city." [45]

There are also the damned. The Jacobins did not feel of their opponents merely that they were wrong, or inconvenient; but that they had sinned. A member at Rodez recalled to the society that just a year before, a deputation from the Tarn had "soiled the precincts of the society with the venom of federalism." The society therefore decided "as *expiation* for that scandalous session, to consecrate a portion of the present session to patriotic songs." [46] At Bergerac the society burned the papal bull condemning the civil constitution of the clergy, in order to purify the paper from "the outrageous blasphemies which insult our sublime Constitution." [47] The club of Toulouse delegated six members, and asked the "peuples des tribunes" (always that distinction, so out of place in an ideal republic!) to delegate six more, to help burn and lacerate certain evil journals.[48] At Beauvais, the club was delighted with a circular from the Committee of Public Safety asking for lists of Jacobins eligible for government places, and especially at the words, "Keep from these lists all these cold, selfish, or indifferent men. . . . The law of Athens would have inflicted death upon them. National opinion among us inflicts upon them political death." [49] The club of Le Havre was told by that of Harfleur "not to receive in its bosom a certain Duclos, priest of the protestant religion. He tried to compromise this society with that of Gaineville, and to ruin the reputation of several patriots." [50]

Some aristocrats at Vesoul having kissed the tree of liberty in mockery, the local club decided to purify it. So, with the president at its head, and with four members carrying vases of pure water and braziers of incense, the club marched in procession to the tree, where, after everyone had sworn to preserve it forever after from all contamination, "the tree was purified with the lustral water, and the president threw on the heated tripods generous handfuls of the most exquisite perfumes."[51] The club at Auch had so strong a conviction of sin that it adapted for its own use the attitude of the Church toward burial in consecrated ground. It proposed to have two town cemeteries, one for good citizens, the other for bad.[52]

Heresy is, of course, one of the easiest ways of falling into sin. The word itself was by no means shunned by the Jacobins. Even under the monarchy, Brissot is found at the Paris club objecting that an opinion of Barnave's is "a great heresy."[53] The rejections of members at the various *épurations* are, of course, usually for heresy of some sort. One man was excluded at Thann because, although at first he had been a good *patriote,* "the corrupting contact of his brother-in-law had completely perverted him"; another, though himself pure, because his maid was not.[54] At Carcassonne one of the questions put was: How long did you lack confidence in Marat and the Mountain? Several were excluded for honestly confessing that they had had a period of doubt on this subject.[55] The pressure of foreign and civil war made the Jacobins more than usually exacting towards their proselytes. One society at least penalized those converted after 1792 by not allowing them to hold office.[56] That of Moulins decided in the spring of 1794 never to admit a new member, except from other towns, and then only when such persons could prove membership in some club before September, 1793.[57] Heretics were apparently not even allowed to repent. Collot d' Herbois at Paris was seeking to get readmitted to the society some of those who had followed the *feuillants* in the schism. "Many of these," he said, "are exceedingly repentant, and would like to efface from their lives the days they spent at the *feuillants*." Yet at Robespierre's insistence they were rejected.[58] And, along with heresy, there is the concept of blasphemy. This is from a report of a session of a Paris club; "An officer, an exchanged prisoner, gives an account of the condition of the French and Austrian armies. But as he reports some violent words used by the enemy general, he is interrupted. Billaud-Varenne reminds the orator that he is repeating expressions which ought not to soil the mouth of a republican." [59]

A little club in Savoy took a milder, and perhaps more modern attitude towards those who disagreed with it. The majority of their fellow citizens they called "the sick ones we have to treat." [60] The club of Toulon, withdrawing its affiliation from the heretics of Pignans, wrote and warned other clubs of this *brébis galeuse*.[61] But the best indication of the theological state of the Jacobin mind is to be found in a circular of the club of Montauban. The class of *émigrés* is to be composed, not merely of those who have gone off, *émigrés de fait*, but also of *émigrés d'opinion*.[62]

No less thoroughly religious a concept than that of regeneration is evident in these proceedings. The taking of the Bastille became the symbolic date, the moment when man was born anew, washed clean of the evils of the old régime. A little provincial society, accordingly, when it celebrates the "holy festival" of July 14, refers to it as the day "when man is resuscitated and born anew in his rights." [63] The society of St. Jean-de-Luz held a festival to celebrate the "abolition of royalty and the *resurrection* of the republic." [64] It is hard to see how the word resurrection can here be taken in any but a theological sense, as the French Republic had never ex-

isted on this earth. Finally, the society at Saverne gave
proof of the most extraordinary faith in the completeness
of the rebirth brought about in 1789, for its secretary
refers to "les ci-devant Juifs." [65]

The Jacobins, then, were a band of the elect, thoroughly aware of their election, and determined to rule
on earth as well as in heaven. The club of Ervy was told
"You must suffer but one caste of men, that of Republicans, Sans-culottes, Montagnards." [66] At Le Havre,
the club voted that those of its members who belonged
to any kind of corporation or brotherhood must choose
between the Jacobin club and such other corporations.[67]
The club of Besançon indignantly refused to open its
doors to all, as "the wicked, mixed with the good, would
predominate."[68] The club of Chablis hesitated before
accepting affiliation with the club of the Ursulines at
Tonnerre, and then turned it down on the grounds that
there couldn't possibly be two clubs in a small town like
Tonnerre.[69] The secretary at Gerberoy apologized to the
club of Beauvais, because everybody passed the *épuration*. Three—their names are duly sent on to Beauvais
—should have been expelled. But the mayor formed a
party among the "little enlightened," packed the club,
and notwithstanding their vices, these three were passed
"by the multitude." The whole letter is filled with a
consciousness of being right and being few.[70]

Finally, it was evident even to some of their number
that the Jacobins were a sect. A member at Ars-en-Ré
remarked that "the moral discourses delivered on *décadis*
are so many dogmas, and consequently, so much religion." He was, it is true, immediately suspended.[71]
The Jacobins held firmly to their final superiority; theirs
was no fanaticism.

CHAPTER VIII

CONCLUSION

I

The Jacobin who figured in our statistical tables as a prosperous middle class person of some standing in his community has turned out to be a religious fanatic. The enlightenment he had acquired in his reading clubs and masonic lodges has become a superstition even more ludicrous than cruel. Yet this Jacobin has been arrived at only by a process of averaging, of eliminating inconsistencies. Again, we cannot escape the fact that language is an inadequate tool, that nothing at the same time true and useful to us can be predicated of the Jacobins that appear in these records. For along with the absurdities like the republican sign of the cross, along with the intolerance of *décadi,* along with the cruelty of dozens of petty provincial Marats are to be found not innumerous examples of moderation, common sense, toleration, humor, of all the riper and more unrevolutionary virtues. While the careers of clubs like those of Nantes or Bordeaux are filled with bloodshed and corruption, in many others—Gray, Breteuil, Vesoul, Guéret—the revolution seems hardly to have altered the decencies of provincial life. A chapter might be written on "Jacobin Moderation" or on "The Jacobin as a Human Being"; for honesty's sake, we must at least indicate some of the material for such a chapter.

Instances of Jacobin moderation are plentiful. We

223

might find many clubs that took literally—and for once therefore sensibly—the famous decree on the freedom of religious worship. The club of Fleurance actually petitioned the municipality at the height of the Terror to reopen the church on the grounds of religious toleration.[1] Another club replied to a complaint that the wife and daughter of a justice of the peace were *fanatiques* (i.e. Roman Catholics) in words perhaps still rather above the average of human disinterestedness "Considering that *M. le juge de paix* is not to blame for the silliness of his family, and that he himself is entirely free to be a *fanatique* too, if he does not disturb order, and if he fulfills his functions properly, the society passes to the order of the day." [2] The club of Dijon, fearing to see the famous *Collège Godran* go down before revolutionary leveling, took up the defense of the older education, and of Greek and Latin in particular. Citizen Baillot, in a speech given in July 1793, could use words not unacceptable to Burke: "Reform, improve, but do not destroy—It is easier to destroy culture and talents than to restore them." [3]

Common sense could reject some of the absurdities of revolutionary ritual. One club scornfully rejected, early in 1794, a proposal that members failing to use the egalitarian "thou" should be fined; [4] another refused to entertain a motion that *Unité, Indivisibilité de la République, Liberté, Egalité, Fraternité ou la Mort* be inscribed over everybody's door.[5] To a member who objected because he wore no liberty cap, the secretary at Bourgoin replied "that patriotism does not consist in any particular way of dress, that a true patriot was to be known only by his actions" and he requested the society to withdraw its decree requiring its officers to wear the liberty cap. The club agreed with him, and voted "that each individual was free to dress as he pleased."[6]

Nor is clemency at all uncommon among the clubs. The clubs of the Haute Saône gladly helped the younger Robespierre in his attempt to put some kind of order into the detention of suspects; at the recommendation of the club of Gray, Robespierre released twenty-one prisoners who had already "been sufficiently punished."[7] The *comité de bienfaisance,* of the club of Thonon intervened in behalf of a citizen arrested for working on *décadi.*[8] At Lille, a member complained to the club that he had caught an individual wantonly mistreating some royalist prisoners; the club sent the individual up before the revolutionary tribunal.[9]

Wit, too, managed to survive in the pages of these records. Probably the Jacobin of Breteuil, who renamed the rue au Loup the rue Marat was a moderate hiding himself in the club.[10] But the secretary of the club of Château-Thierry, who, after describing how some club missionaries had been roughly treated by peasants, continued "Bezu n' a échappé que par un excès de prudence et de bonheur" may have been a good Jacobin for all his malice.[11] As for the Rouennais who proposed "that young and middle aged priests be required to marry, and the older ones to do what they can," his Jacobin orthodoxy is unquestionable.[12]

The Jacobins were even capable of being bored, a characteristic most remote from the true religious temperament. The rules of the club of Porrentruy contain this useful provision: "If an orator wanders or tires his auditors, they may stand up; if twelve stand up, the whole society must be consulted, and if the majority wishes the orator to be silent, he must descend from the tribune."[13] Here is a passage from the proceedings of another club: "The order of the day brings next the reading of the report of M. Robespierre on the connection between religious and moral ideas and republican principles; and hardly does the reader achieve the middle of the report when, the room being quite deserted, the president adjourns the meeting." [14]

Now it is possible that if we could restore to life every Jacobin, if we could successfully get inside them all, and if finally we could bring ourselves to sort them into two groups, sensible men and foolish men, we might find the first group numerically larger than the second. It is even barely possible that, if we had access to all the records of all the clubs, we might finally decide that they contained more entries of the kind just cited than of the kind so frequently brought forward in previous chapters. Yet rightly we take the fanatical Jacobin, the virtuous republican with his rites, his dogmas, and his political theology to be the Jacobin with whom history must concern itself.

For the simplest rule of logic would tell us that those characteristics of the Jacobin wherein he differs from other human beings are the characteristics we must attach to the name Jacobin. Only if these characteristics seem quite accidental, quite infrequent, have we a right to neglect them; and they are far too numerous to be accidental. Even if we think so highly of human beings that we are persuaded that the bulk of Jacobins could never have accepted Jacobinism, that our hundreds and hundreds of Friends of the Constitution, or Friends of Liberty and Equality were really intelligent hypocrites, playing the Jacobin for safety's sake, the fact remains that they acted like Jacobins. For those of us who must live under the Volstead act, it does not very much matter whether that great American folk-figure, the wet-living, dry-voting Congressman exists in numbers or not. For Frenchmen of 1794, the Jacobin dispensation under which they lived was important, and not the sincerity of individual Jacobins. Nor need we assume that the absurdity of the Jacobin cult was evident to the nameless Jacobins of our statistics. After all the Jacobins, at their best, were but a minority; and history is full of the madness of minorities. One need not even consult the history of religious sects, with whom the Jacobins nevertheless had so much in common. Sober commercial history is full of Mississippi and South Sea bubbles, of California gold rushes and Florida land booms. To many an obscure Jacobin the Faith must have been as real as it unquestionably was to Robespierre. For deliberate, conscious hypocrisy is surely one of the rarest of human characteristics. Tartuffe is no ordinary man. Few men can separate their beliefs from their actions. When the one seems inconsistent with the other, we can be almost sure that the person is not aware of the inconsistency. Self-delusion is as common as hypocrisy is rare.

If then we are in the last resort to accept the definition of Jacobinism as a new sort of religious faith we are faced with certain questions necessary to any conclusion of this study. How did the Jacobins succeed in establishing themselves as rulers of France in 1793-1794, and in making their religion the state religion, so to speak, for that period? Why, having established themselves, were they overthrown in thermidor? Why did the democratic republic of the Jacobins have so brief a course? The answer to these last questions seems simpler, and we may begin with it.

The answer is partly, of course, that Jacobinism never did die out in France. Its political platform was almost wholly realized in the Third Republic, after having inspired radicals throughout the world for a century. Its symbolism survived in a hundred ways. As a form of the religious temperament it was familiar to all who knew nineteenth century France. Flaubert's M. Homais is almost too good a Jacobin. As for contemporary France, if the Cartel obviously inherited something of the effective Jacobin tactics, it also inherited something of Jacobin ideas about the Roman Catholic Church and about the undesirability of large fortunes which are a bit too thoroughly eighteenth century to be quite effective nowadays.

But the First Republic undoubtedly fell, and with it the pure Jacobin faith. M. Mathiez has laid his finger on the chief reason for its fall. The Jacobin heaven was inescapably on earth. The club of Beauvais, at the planting of its tree of liberty, sang:

> L'arbre planté sur le calvaire
> Est pour les Chrétiens le signe salutaire
> Qui promet dans les cieux un bonheur éternel!
> L'arbre que vous plantez dans ce jour solennel,
> Est pour les citoyens que la raison éclaire
> Le signe heureux du bonheur sur la terre!"[15]

The blessed sign of happiness on earth! But what did Jacobin rule bring? War and high prices, then the *maximum* and scarcity. Hunger, cold, and in those days of arbitrary rule, even prisons were often the lot of those who joined the Jacobin cause. It is small wonder that the number of true Jacobins diminished. And as for the lower classes, the *peuple des tribunes* on whom the Jacobins were forced to lean, the promised heaven seemed more and more remote. It was useless for the Jacobins to enact the *maximum,* to promise social justice by a redistribution of property confiscated from the *émigrés.* What was the good of being a virtuous *sans-*

culotte if one were to remain as ill-clothed and as ill-fed as before?

Yet men are perhaps less exacting about such matters than more hopeful materialists will admit. Certainly the devoted Jacobins were hardened and confirmed by adversity. But for the ordinary man Jacobinism gave none of those vicarious satisfactions which permit the Christian to endure suffering. Even in prosperity, it is fairly clear that Jacobinism was too abstract, too heroic a faith to have held the common man. Its ritual, as we have seen, was an unskillful mixture of pseudo-classic elements quite beyond the comprehension of the uneducated, and of Christian practices too obviously deformed to fool the dullest for long. The most practical and the most effective of their canons of faith, nationalism, could, as the nineteenth century was to show, hold the imaginations of many men, discipline them even into accepting privation. But the Jacobins never made good their claim to a monopoly of French nationalism; and moreover, they insisted far too much on virtue, on a virtue curiously compounded of humanitarian and puritanical elements, for the true lover of his country. Love of country, like love of virtue, may be its own reward; but one's country is at once a less exacting and a more immediately present mistress than virtue.

Again, it must not be forgotten that the bulk of the Jacobins were respectable and prosperous *bourgeois*. Under pressure of revolutionary excitement, and under the influence of eighteenth-century philosophy, they might at times talk like socialists. Moreover, their allies the common people were exacting, and so too was the economic situation caused by the war. The necessity for rationing brought on the *maximum,* and the *maximum* was perhaps the first step towards an enforced economic equality. Is it surprising that many a Jacobin business man, many a big Jacobin landowner, began to draw back in 1794? Too much is perhaps not to be concluded from the almost universal acceptance by provincial clubs of the overthrow of Robespierre. By that time, the provinces were willing to accept almost any Parisian *coup d'état*. Yet unless all our commonly accepted notions of human nature are faulty, it is too much to expect that property owners will lead a revolution against their particular form of ownership of property. Orthodox Jacobinism—the Jacobinism of Robespierre and St. Just —was verging on what we now call socialism. Therefore the bulk of Jacobins ceased to be orthodox, and the Jacobin rule was over.

Finally, as we have seen, the revolutionary government of the Terror rested entirely on the *sociétés populaire*. It could not even make the claim of modern parliamentary governments to rest ultimately upon a majority vote of qualified citizens. Once the active participation of the societies ceased, there was left nothing but a group of professional politicians—better described by the expressive French *fonctionnaires*. Now the societies clearly began to tire of their rôle long before thermidor. We have seen how exacting were the self-imposed duties of these Jacobins of 1794—the committees, the missions to the infidel peasantry, the commissions, the clerkships, the investigations into markets, army supplies, hospitals. It is too much to expect citizens of a modern state already in the beginning of the industrial revolution to take self-government in the Athenian sense. Even before thermidor, then, the Jacobin government was increasingly a government of *fonctionnaires;* and such a government has no need of the elaborate religious forms of high Jacobinism. Nothing can be more illuminating in this

respect than a study of the after careers of the more
active local Jacobin leaders. Man after man assumes an
appointive position under the Directory, and ends up
as a Napoleonic official—prefect, sub-prefect, mayor,
judge. Napoleon was as indebted to the Jacobin government for his civil administration as he was to the revolutionary armies for his military leaders. Jacobinism and
the *sociétés populaires* had been for men like these incidents in their professional careers. For the rank and file,
the societies had been for a time an extremely interesting
diversion, all the more diverting, indeed, because of its
seriousness. But economic necessity alone is enough to
keep large numbers of men from following an avocation
at the expense of a vocation; and in the long run personal matters, family matters are probably more interesting to most men than affairs of state. Even had they
not been suppressed, the *sociétés populaires* must have
become what they were fast becoming in 1794, mere
syndicates of civil servants.[16]

II

The fall of Jacobinism, then, can be quite plausibly
accounted for; an explanation of its rise is a far more
difficult matter. It is not that the actual triumph of the
Jacobins over other groups during the Revolution is at
all hard to understand. Given Jacobin organization and
Jacobin faith, their triumph was almost inevitable. Our
chapter on Jacobin tactics ought in itself to be an adequate account of this triumph. Indeed, it is tempting to
assert that the ultimate, if brief victory of well-organized
extremists can be accepted as a kind of sociological law
applicable to all great revolutions. The really interesting
and subtle problem is, how did the Jacobins themselves

come to be what they were? If the conclusions of
chapter III have any value, the Jacobins were not predominately failures before 1789, frustrates, victims of
maladjustment; nor were they members of a lower class
struggling against oppression by their masters, and held
together by economic solidarity. They were in the main
ordinary, quite prosperous middle-class people. And yet
they behaved like fanatics. The Reign of Terror was
marked by cruelties and absurdities which the greatest
of misanthropes will hardly maintain are characteristic
of ordinary human beings. The heart of our problem
then, is this: how did the Jacobins come to produce, at
least to accede to, the Terror?

Augustin Cochin saw with admirable clearness that
all explanations of the Terror have fallen into two
classes: that represented by Taine, which Cochin calls
the *thèse du complot*, and that represented by Aulard,
which he calls the *thèse des circonstances*.[17] Taine in a
famous metaphor asks what a spectator must think if
he sees a man in apparently sound health take a drink,
and suddenly fall down in a fit. The drink, obviously,
contained a poison. The drinker was the Jacobin, and the
poison was the philosophy of Rousseau. The Jacobins,
then, were a group of madmen bent on realizing an impossible Utopia. The Revolution was plotted by these
men, made irresponsible by fanatic devotion to their
ideal. Their lack of principle made it easy for them,
though in a minority, to overcome the good sense of the
majority, and establish themselves in power. Once in
power, they could maintain themselves only by the Terror. Cochin himself accepts a variant of this explanation.
According to him, the Jacobins formed a "petite ville,"
a society of unpractical idealists, fanatics bent on imposing upon their fellows of the "grande ville" a rigid

code governing all human actions, a code quite inconsistent with normal human conduct, as we know it from
tradition and from observation.[18]

Now it is impossible not to accept much of this explanation. The Jacobins were certainly fanatics of the
religion of humanity. It is tempting to maintain that the
acceptance of certain tenets of eighteenth century philosophy—the essential equality of men, the natural goodness of men—lead in action straight to the Terror. The
trouble is that the acceptance of just these tenets by
Thomas Jefferson, for instance, led to consequences so
very different from those following their acceptance by
Maximilien Robespierre. Moreover, granting to Cochin
that the Jacobins formed a "petite ville," where are we
to look for the "grande ville"? Cochin himself probably
thought of decent, non-socialist Frenchmen of the Third
Republic as the citizens of the "grande ville." But even
in the fairly stable nation-state of the nineteenth century, the realist will discern numerous "villes," numerous groups of men with different aims and different ways
of life struggling to maintain themselves, and achieving
only a precarious equilibrium. And during the Revolution, when this equilibrium was completely destroyed,
this "grande ville" did not exist in France. Surely it
was not the royalists, nor the Catholics, nor the Feuillants, nor the Girondins. And if the citizen of the "grande
ville" is simply the ordinary man who acts reasonably,
and in accordance with traditional ways, then he hardly
exists in the French Revolution. Any study of the various groups just mentioned should convince the impartial
observer that their state of mind was almost as abnormal,
as much inclined towards extremes of cruelty or absurdity as the Jacobins'. The White Terror was as real
as the Red.

It is perhaps too easy here to make a synthesis of Taine and Aulard. The Jacobins were an organized minority bent on imposing their way of life on their fellow Frenchmen; so much for the *thèse du complot*. But circumstances—the inheritance of the *ancien régime,* the pressure of war from without, of civil disturbances and food scarcity from within—put such obstacles in their way that they were driven to extremes. In order to exist at all, they were obliged to be cruel and intolerant. Even in their factitious ritual, their republican catechisms and decalogues, the Jacobins appear beleaguered; the touch of Hebraic fury one finds from time to time in their records is not wholly artificial. The revolutionary government was a government of national defense. No fair-minded person need deny the value of Aulard's life-work. The war, at least as much the product of traditional European high politics as of anything Jacobin, made the Jacobin more righteous, and more bitter, and saved him from any chance of appearing ridiculous in his own eyes. Moreover, the introduction of circumstances at least disposes of the difficulty with Thomas Jefferson. But it gives little comfort to the sociologist seeking from history laws permitting human beings to adjust their actions to conditions in the present—little comfort, in short, to the new historian. For the circumstances of a great event like the French Revolution are unique—unique, if not to omniscience, at least in their extreme complexity unique to the historian. The fatal "ifs" of history in the conditional—if Mirabeau had not died, if the king had not fled to Varennes—enter in, and make scientific induction impossible. Men's beliefs are, for a given group, held in common and relatively easy to arrive at; so too a given group may have certain similar and perfectly describable characteristics in common

—rank, occupation, social standing, wealth. Yet we have no right to assume that their actions can be predicted from these data.

For the whole point of our study is just this: when one considers the material facts about the Jacobins— their social environment, their occupations, their wealth —one finds sufficient evidence of their prosperity to justify predicting for them quiet, uneventful, conservative, thoroughly normal lives. When one studies the records of their proceedings, one finds them violent, cruel, intolerant, and not a little ridiculous. The antithesis, it must be insisted, is real. Where material evidence indicates normality, we find abnormality. Rightly enough, no doubt, this material evidence seems real and important. Therefore the Jacobins present a genuine paradox. Their *political* being seems quite inconsistent with their *real* being. Their words and their acts *qua* members of the clubs are not what we should expect from them *qua* members of civil society. Or to put it as crudely as possible, the Jacobins present for a brief time the extraordinary spectacle of men acting without apparent regard for their material interests.

This, of course, will never do. The economic interpretation of history would tell us that we are either mistaken in our facts (which is always possible) or that there is an explanation which will show men properly and decently following their material interests. Yet perhaps after all the economic interpretation of history is not the whole explanation of the Terror. We are in a realm of thought where the professional psychologist could no doubt add greatly to the precision of our argument. But to a layman it would appear that voluntary human action must have either a more or less directly physical, bodily source (desire, habit, desire partly intellectualized into interest) or a more or less immaterial and intellectual source (principal, idea, desire thoroughly intellectualized into ideal) or finally, must have its source in mere chance. Now if certain important Jacobin actions did not originate from interest, they must have originated from principle or from chance. The first alternative suggests the old-fashioned belief that men act on principle, and leads us back to the school of Taine. If it can be shown that Jacobin ideas logically produce Jacobin actions in 1794, then we need not worry because Jacobin interests and Jacobin habits would not produce such actions. There is just the possibility that the old-fashioned belief about the importance of ideas is justified, at least for certain historical crises, and for certain groups of men. It is not even necessary to refer to such examples of corporate madness as the Children's Crusade; one need only reflect on how much the *interests* of the average man were at stake in the late highly popular war. But to accept this explanation would lead to the restoration of ideas to their active rôle in human life, and would put the history of ideas, at least during times of crucial change, on a level with the history of institutions, customs, commerce, and the rest of man's material environment. This will hardly content the new historian, for whom intellectual history is largely a reflection of social history, for whom ideas are most decidedly born of, and consistent with, material interests.

There is the final possibility of accepting chance as the determining factor in human conduct. This need not be as shocking as it seems. Chance may merely stand for a complexity unfathomable to human beings; or it may mean that historical events—that is, of course, human actions——are really unique and exempt from the play of cause and effect as nineteenth century science

understood it. That would still leave the play of cause
and effect as the artist, and perhaps even the philosopher,
have always understood it. It would still leave narrative
history; it would merely destroy the new history.

III

Our enterprise in retrospective sociology has not perhaps been altogether satisfying. The kind of information
about the Jacobins available to the social scientist has not
provided us with any fashionable explanation of why men
take part in revolutions. The Jacobins seem not to have
been crudely at odds with their environment before the
revolution; they certainly were not starving; they were
hardly a social or an economic class. They were certainly
a collective body—a group—of more than ordinary co-
hesion, reasonably well disciplined, active, with a definite program, a ritual of their own, a faith charged with
emotion, and a pertinacity, a vitality that has enabled
the group to survive under changing forms into the Third
Republic. Yet so disparate were the social and economic
origins of these revolutionaries that we have been driven
to the conclusion that large numbers of them, by espous-
ing the Jacobin cause, acted against what they must have
been aware were their true selfish interests. Before so
surprising a conclusion sociology rightly recoils. The ex-
ploded intellectualist fallacy is obviously trying to creep
in, and we had better not open the door any wider.

But if we have not got far with the applications to
French Revolution of a science of social dynamics, can
we not at least give a clearer definition of Jacobin at
the end of this enquiry than at the beginning? Here,
however, as with so much of modern history, the trouble
is that we know too much. A fragment of the rules of

one of the clubs would be illuminating to the historian at work in the dark; the records of hundreds of them are blinding. Where statistics fail—and they fail very soon —there is no way of arriving at what is common to the Jacobins. No classification of the complete records of these clubs can be so made that the members of each class can be counted. One might count the number of references to Rousseau; but would such a count serve to weigh the influence of Rousseau on the clubs? The historian must fall back on the normal functioning of his mind, which classifies loosely and pragmatically enough what he experiences in daily life, and which with urging can so classify the matter of his historical studies. But no matter how honest he is, into the making of this classification will come much of his own personal history. What one finds in the Jacobin clubs is what one finds important; and importance, when it is not mathematical, is as subjective as good and bad or sweet and sour.

And yet perhaps the true Jacobin is the rare and perfect Jacobin of the imagination—the Jacobins, let us say, of Anatole France's *Les Dieux ont soif.* One rarely meets an American like Uncle Sam or an Englishman like John Bull, and never a Frenchwoman like the cartoonist's Marianne. Indeed, just as a mass of unbarbered and untailored human animals, Englishmen, Frenchmen, and Americans are probably more alike than we are apt to think. Yet national types do exist, if only in our minds and aspirations. To define them is in a measure to create them; whether we create scarecrows or flesh-and-blood will perhaps not suffer ultimate determination.

This true Jacobin, who may be a scarecrow, but who we hope will be of flesh and blood, is then of no one occupation, of no one social class, of no determinable rank and wealth. He has no ordinary, daily, selfish human interests. He is a religious fanatic, a man inspired and possessed, a man bent on changing overnight this earth into his heaven. What his notion of heaven was we have tried to learn. It was not an uncommon notion of heaven, not one that many men of modern times, if they entertained at all the notion of heaven, would reject—a place where pain and strife could not exist, where the traditional Christian virtues had banished forever the traditional Christian vices, where men were free and equal, and contented with their freedom and equality. The Jacobin was not a revolutionary in that he believed in heaven, or even in that he believed in a special kind of heaven, but in that he attempted to realize his heaven here on earth. That attempt led to the Terror. You cannot have disagreement in heaven. When the Jacobin found he could not convert those who disagreed with him, he had to try to exterminate them. *La sainte guillotine* was not so christened in the spirit of Villon or of Rabelais, but in the spirit of Calvin.

Now common sense, to say nothing of the social sciences, would tell us that most of our five hundred thousand Jacobins were not of this heroic mold. Yet the Terror was a reality, a reality not to be diminished by statistical proof that even in 1794 violence was the exception, not the rule. The slightest document of the period—a theater program, a fashion plate—is no ordinary document, but a sign from another world. Most men in 1794 no doubt ate, drank, slept, and went about most of their business as they had in 1784; most men were no doubt as stupid, as selfish, as kindly, as good in 1794 as in 1784. But into the whole lives of some Frenchmen, into some part of the lives of all Frenchmen, had come this indefinable, incredible pattern of action and feeling we have called Jacobinism. Very real, very earthly grievances had gone into making the pattern; wise, selfish, ordinary men had helped make the pattern to achieve wise, selfish, ordinary purposes. But a few foolish, unselfish (as the world uses the term) and extraordinary men—with circumstances aiding—had by 1794 turned the pattern into the madness of true Jacobinism. Yet still most Jacobins were normal men. They were still of respectable middle class origins. What had happened to them? Were 499,000 of them hypocrites, trembling before a thousand fanatics? Probably not. It seems more likely that, for a few short months, these ordinary men were possessed by a faith, a contagion, an unearthly aspiration. Jacques Dupont, the man in the street, the economic man, the sociological man, the psychological man, ceased for a brief while to behave in the orderly fashion laid out for him by these sciences, and took instead to the ways of Carlylean heroes or Emersonian representative men.

Jacobinism is, then, first of all a faith. Were they not believers, the Jacobins would be unintelligible to us. As it is, the Jacobin may be strong or weak, tall or short, rich or poor, gentleman or vagabond; what makes him a Jacobin is none of these varying and individual attributes, but a fixed faith. "Liberty, Equality, Fraternity," as words, may be subject to definition and contain the seeds of infinite dispute; as symbols, they were to the Jacobins a common property above logic. The emotions which they evoked allowed the Jacobins to form, for the moment, one body; they provided a common fund of pooled emotions, an inexhaustible and immaterial fund.

Now, in time, this very immateriality of the fund began to pall on many Jacobins. Tough-minded philoso-

phers who, from the utilitarians to the economic inter-
pretationists have perhaps thought a little too highly
of their fellow men, would of course maintain that the
fund must have been material, or held out the promise
of materiality, ever to have held human beings at all.
To them, there must somehow be a connection between
the individual's standing, and the position he takes in
politics. Perhaps they are right as a general rule, right
in the long run and in normal times. Yet our study of
the Jacobin clubs has failed to establish such a connection for the French Revolution. Neither the class struggle
theory nor the maladjustment theory seems in itself
to account for the extraordinary diversity of membership
in the clubs, nor for the extraordinary variety of things
the clubs endeavored to do.

What was meant sincerely as a study in the new history has come to a conclusion strangely like that of very
old-fashioned history indeed. If the subject matter of
the social sciences be natural man, then the Jacobin appears to have a touch of the supernatural. The French
Revolution appears, as it did to Maistre, to Wordsworth,
and to Carlyle, as utterly inexplicable in terms of daily
life, of common sense, of scientific causation. Yet perhaps
we need not call the Revolution a miracle. Only if man
is wholly at the mercy of his simpler appetites need we
have recourse to the miraculous to explain Jacobin aber-
rations. If the incredibly complex world which human
thought has added to the world of our simpler appetites
can at times give ordinary men motives for action even
stronger than these simpler appetites, then the French
Revolution is explicable. It seems too bad to have to
conclude that sometimes some men—or even many men
—believe for no more apparent reason than that they
want to believe, that their beliefs have, at least in part,

independent and immaterial lives. Yet, if only in his capacity for adjusting his conduct to illusion and not to fact, man is most obviously an animal apart. Surely there is nothing surprising if a study of the Jacobins forces us to the conclusion that man cannot live by bread alone?

NOTES

NOTES

CHAPTER I

1. Limoges, p. 206. (For references in this form see Appendix I, p. 281.)
2. See Chapter III.
3. The best are those which reproduce the minutes and membership lists of a club *in extenso*, with data on the leaders, relations with governing authorities, correspondence, and publications. Particularly good are the monographs on the clubs of Colmar, Bergerac, Rodez, Limoges, Tulle and Lons-le-Saunier (see Appendix I, under the above place-names). Aulard's great collection on the Paris Jacobins, though it must be used with caution, shows how much can be learned about a club even when its minutes have entirely disappeared. For a recent synthesis of Jacobin history see de Cardenal, L., *La Revolution en province: Histoire des clubs jacobins* (1929).

CHAPTER II

1. *Les Sociétés de pensée et la démocratie: Etudes d'histoire révolutionnaire* (1921).
2. Crépin-Leblond, M., and Renaud, C., *Ephémérides moulinoises* (Moulins, 1926), p. 58 note.
3. Castres, p. 393. (For references in this form see Appendix I, p. 281.) These social activities were often carried over into the Jacobin clubs. As late as 1791 the Jacobins of Perpignan voted not to allow bets of more than one *sou* per *tableau* at lotto played in the club rooms. *Arch mun. Perpignan* I 348. (For references in this form see Appendix I, p. 281.)
4. *Les Sociétés de pensée et la Révolution en Bretagnè* (1925), 2 vols.
5. p. 449. (For references in this form see Appendix I, p. 281.) *Tabagie* is literally a "smoking club."

6. *Journal des Amis de la Constitution* (Paris), no. 7, 11 Jan. 1791 (hereafter *Jour.* A.-C.)

7. III, p. 359.

8. p. 11.

9. p. 53.

10. p. 330.

11. I, p. 435.

12. p. 5.

13. Auch I, p. 158.

14. p. 27.

15. *Arch. Haute Garonne* L 740.

16. Auch I, p. 159. And at Noyers "even outside the meetings the brothers will love one another like good and true friends." *Arch Yonne* L 1142.

17. Epinal, p. 199.

18. *La franc-maçonnerie française et la préparation de la Révolution* (1926).

19. As for example in Montauban, i, p. 132.

20. Indre-et-Loire, p. 367.

21. Babeau, A., *Histoire de Troyes pendant la Révolution* (1873), i, p. 433.

22. xx, p. 24.

23. *Arch. Haute Garonne* L 740.

24. See Funck-Brentano, F., *The Old Régime in France* (New York and London, 1929) pp. 11-72.

25. For the Club Breton in general see Paris I, i, Introduction, and Paris IV.

26. Paris IV, p. 28.

27. The *réglement* of the Paris club is printed in full in Paris I, i, pp. xxviii-xxxiii. For an example of its imitation by a provincial club see Montauban, x, p. 7. As the larger clubs modeled themselves on the Paris club, so the smaller clubs followed the lead of provincial capitals. The club of Nuits-St.-Georges, finding the rules of the club of Dijon "établi sur des bases pleines de justesse, il a été délibéré unanimement que ce réglement est adopté pour la Société, sauf des retranchements ou modifications en raison de la moindre population de cette ville." *Arch. Côte d'Or L IV b.* 14 *bis* f. 1.

28. *Arch Oise L IV*, first of four unclassified registers of the club of Senlis, f. 34.

29. p. 27.
30. p. 331.
31. *Arch. mun. Perpignan* I 353.
32. x, p. 8.
33. p. 5.
34. p. 10.
35. I, i, p. xxix.
36. Galley, *St. Etienne et son district pendant la Révolution* (St. Etienne, 1903), i, p. 191.
37. p. 12.
38. *Arch. Aveyron* L, unclassified register of the club of Sauveterre, at date 31 May, 1791.
39. Eight sponsors instead of four were required for out-of-towners at Lunéville: but "farmers" not resident at Tulle could be voted in without the customary delay and posting of their names on the bulletin board. Lunéville, p. 338; Tulle, p. 9.
40. p. 6.
41. III, p. 527.
42. i, p. 88.
43. I, ii, p. 267.
44. p. 293.
45. As, for instance at Montauban, where the personnel of the eight committees of correspondence, finance, relations, admission, military affairs, policy, reading, and charity was renewed one-half every month. Montauban, x, p. 10.
46. II, p. 101.
47. *Arch. Corrèze* L 779.
48. p. 118.
49. p. 386.
50. *Journal des Débats de la Société des Amis de la Constitution séante à Paris* (hereafter *Journ. Déb. Jac.*) no. 149, 26 Feb. 1792.
51. *Arch. mun. Perpignan* I 348.
52. *Arch. Haute Garonne* L 752, 756. (The last is the register of the Committee on Public Charity).
53. *Arch Haute Garonne* L 752, 19 germinal, an II.
54. Montauban x, p. 6; Paris I, i, p. xxxiii.
55. Aulard, A. *Actes du comité de salut public* (1889-1923), ix, p. 146.
56. Dreux, p. 242.

57. Thonon, p. 90.
58. Bourgoin, p. 458.
59. Eymoutiers, p. 305, note.
60. *Arch. Meurthe-et-Moselle* L 3137 f. 111.
61. *Arch Haute Garonne* L 756 f. 305.
62. p. 20.
63. *Arch. Seine Inférieure* L 5643, 3 May 1792.
64. Breteuil, p. 482; Cherbourg (1908), p. 382.
65. See for instance Béziers p. 315, Cherbourg (1906), p. 331; Lille, p. 18; Montpellier, p. 548.
66. i, p. 140.
67. p. 65.
68. See for instance St. Jean-de-Luz, pp. 128-129.
69. p. 11.
70. Lunéville, p. 339; Villenauxe-la-Grande, p. 47; Beauvais II, p. 139; Dreux, p. 7; Vire, p. 308.
71. p. 482.
72. p. 243.
73. Auch I, p. 160; Vouneuil-sur-Vienne, p. 148; Romans, p. 37; Agen, p. 150.
74. *Arch. Yonne* L 1140 f. 3.
75. p. 131.
76. x, pp. 16-17.
77. St. Jean-de-Maurienne, p. 10.
78. *Arch. Meurthe-et-Moselle* L 1327, 2 floréal, an II. Here is another example, literally transcribed from a little Alsatian club: niemand solle bedrunken in der Gesellschaft erscheinen, und im fall einer sich der Ehre der Gesellschaft nachtheilige Auffuhrungen in der Bedrunkenheit erlaubte, so soll ihm von seiten des präsidenten die Entfuhrung angerathen und fürs zweitemahl sein Namen aus der Verbrüterung ausgestriefen werden und muss alsobald sein Billet zurückgeben." *Arch. Haut Rhin* L 119.
79. See above, p. 22.
80. *Arch. Yonne* L 1140, f. 95, 24 Sept. 1793.
81. *Ibid.*, 9 nivôse, an II.
82. III, p. 520.
83. p. 56.
84. Beaufort-en-Vallée, p. 73.
85. p. 36.

86. *Arch. Seine Inférieure* L 5600. Papers of the club of Bacqueville.

87. p. 466.

88. The first proceedings of the newly-formed club of Orthez go so far as to say that "the assembly, recognizing that the society which it has formed will not have a *legal character* until it has been affiliated with that of the Jacobins of Paris," takes steps to procure that affiliation. Orthez, p. 7.

89. Lille, p. 34.

90. Paris I, v, p. 517.

91. *Ibid.*, v, p. 57.

92. *Ibid.*, iii, p. 618.

93. Beauvais III, p. 536.

94. *Ibid.*, p. 548.

95. Villenauxe-la-Grande, p. 52. Villenauxe is a village, Sézanne a market town.

96. p. 201.

97. Crest, p. 343.

98. Tulle, p. 36.

99. *Ibid.*, pp. 129-150. The towns were Dijon, Montauban, Chartres, Poitiers, Marseilles, Carcassonne, St. Germain-en-Laye, Bordeaux, Landau, Orléans, Juillac, Aubusson, Tours, Castelnaudary, Cambrai, Limoux, Strasbourg, Toulouse, and Romans.

100. In addition to near-by towns, visitors came from societies in Pontarlier, Dijon, Amiens, St. Malo, Montargis, Colmar, Pithiviers, Brest, St. Valéry-sur-Somme, Metz, Narbonne, Paris, Dunkirk, Villeneuve-sur-Yonne, and Le Mans. *Arch. Seine Inférieure* L 5654.

101. M. Chobaut's figures follow:

Vaucluse	139	societies	154	communes
Gard	132	"	382	"
Drôme	258	"	355	"
Basses Alpes	117	"	260	"
Var	104	"	151	"
Bouches du Rhône	75	"	107	"
		"		"
Totals	825	"	1409	"

See *Annales historiques de la Révolution française* (Sept.-Oct., 1926), Vol. iii, pp. 450-453.

102. de Cardenal, L., *La Révolution en Province* (1929), p. 42.

103. The following table is constructed from material in these
sources: Bergerac, p. 4; Ervy, p. 440; Basses-Pyrénées, p.
492; Toreilles, P., *Histoire du clergé des Pyrénées-Orientales
pendant la Révolution* (Perpignan, 1890); Indre-et-Loire, x, p.
31; Peuchet, J., *Statistique élémentaire de la France* (1805);
Almanach royal for 1792. For the Basses-Pyrénées and the
Aube figures for the whole department are inferred from statistics on certain districts only.

Dordogne	79 societies	410,000 population
Aube	78 "	240,000 "
Basses Pyrénées	96 "	385,000 "
Pyrénées Orientales	60 "	117,000 "
Indre-et-Loire	75 "	278,000 "
Totals	388 "	1,430,000 "

Taking a round figure of 25,000,000 as the population of
France at the period, this proportion applied to the whole
country would give 6783 societies.

104. This is in agreement with M. Chobaut's latest opinion. He
writes that the number of societies "may have attained six or
seven thousand and perhaps more." *Annales historiques de la
Révolution française* (July-August, 1929), Vol. vi, p. 407. Research will hardly add to this.

105. Chobaut, H., in *Annales historiques de la Révolution française*
(Sept.-Oct. 1926), Vol. iii, p. 452.

106. There is a register in the national archives at Paris inscribed
"Etat des Sociétés populaires d'après les Etats envoyés par
les municipalités des chef-lieux de canton et celui remis par les
Jacobins de Paris," obviously very incomplete, but listing
1897 societies, representing every department. It is especially
to be noted that the important administrative centers are all
represented by Jacobin clubs. All *chef-lieux de departement*,
and nearly all *chef-lieux de district*, have clubs. Even La
Vendée has nine clubs. The document is undated, but as Lyons
appears as *Commune Affranchi,* and the department of Mont
Terrible is included the compilation was probably not ended
before the spring of 1794, *Arch. nat.* F la. 548.

107. See Table I, Appendix II, p. 299.

108. Colmar, pp. 456-478.

109. See Table II, Appendix II, p. 300.

110. See Table III, Appendix II, p. 300.

111. This appears to be true of the Indre-et-Loire as well. The following gives membership for thirteen clubs in the district of Tours in 1794, with the population of the towns in parentheses. The source for membership is Indre-et-Loire, x, p. 31. I could not conveniently find population figures for the period, but have used figures from the *Dictionnaire des postes et télégraphes* for 1898-99. Few of these rural communities can have grown much in the interval—the movement was rather the other way. But even were these places only half as large in 1794 as in 1894, it is still true that their proportion of Jacobins is smaller than in the Haute Saône or in the Gard. Joué, 64 (2462); Azay-sur-Cher, 22 (1107); St. Avertin, 28 (1723); Luynes, 31 (1948); Vouvray, 54 (2361); Montbazon, 47 (1143); Rochecorbon, 52 (1544); St. Christophe, 54 (1103); Montlouis, 43 (2053); Véretz, 23 (787); Fondettes, 22 (211); Sorigny, 28 (1080).

112. Malouet estimated the total number of Jacobins at 300,000; Grégoire at the same figure; M-J. Chénier at 400,000. These are all quoted in Taine, *Origines de la France contemporaine*, 12th ed. (1885), Vol. III, p. 63. Taine himself chose the smaller number. Yet in view of the figures given above as to the number of clubs, I do not feel that a total of 500,000 enrolled Jacobins during the Terror is too high.

113. *Arch. mun. Avallon* I.2.23.10.

114. *Arch. Côte d'Or* L IVb. 14bis.1.

115. *Arch. Côte d'Or* L IVb.14.1.

116. *Arch. Oise* L, first of four unclassified registers of the club of Senlis.

117. *Arch. Seine Inférieure* L 5641, 27 July 1791; L 5645, 30 frimaire, an II.

118. *Arch. Seine Inférieure* L 5647, 2 floréal, an II.

CHAPTER III

1. By the law of 25 vendémiaire, an III, passed during the thermidorean reaction as a police measure for the better control of the clubs, each club was obliged to draw up a list of its members, giving age, Christian names, occupation, birthplace, residence before and after 1789, and date of election to the club

for each member. These lists are often badly drawn up, but at any rate many of them have survived. Where there are no such lists, fairly complete records of membership can often be obtained from the minutes themselves. It is true that after thermidor some of the clubs actually became instruments of reaction (see Lefebvre, Guyot, and Sagnac, *La Révolution Française* (1930), p. 262). But I think most of the lists used in this study are lists of good Jacobins.

2. Tables IV, V, and VI, Appendix II, pp. 301-304 give the detailed figures for these groups town by town.

3. Saverne, pp. 23 ff.

4. These villages are Faverney, Gaillefontaine, Manneville-la-Goupil, Mareuil, Pechbonnieu, St. Doulchard, St. Saëns, Vauvert, Villemur, Vilquiers.

5. See Tables VII, VIII, and IX, Appendix II, pp. 305-308 for details.

6. For instance, a certain Ricard appears in the records of the club of Libourne as a *marin* (*Arch. mun. Libourne*, unclassified register of Jacobin club), which can hardly be translated other than as "sailor," a very humble occupation; yet in the roll of the *taille* (*Arch. Gironde* L 842) he appears as a *"maître de barque"* and is assessed 39 livres, where the average for all male inhabitants is 16 livres.

7. *Arch. Aveyron* C 597 f.43.

8. The *capitation* of the *privilégiés* was usually on a separate roll. Such rolls I was usually unable to find.

9. In Toulouse, for instance, a large city with a considerable population on the margin of poverty, I was able to find but a scant dozen of Jacobins listed as paying no tax. For page after page of the rolls of the *capitation*, when the poorer quarters were listed, and occupations like *travailleur, matelot, rapeur de tabac, manoeuvre, fondeur de suif, mendiant, portefaix* and *journalier* kept recurring, names of Jacobins almost never cropped up.

10. Authorities for the materials on which these statistics are based will be found under the appropriate place-names in Appendix I.

11. See Table X, Appendix II, p. 309.

12. See Table XI, Appendix II, p. 310.

13. Albi, Belfort, Bourges, Gaillefontaine, Lunéville, Nuits-St. Georges, Rambouillet, St. Saëns, Thonon, Ventes d'Eawy.

14. Beauvoisin, Belfort, Beynat, Billac, Bourges, Brive, Castres, Dieuze, Gaillefontaine, Giromagny, Lescure, Londinières, Lunéville, Manneville-la-Goupil, Martres-Tolosane, Pont-à-Mousson, Rabastens, St. Saëns, Thann, Turenne, Vauvert, Verfeil., Villemur.

15. Belfort, Beynat, Billac, Bourges, Brive, Castres, Dieuze, Giromagny, Lescure, Lunéville, Manneville-la-Goupil, Martres-Tolosane, Pont-à-Mousson, Thann, Turenne, Villemur.

16. See above, note 1, p. 251.

17. Such lists, or at least *dossiers* of many of the terrorists, can often be found in departmental archives of the series L, usually classified under *police générale*.

18. See Appendix II, p. 311.

19. See Appendix II, p. 311.

20. See Appendix II, p. 312.

21. See Appendix II, p. 312.

22. M. Chobaut calls attention to the complexity of this problem of the variations in the personnel of the clubs in the *Annales historiques de la Révolution française* (July-August, 1929), Vol. vi, p. 407. He seems convinced that for parts of France at least the *sociétés populaires* were really recruited in a great measure from the *peuple*.

23. Albi, Auterive, Auxerre, Avallon, Beauvais, Blagnac, Bourges, Dijon, Frouzins, Grenoble, Lavalette, Lille, Montjoire, Nancy, Nîmes, Rieumes, Rodez, Rouen, Toulouse, Tulle. For the sources, that is, lists of terrorists and tax-lists, see under the above place names in Appendix I.

24. Albi, Auterive, Beauvais, Blagnac, Bordeaux, Bourges, Dijon, Frouzins, Grenoble, Lavalette, Lille, Montjoire, Rieumes, Rodez, Toulouse, Tulle.

25. Those put under police guard at Lille as partisans of Robespierre included six prosperous business men, one lawyer, three of the liberal professions, twelve army officers (*no* privates), two civil servants, and one working man. Lille, p. 216. For a more detailed account of the social position of the terrorists see the present writer's article "Les origines sociales des terroristes" in *Annales historiques de la Révolution française* (Nov.-Dec. 1928), Vol. v, pp. 521-529.

26. p. 18.

27. pp. xxx-xxxvii.

28. pp. 325 ff.

29. I, p. 77.

30. p. 339 note 2.

31. p. 36 note.

32. p. 151.

33. pp. 507-508.

34. p. 47.

35. II, pp. 266-268.

36. Lille, p. 71, p. 79.

37. pp. 60-61.

38. *Arch. mun. Beauvais*, I 45.

39. p. 82.

40. Charnècles, Oct. 5.

41. *Arch. Haute Garonne* L 740-749.

42. *Arch. Allier* L 901.

43. *Arch. Gironde* L 2160 bis.

44. An interesting list of what M. de Cardenal calls "ces conduc-
teurs de petites masses, des escouades de la Révolution" is
given in his *La province pendant la Révolution*, p. 57.

45. *Annales historiques de la Révolution française* (Jan.-Feb.
1928) Vol. V, p. 76.

46. See Tables IV, V, and VI in Appendix II. The tables show 4%
of the membership priests in 1789-1792 and 2% in 1793-1795.
But it must be remembered that in the later period ex-priests
took care to conceal as far as possible their former status, and
that therefore the total number of men educated as priests in
the 42 clubs of Table VI (136 out of a membership of 8,062)
is considerably greater than would appear.

47. Compare the list of members of the club of Rodez in Combes
de Patris' monograph with the faculty of the *collège de Rodez*
and with the chapter of the cathedral, both of which are listed
in the tax-rolls for 1788-1789, and it will be seen that the college is heavily represented in the club, the chapter hardly at
all. *Arch. Aveyron* C 597, 598.

48. Blois, p. 16 and note.

49. *Arch. Gironde* L 2108.

50. *Arch. Allier* L 901, 10 ventôse, an II.

51. *Arch. Haute Garonne* L 752, 7 floréal, an II.

52. *Arch. Gironde* L 2160 f. 255.

53. *Arch. Côte d'Or* L IVb.9.2.

54. Paris I, vi, p. 79.
55. *Arch. Aveyron* L 304.
56. La Garde-Freinet, p. 46.
57. *Arch. Haute Garonne* L 752, 1 germinal, an II.
58. Labroue points out that for Bergerac, as early as 1791, the prosperous founders have admitted large numbers of less prosperous petty *bourgeois*, that, in fact, the personnel of the club was by the end of 1791 as democratic as it was ever to be. Bergerac, p. 21 and note.
59. See especially Table X, Appendix II.
60. At Le Havre, for instance (*Arch. Seine Inférieure* L 5641), and at Libourne (*Arch. mun. Libourne*, unclassified).
61. For its papers, see *Bibl. Bordeaux* MSS 1037.
62. *Ibid.*, f. 3.
63. "L'orateur a eu l'honneur ensuitte de presenter le droit de l'homme et du citoyen, encadré et sous glace. A cest hommage bien cher a nos coeurs, le fruit de la saine Reson et de la philosophie du dix-huitième siecle, la societte a temoigné sa reconnaissance." *Ibid.*, f. 9.
64. See Chapter V for a discussion of this same point, as part of the question as to how far the Jacobin program was "socialistic."
65. p. 368.
66. p. 89.
67. p. 94.
68. p. 37.
69. This is obvious from such works as those of Mortimer-Ternaux and Wallon; but it comes out most strikingly from the kind of local history assembled in the reports of the *représentants en mission* in Aulard's *Actes du comité de salut public.*

CHAPTER IV

1. This subject is treated in Paris I, i, pp. xc-ciii and in Coutances I, pp. 4-31. The following summary is therefore very brief.
2. See for instance Montauban, i, p. 125. At Toulon the municipality was obliged to forbid the club specifically to continue to receive "passive" citizens. Toulon, p. 11.
3. See particularly Blois, Montauban, Colmar.

4. See for instance the "pétition individuelle des citoyens actifs réunis conformément a la Loy," obviously from the club of Metz. *Arch. nat.* C 174 1.446. There are many similar petitions to be found under *Arch. nat.* C 173. 174.

5. Paris VII, p. 8.

6. Here is the list for the club of Montauban on 7 Nov. 1791: *Moniteur, Journal de Paris, Chronique de Paris, Annales patriotiques* (Mercier), *Gazette universelle, Patriote français* (Brissot), *Feuille villageoise, Journal des Débats des Amis de la Constitution de Paris, Journal des Débats de l'Assemblée nationale, Ami des Citoyens* (Tallien), *Courrier des Pays Bas, Journal patriotique* (Marandon of Bordeaux), and a local paper, the *Nouvelles Intéressantes.* Montauban, x, pp. 13-14.

7. Cherbourg (1906), p. 334.

8. *Arch. Haute Garonne* L 755.

9. *Arch. Yonne* L 1140, 25 messidor, an II.

10. The club of Tours. *Jour. A.-C.*, no. 20, 12 April, 1791.

11. x, p. 12.

12. I, ii, p. 605.

13. I, iii, pp. 323-331.

14. I, iv, p. 431.

15. I, iv, p. 620.

16. Toul, p. 81.

17. Bergerac, p. 97. All this was apparently received on 27 Feb. 1791.

18. See above, note 6, for a typical list. After 1791, of course, the *Ami du Peuple* of Marat, and later even the *Père Duchesne,* became part of Jacobin orthodox reading.

19. For the complicated history of newspapers officially patronized by the Paris Jacobins, see Paris I, i, pp. cviii-cxxiii and Tourneux, M., *Bibliographie de l'histoire de Paris pendant la Révolution* (1894), vol. ii, pp. 377-379.

20. *Arch. Haute Garonne* L 740, 3 Nov. 1790.

21. p. 162.

22. Nantes I, p. 270; Châlons-sur-Marne, p. 268.

23. *La Vedette, ou Journal du Département du Doubs,* no. 1, November, 1791 (hereafter, *Ved.*).

24. See above, p. 78.

25. Tourneux, *op. cit.*, vol. ii, pp. 380-432.

26. Epinal, p. 198.

27. Thann, xiii, p. 224.
28. p. 122.
29. *Jour. Déb. Jac.*, 29 Nov. 1791.
30. Delon, P., *La Révolution en Lozère* (1922), p. 566.
31. *Le Spectateur du Sud de la France* (Toulouse), 1 Jan. 1791.
32. II, p. 147.
33. p. 206 ff.
34. Beauvais III, p. 988.
35. Barbé, J., "Le théâtre à Metz pendant la Révolution," *Annales historiques de la Révolution française* (July-Aug. 1927) Vol. iv, p. 386.
36. p. 34.
37. See for instance Aix-en-Provence, xiii, pp. 289-290.
38. p. 360.
39. Trets, p. 219.
40. Bergerac, pp. 199-202. Dorfeuille can be further traced in Paris I, iv, pp. 553, 567, 620, 632; v, 3, 18.
41. p. 419.
42. *Arch. mun. Avallon*, I. 2. 23. 8.
43. p. 25.
44. p. 140.
45. Aulard, *Le culte de la Raison et le culte de l'Etre Suprême* (1892), p. 127.
46. *Arch. mun. Avallon* I. 2. 23. 9, 11 Jan. 1792.
47. p. 144.
48. Saverne, p. 84.
49. II, p. 536.
50. Strasbourg, p. 167; Lons-le-Saunier, p. 63; Bergerac, p. 93.
51. *Arch. Gironde* L 2160, 14 June 1791.
52. *Arch. Haute Garonne* L 740, 1 Dec. 1790.
53. Rodez, p. 24.
54. *Arch mun. Avallon* I. 2. 23. 8.
55. Paris I, ii, p. 520.
56. Election pamphlet of the club of Bordeaux, in the papers of of the Rodez club. See Rodez, p. 631.
57. i, p. 167.
58. *Journal des Clubs*, no. 2, 25 Nov. 1790.
59. pp. 103, 138, 120.
60. p. 173.
61. p. 35.

62. Poitiers, p. 469.
63. pp. 512-513.
64. *Arch. Haute Garonne* L 740, 9 July 1793.
65. I, iv, p. 225.
66. Eymoutiers, pp. 306-307.
67. Aix-en-Provence, xiv, pp. 267, 470; xv, 16-24.
68. p. 260.
69. p. 80.
70. pp. cii ff.
71. *Journal des Clubs*, no. 13, 22 Feb. 1791.
72. *Arch. Deux-Sèvres* L 171.
73. p. 370.
74. Poitiers, pp. 422-428.
75. Paris I, ii, p. 134 and, for Parisian monarchical clubs in general, Paris X.
76. Poitiers, p. 298.
77. p. 129.
78. Paris I, ii, p. 318.
79. (1908), p. 381.
80. See Béziers, p. 266; Montauban, x, p. 292; Gray, p. 50; Indre-et-Loire, p. 382; Monpazier, p. 17; *Jour. Déb. Jac.*, no. 64, 21 Sept. 1791; *Arch. mun Avallon* I. 2. 23. 9, 23-25 Oct. 1791.
81. *Arch. Haute Garonne* L 740, 4 Dec. 1790.
82. Morbihan, v, p. 259.
83. Paris I, i, p. 60.
84. pp. 9-11.
85. For example, Indre-et-Loire, p. 379; Chateauroux, p. 34; Chauny, p. 8.
86. p. 85.
87. *Arch. mun Avallon* I. 2. 23. 9, 1 Jan. 1792.
88. *Arch. nat.* C 173. 1. 436.
89. See above, p. 74.
90. At Blaye. *Arch. Gironde* L 2160 f. 186.
91. At Le Havre. *Arch Seine Inférieure* L 5643, 26 Aug. 1792.
92. *Ved.*, no. 42, 30 March 1792.
93. *Arch. mun. Perpignan* I 353. f. 35.
94. Something of the sort seems to have happened at Bergerac. See Bergerac, p. 185.
95. p. 360.
96. *Arch. Gironde* L 2160 f. 18.

97. Paris I, i, p. 42.
98. *Ibid.*, i, p. 28.
99. *Ibid.*, iii, p. 146.
100. Sisteron, pp. 14-32.
101. Paris I, i, p. 120.
102. *Moniteur*, no. 319 15 Nov. 1790; *Révolutions de France et de Brabant*, no. 54, Nov. 1790.
103. Indre-et-Loire, p. 381.
104. pp. 66-68.
105. p. 77.
106. *Jour. Déb. Jac.*, no. 87, 31 Oct. 1791.
107. *Arch. Haute Garonne* L 746, 13, 16 May 1793.
108. Poitiers, pp. 506-519.
109. *Arch. Yonne* L 1140, 30 June, 11 Aug. 1793.
110. Limoges, p. 65.
111. Paris I, iii, p. 360.
112. *Arch. Seine Inférieure* L 5641, 4 July 1791.
113. p. 114.
114. *Arch. Seine Inférieure* L 5672 f. 3.
115. *Jour. A.-C.*, no. 11, 8 Feb. 1791.
116. See Paris I, i, p. 111 for numerous petitions on this subject from the provinces.
117. Paris I, ii, p. 336.
118. *Tableau des évènements qui ont eu lieu à Bordeaux* (1794). *Bibl. Bordeaux* 713. 2. 48.
119. As early as March 1792 Hyon told the Paris club that to achieve its ends "the principal points consist in making public the section meetings, in passing in these meetings decrees which shall be communicated to other section meetings by special delegates who shall meet together at the city hall." *Jour. Déb. Jac.*, no. 159, 14 March 1792.
120. I, iii, p. 335.
121. I, iii, p. 345.
122. IV, p. 86.
123. See for instance I, iv, p. 143 and *Moniteur*, no. 211, 29 July 1792 (Denunciation of Bulté); I, iv, p. 124 and *Moniteur*, no. 206, 24 July 1792 (Delegation from Orléans); I, iii, p. 436 and *Moniteur*, nos. 82 and 84, 22 and 24 March 1792 (Employees of *Fermes*). Citation of such instances could be multiplied indefinitely.

124. See the copy of the minutes of the town council of Sierck, sent the club in October 1791. I, iii, p. 183.
125. I, ii, p. 303.
126. I, ii, p. 220.
127. I, i, p. 60.
128. *Arch. Gironde* L 2160 bis, 10 prairial, an III.
129. *Arch. nat.* D III. 305.
130. *Arch. Yonne* L 1140, 5 germinal, an II.
131. *Arch. mun. Avallon* I.2. 23. 10, 3 frimaire, an II.
132. p. 23 and note.
133. pp. 41-45.
134. p. 83.
135. p. 492.
136. p. 35.
137. p. 204.
138. p. 14.
139. I, iii, p. 595.
140. p. 323.
141. Coutances I, p. 45; Vannes, p. 498.
142. *Arch. Seine Inférieure,* L 319, 18 prairial, an III.
143. *Jour. A.-C.,* no. 17, 22 March 1791.
144. St. Amand, p. 456.
145. p. 547.
146. I, p. 184.
147. Auch I, p. 191.
148. p. 187.
149. *Ved.,* no. 40, 23 March 1792.
150. Thonon, p. 107.
151. Châlons-sur-Marne, p. 68.
152. p. 114; see also Lescar, p. 487; Strasbourg, p. 257.
153. p. 185.
154. p. 161.
155. p. 137.
156. p. 11.
157. p. 20.
158. *Ved.,* no. 13, 18 Dec. 1792.
159. Bergerac, p. 92. It would be interesting, though very difficult, to follow up in detail petitions, requests, "invitations" and other steps of a given club, and see just how the governing authorities dealt with them. I have very roughly attempted this

from printed sources, merely to show what could be done, with time and patience, in the archives. From the notes in the excellent monograph of Libois on Lons le-Saunier, it would appear that of 46 requests to the city government, 11 to the district, 26 to the department, and 13 to miscellaneous authorities, that is, 96 in all, 30 were granted, 5 refused, 12 tabled, postponed or otherwise put off, 3 already anticipated, and of the other 46 there is no trace. From Planté's account of the club of Orthez, it appears that of 23 petitions to the city government, 10 to the district, 12 to the department, 21 to other authorities, that is, 66 in all, 17 were accepted, 2 refused, 8 postponed, and of 39 no trace is found. At Auxerre, to judge from the records of the city government (Demay, *Procès-verbaux de l'administration de la ville d'Auxerre*), up to 1792 14 requests from the club were granted, and 2 refused.

160. Paris V, p. 30.
161. Paris I, iii, p. 196.
162. I, iii, p. 384.
163. I, i, p. 404.
164. I, iii, p. 225.
165. I, iii, p. 410.
166. Authorities: for Moulins, *Arch. Allier* L 901; for Toulouse, *Arch. Haute Garonne* L 750. 751; for Castres, *Arch. Tarn*, L unclassified; for Albi, *Arch. Tarn* L unclassified; for Brive, *Arch. Corrèze* L 760; for Metz, Metz, pp. 94-99; for St. Jean-de-Maurienne, St. Jean-de-Maurienne, p. 79.
167. p. 129.
168. The clubs were not nearly so uppish in their relations with the representatives on mission in 1793-1794 as they had been with almost all authorities in 1791-1792. For instance: "Vilestivaud replies that the society is not judge of the conduct of civil servants; its duty is to limit itself strictly to describing the facts concerning them to the representative on mission." Limoges, p. 160.
169. The French phrases "épurer une administration" and "épuration" are really quite untranslatable. They mean, of course, the weeding out of the opponents of the party in power. During the Terror, this was done with no pretense at legality, beyond the almost unlimited powers assigned by the Convention to its representatives on mission.

170. Aulard, *Actes du Comité du Salut Public*, x, p. 265.
171. *Ibid.*, x, p. 327.
172. *Ibid.*, ix, p. 309.
173. *Ibid.*, x, p. 253.
174. *Ibid.*, xiii, p. 144.
175. *Ibid.*, x, p. 599.
176. *Ibid.*, ix, p. 68. (Italics mine.)
177. *Ibid.*, x., p. 310.
178. The career of Lakanal in Périgord is a good example of the way an able deputy could have the clubs under his thumb. See Bergerac, pp. 297 ff. and Labroue, H., *La mission du Conventionnel Lakanal dans la Dordogne* (1913).
179. *Documents pour servir à l'histoire de la Révolution française dans la ville d'Amiens* (Amiens, 1897-1900), vii, pp. 466-471.
180. Carcassonne, p. 311.
181. *Ibid.*, p. 314.
182. Nantes II, p. 114.
183. *Arch. Yonne* L 761, 7 ventôse, an II.
184. p. 127.
185. *Arch Seine Inférieure* L 5647, 17 ventôse, an II.
186. *Arch. Yonne* L 1130 f. 1 and f. 5.
187. *Arch. Côte d'Or* L IVb. 14. f. 4.
188. p. 164.
189. p. 452.
190. p. 30.
191. *Arch. Seine Inférieure* L 5647, 7 germinal, an II.
192. Thann, xv, pp. 386-388.
193. Dreux, p. 212.
194. *Arch. Haut Rhin* L 119 f. 13.
195. *Arch. Haute Saône* L 359. 1.
196. p. 7.
197. Chobaut, H., "Le nombre des Sociétés populaires du Sud-Est en l'an II," *Annales historiques de la Révolution française* (1926), iii, p. 454.
198. For other examples of rural societies see Villenauxe-la-Grande, Villecroze, Callas, Artonne, Vouneuil-sur-Vienne, La Garde-Freinet, St. Arnoult, Larche. The most aggressive rural societies I have encountered have been in Normandy, that of Bacqueville, for instance (*Arch. Seine Inférieure* L 5600), or that of Manneville-la-Goupil (*Ibid.*, L 5672).

199. For an analysis of the economic activities of the clubs, see de Cardenal, *La Révolution en province* (1929), Book IV, Chap. VI.

200. *Arch. mun. Avallon* I. 2. 23. 10, 21 prairial, an II.

201. *Arch. Yonne* L 1140, 14 June 1793.

202. *Ibid.*, 6 brumaire, an II.

203. *Arch. Seine Inférieure* L 5644, 18 Sept. 1793.

204. *Arch. Haute Garonne* L 752, 8 ventôse, an II.

205. p. 84.

206. *Arch. Aveyron*, L unclassified, register of the club of Millau.

207. *Arch. Haute Saône* L 359. 1, 19 pluviôse, an II.

208. *Arch. Côte d'Or* L IVb. i4. f. 28.

209. Ste. Marie-aux-Mines, p. 280.

210. *Arch. Gironde* L 2160 f. 186.

211. *Arch. Seine Inférieure* L 5647, 17 floréal, an II.

212. p. 260.

213. *Arch. Haute Garonne* L 756, 8 ventôse, an II. Again, from the minutes of another club: "La société a nommé deux commissaire pour engager la municipalite d'enjoindre a tous les oberjistes, caffetiers, etc., de placer un baquet chez eux propre a recevoir les urines des citoyens qui fréquentent leurs maisons, et d'inviter en meme temps cette otorité de prendre pareille mesure dans tous les cartiers de la commune, ainsi qu'a l'hopital." Crest, p. 331.

214. *Arch. Meurthe-et-Moselle* L 3137.

215. See for instance Ste. Marie-aux-Mines, p. 282.

216. *Arch. Seine Inférieure* L 5647, 10 floréal, an II.

217. *Arch. Allier* L 901, 10 germinal, an II.

218. *Arch. Haute Garonne* L 756; L 752, 29 ventôse, an II.

219. *Arch. Seine Inférieure* L 5647, 26 germinal, 24 floréal, 1 frimaire, an II.

220. Castelnau-Rivière-Basse, ii, p. 403.

221. *Arch. Allier*, L 901, 9 thermidor, an II.

222. *Arch. Haute Garonne* L 756, 16 ventôse, an II.

223. *Arch. Haute Garonne* L 752.

224. *Ved.*, no. 65, 26 thermidor, an II.

225. Thonon, p. 166. Also: "A member requests that the resolutions taken by the society not be allowed to remain buried in the registers, and that our decrees be put into execution." Rouen, p. 182.

226. Paris I, v, pp. 344, 346.
227. p. 252, note 3.
228. p. 259, note 1.
229. *Arch. Seine Inférieure* L 5647 14 floréal, an II.
230. *Arch. Côte d'Or* L IVb. 14. 1 f. 46.

CHAPTER V

1. *Secondes réflexions sur l'institution du pouvoir exécutif par Jean Henri Bancal, lues a la Société des Amis de la Constitution de Clermont-Ferrand, le 3 juillet 1791*, p. 6. Bancal des Issarts, later elected to the Convention, was not an orthodox Jacobin, but his views here are typical enough.
2. Neuilly-St. Front, p. 117.
3. There is a curious phase of Jacobinism, just before the Terror, when women were accepted in some clubs as equals, or encouraged to form clubs of their own. The subject is well treated in de Cardenal, *La Révolution en province*, pp. 65-74. The important thing is that Jacobin women were always in a small minority among their own sex, and subject to social scorn. At Senlis, for instance, where women were admitted on absolute equality with men, and addressed as "soeur," I find only five women who accepted membership, and only two or three in habitual attendance. (*Arch. Oise* L, unclassified registers of the club of Senlis, between 5 Feb. 1792 and 16 April 1793). A decree of the Convention (9 brumaire, an II) forbade female membership and female clubs. No doubt women were more and more identified as of the clerical party, and the characteristic French hostility to woman's suffrage was already taking root. Something of this feeling, I think, comes out in the following passage: "The religion of a republican is in the observance of laws emanating from sane reason, the religion of a republican is to open the eyes of all those whom persecuting religions still render unjust and cruel. Do not permit men to entice you into receiving into our society women, or rather certain women, whom their duty calls rather to the care of their household." (St. Jean-de-Luz, p. 119).
4. I, ii, p. 341.
5. I, i, p. 149.

6. I, i, p. 145.

7. *Journ. A.-C.*, no. 15, 8 March 1791.

8. Tulle, p. 95.

9. *Journal du Club des Cordeliers*, no. 1, 28 June 1791.

10. "All members of the society took an oath never to permit the establishment of two chambers." Lons-le-Saunier, p. 46.

11. *Journal des Clubs*, no. 5, 16 Dec. 1790. Note how early a date this is for such strong Jacobin language.

12. p. 121.

13. *Arch. mun. Libourne*, unclassified register of the club of Libourne, 6 August 1793.

14. Ars-en-Ré p. 36. The earlier clubs were at least verbally insistent on their rôle as defenders of the law. "Let each member, gentlemen, consider himself invested with the honorable mission of recommending to his brother citizens obedience to the law and to constituted authority." Sedan, p. 230.

15. "The judge is but the organ of the law, and he cannot apply to it more of his intellectual faculties than the attention which apprehends without deciding anything itself. In this point of view, man is given back to his own real nature, as soon as it is to the law which he himself has made that he is obliged to conform." Paris I, i, p. 46.

16. Melun II, p. 335.

17. Garnier (of Saintes) in Paris I, vi, p. 47.

18. Dufourny, in Paris I, v, p. 518.

19. Paris I, v, p. 492.

20. Rivalry between neighboring towns was often extremely acute. The club of Chablis refused to admit that the club of Auxerre had any rights over other clubs in the department merely because Auxerre was the capital city. There was much bitter talk about Auxerre in this club. (*Arch. Yonne* L 1140 f. 98.) Le Havre never forgave the smaller town of Montivilliers for winning the position of district capital, even after revolutionary enthusiasm had christened one Havre-Marat and the other Brutus-Villiers. (*Arch. Seine Inférieure* L 5647, 12-20 ventôse, an II.)

21. See Aulard's collection of the acts of the Committee of Public Safety, especially vols. viii-xi.

22. At Bergerac the American, English, and Polish flags were draped with the tricolor behind the president's chair (p. 192).

23. p. 245.
24. p. 246.
25. p. 429.
26. Epinal, p. 133.
27. *Journal républicain des deux départements de Rhone et de Loire*, no. 15, 20 pluviôse, an II. (hereafter *Jour. rép. R. & L.*)
28. Morbihan, p. 464; St. Jean-de-Luz, p. 200; Nice, p. 405.
29. Colmar, p. 44.
30. Callas, p. 496.
31. Lunéville, p. 350.
32. Strasbourg, p. 303.
33. p. 331.
34. Ste. Marie-aux-Mines, p. 229.
35. Monpazier, p. 27.
36. p. 184.
37. p. 151.
38. *Arch Seine Inférieure* L. 5647, 18 ventôse, an II.
39. *Arch. Haute Garonne* L 746, 14 April 1793.
40. Artonne, p. 76.
41. *Ved.*, no. 23, 24 Jan. 1792.
42. *Le Spectateur du Sud de la France*, I Jan. 1791.
43. *Jour. A.-C.*, no. 16, 15 March 1791.
44. See above, p. 65.
45. *Arch Yonne* L 1140 f. 233.
46. *Arch. Haute Saône* L 359.1, 19 pluviôse, an II.
47. p. 321.
48. *Arch. nat.* C 174 1. 446 f. 5.
49. Auch I, p. 185.
50. p. 129.
51. p. 20.
52. *Arch. Haute Garonne* L 752, 12 ventôse, an II.
53. *Arch. mun. Avallon* I 2. 23. 8. A good example of the unreality of the economic motives alleged. The society would let an ex-priest be idle, if he were married. It was the priest they disliked, not the non-producer.
54. Larche, p. 58.
55. p. 80.
56. Trets, p. 223.
57. p. 33.
58. I, v, p. 430.

59. Unless, indeed, we take the society of Noyon at its word, and assume virtue and talents to be unnatural. "Equals in the eyes of the law as in the eyes of Nature, there exist between Frenchmen no differences save those of virtue and talents." Noyon, p. 421.

60. Thonon, p. 191.

61. p. 200.

62. *Moniteur* (réimpression) xviii, p. 651.

63. *Ibid.*, xvii, p. 738.

64. p. 76.

65. p. 161.

66. p. 293.

67. Carcassonne, p. 167.

68. Villeneuve-sur-Yonne, p. 479.

69. p. 311.

70. See for instance St. Omer, p. 19, where in 1791 the club calls on all citizens to obey the law during a strike.

71. Monpazier, p. 8.

72. Rouen, p. 214.

73. p. 118.

74. p. 178.

75. Auch I, p. 157.

76. Lille, p. 50.

77. *Arch. Gironde* L 2160 f. 28.

78. Morbihan, v, p. 239; Paris I, vi, p. 347 (The club of La Teste-de-Buch reports that it excludes bankrupts.)

79. Paris I, vi, p. 223.

80. See above, Chapters II and IV.

81. "Ah! The unfortunate man whom fate overwhelms is, in the eyes of the Gods themselves, a respectable man." Dreux, p. 167.

82. Sainte-Marie-aux-Mines, p. 250. Next week another member protested that workmen for the municipality were not earning their 30 *sous* a day. The whole protest sounds like a modern business man attacking governmental inefficiency. *Ibid.*, p. 255. All this is in germinal, an II.

83. *Arch. Seine Inférieure* L 5644, 10 Sept. 1793.

84. Castelnau-Rivière-Basse, p. 407.

85. *Arch. Seine Inférieure* L 5647, 22 germinal, an II.

86. Paris I, i, p. 122.

87. p. 58.

88. *Arch. Allier* L 901, 9 ventôse, an II.
89. p. 17.
90. *Arch. Haute Garonne* L 756 f. 10.
91. p. 331.
92. p. 248.
93. *Arch. Haute Garonne* L 752, 14 ventôse, an II.
94. *Arch. Seine Inférieure* L 5647, 5 floréal, an II.
95. p. 309.
96. Romans, p. 37, 13 pluviôse, an II.
97. *Arch. Yonne* L 1140, 12 floréal, an II.
98. Aiguesmortes, p. 245.
99. Crest, p. 339.
100. *Arch. Haute Saône* L 359. 1 f. 2.
101. *Arch. Côte d'Or* L IVb. 14. 4.
102. p. 151 and note 2.
103. *Arch. Yonne* L 1140 f. 292.
104. *Arch. Allier* 901, 10 ventôse, an II.
105. See, for instance, Bergerac, p. 288.
106. Châlons-sur-Marne, p. 265.
107. *Rapport sur le rachat des droits féodaux, et arrêté pris dans la Société des Amis de la Constitution d'Ambert* (Clermont-Ferrand, 1790), p. 2.
108. Neuilly-Saint-Front, p. 123.
109. *Arch. Seine Inférieure* L 5645, 26 frimaire, an II. From the minutes of the club of Le Havre. There is no indication that the club paid any attention to this letter.
110. *Arch. Yonne* L 1141, 26 fructidor, an II. See also Saint-Omer, p. 94; Beauvais III, p. 518.
111. pp. 183-184.
112. p. 238.
113. p. 337.
114. *Arch. Côte d'Or* L IVb. 14. 4.
115. I, v, p. 457.
116. The decrees of ventôse were apparently well received in the clubs. But the real test, their application, can hardly have been made for lack of time. More studies like that of M. Schnerb on the application of these decrees in the district of Thiers (*Annales historiques de la Révolution française* (Jan.-Feb., 1929), vi, pp. 24-33) are needed before we can generalize.
117. *Arch. Yonne* L 1140, 12 frimaire, an II.

118. Paris I, v, p. 73. The Paris club, of course, heard all sorts of proposals during its long career. After thermidor it was driven into extreme radicalism. There is an amusing and very collectivist debate on education in October 1794. One citizen "wishes children brought up in common as in Sparta—minus the helots." *Ibid.*, vi, p. 612. But in economic questions Paris is not typical.

119. There are occasionally amusing examples to be found. At Limoges, in the spring of 1794, a club member "denounced the remark of a servant attached to the special jail for suspects; bargaining for chickens in the market, he is said to have remarked that he was buying them for the Marquis of Mérinville, who was made for eating them." The servant was of course arrested. Limoges, p. 282.

120. At Chablis as early as June 1793 dues were remitted to the poor; yet there are no signs of the poor joining. (*Arch. Yonne* L 1140, 20 June 1793 ff.) M. Leleu writes of the use by the club of Lille of the phrase "sans culotte" as "an affectation of democratic sentiments." The club itself was composed almost entirely of rich *entrepreneurs*. (Lille, pp. 111, 153.) See also St. Jean-de-Maurienne, p. 9.

121. The club and the "peuple des tribunes" were usually working for common ends. At Le Havre "the club decrees that all citizens, even in the *tribunes*, can give their opinions on condidates for the society." (*Arch. Seine Inférieure* L 5647, 16 floréal, an II). The same club granted citizen Thomasset, at his own request, a certificate stating his constant attendance at meetings. But he was not a member, and had attended in the *tribunes*, where such humble men belonged. (*Ibid.*, 16 germinal, an. II.)

122. Callas, p. 492.

123. p. 123.

124. II, p. 265.

125. This brief rule of extremists is reported, very much exaggerated, in the *dossiers* of terrorists disarmed in the year III. For a good example, see the account of the extremists at St. Romain in Normandy, *Arch. Seine Inférieure* L 319.

126. p. 396.

127. III, p. 988.

128. *Journal des Clubs*, no. 12, 15 Feb. 1791.

129. Beauvais III, p. 993.
130. Morbihan, p. 363.
131. I, v, p. 242.
132. *Arch. Corrèze* L 779 f. 5.
133. p. 426.
134. p. 141.
135. *Arch. mun. Perpignan* I 348, 26 Jan. 1791.
136. *Arch Haute Garonne* L 740, 26 Nov. 1790.
137. p. 310.
138. Digne, p. 423.
139. Cognac, p. 422.
140. p. 214.
141. Morbihan, p. 263.
142. p. 63.
143. *Ved.*, no. 83, 4 brumaire, an II.
144. p. 49.
145. *Arch. Haute Garonne* L 752, 11 ventôse, an II.
146. *Arch. Seine Inférieure* L 5647, 27 germinal, an II.
147. p. 88.
148. p. 278.
149. Rouen, p. 145.
150. I, vi, p. 124.
151. p. 117.
152. Chateau-Thierry II, p. 204.
153. I, iv, p. 136.
154. *Jour. A.-C.*, no. 1, 1 Dec. 1790.
155. Beaufort-en-Vallée, p. 71.
156. Paris I, vi, p. 146.
157. Coutances I, p. 83.
158. II, p. 339.
159. Le Havre, *Arch. Seine Inférieure* L 5647, 7 germinal, an II.
160. Aulard, *Le culte de la Raison et le culte de l'Etre Suprème* (1892), p. 129, note 1.
161. p. 138.
162. p. 157. This is of course nothing unique. Social revolutionaries have always appealed to the real Jesus. The club of St. Etienne accepted a motion to ask the Convention to put a "bust of the *sans-culotte* Jesus" in the Pantheon along with those of Marat and Lepelletier. Galley, *St. Etienne et son district pendant la Révolution* (1903), ii, p. 179.

163. Dreux, p. 6.
164. II, p. 339.
165. Thonon, p. 196.
166. p. 268.
167. p. 120.
168. St. Amand, p. 460.
169. Béziers, pp. 298-300.
170. *Arch. nat.* D III. 304 l. 7.
171. p. 93.

CHAPTER VI

1. See on the general subject of the revolutionary cults Aulard, *Le culte de la Raison et le culte de l'Etre Suprème* (1892); Mathiez, *Les origines des cultes révolutionnaires* (1904); *La Théophilanthropie et le culte decadaire* (1904); Dommanget, *La déchristianisation à Beauvais* (1921).
2. See for instance Paris I, iii, p. 291; Rouen, p. 10.
3. *Arch. Yonne* L 1140, 29 brumaire, an II.
4. p. 181.
5. *Arch. Yonne* L 1140, 26 Sept. 1793.
6. The Jacobins did not wholly despair of their American brothers. There is a curious account of a festival at Bordeaux in the summer of 1794 in *Bibl. Bordeaux, Collection Bernadau*, 713. 2. 9. Ysabeau and the American consul, followed by French and American sailors, walked in a procession, holding olive branches, climbed a symbolical Mountain hand in hand, and swore friendship before the altar of the fatherland. Afterwards there was a *repas civique*, and toasts beginning "To the union of the French and American peoples" and ending "To the destruction of London." On this old pamphlet a firm hand has written the comment, which perhaps deserves to be printed for the sake of a Franco-American friendship based apparently upon many similar misunderstandings: "People indulged the Americans at that time because they brought to Bordeaux flour for our bread—fraudulently adulterated flour at that."
7. *Arch Aveyron* L unclassified register of the club of Sauveterre.
8. *Jour. Déb. Jac.*, no. 158, 11 Mar. 1792. Doppet rather ingenu-

ously claims in his memoirs that the whole thing was an accident. Doppet, *Mémoires politiques et militaires*, (1797), p. 45.

9. p. 37. A good description of a Jacobin *salle* is to be found in
Louhans, p. 108. "The *salle des séances* of the society was
ornamented with medallions, statues of Rousseau and Voltaire,
to which were added later those of Marat and Lepelletier, a
copy of the Rights of Man, and various republican symbols,
pikes surmounted by red liberty caps, patriotic inscriptions and
mottoes. The names of the deputy Guillermin, who died in
Paris in April, 1793, and those of defenders of the Fatherland
who had died in service, were inscribed on columns. On the
walls were to be seen the *oeil de surveillance* and ferocious
warnings like 'Tremble, scoundrels.'

10. xiii, p. 280.
11. p. 136.
12. p. 22.
13. p. 252.
14. *Arch. Seine Inférieure* L 5672 f. 1.
15. xiii, p. 464.
16. This text is from *Arch Seine Inférieure* L 5647, 13 ventôse, an
II, but a copy of the oath is to be found in the papers of many
clubs, and is printed in *Annales historiques de la Révolution
française* (1924), i, p. 463.
17. p. 191.
18. p. 322.
19. Vire, p. 318.
20. II, p. 187.
21. p. 364.
22. Cherbourg (1906), p. 333.
23. Ars-en-Re, p. 191.
24. II, p. 228.
25. For examples see Indre-et-Loire, p. 369; Agen., p. 512 (it is
headed "Sinaï des Français"); Bourgoin, p. 462. The latter follows:

> Français, ton pays défendras
> Afin de vivre librement.
>
> Tous les tyrans tu poursuivras
> Jusqu' au delà de l'Indostan.
>
> Les lois, les vertus soutiendras
> Même, s'il le faut, de ton sang.

Les perfides dénonceras
Sans le moindre ménagement.

Jamais foi tu n'ajouteras
A la conversion d'un grand

Comme un frère soulageras
Ton compatriote souffrant

Lorsque vainqueur tu te verras
Sois ferme, mais sois compatissant.

Sur les emplois tu veilleras
Pour en expulser l'intrigant.

Le dix-août sanctifieras
Pour l'aimer eternellement

Le bien des fuyards verseras
Sur le sans-culotte indigent.

The last commandment is particularly interesting. This decalogue originated in the section of the Quinze-Vingts at Paris.

26. Chateau-Thierry II, p. 229.
27. p. 336.
28. p. 161. Robert Raikes, regarded as the founder of the modern
    Sunday school movement, established his first school in 1782.
29. *Arch. mun. Avallon* I 2. 23. 10, 30 prairial, an II.
30. *Arch. Seine Inférieure* L 5647, 27 germinal, an II.
31. I, i, p. 406.
32. *Ved.*, no. 82, 1 brumaire, an II.
33. See for instance Louhans, p. 121; Guéret, p. 344; Chaumont,
    p. 50.
34. Tulle, p. 48.
35. *Journal du département de la Haute Vienne*, no. 19, 29 fri-
    maire, an II.
36. Provins, p. 131.
37. p. 148.
38. p. 179.
39. I, p. 182.
40. *Arch. Seine Inférieure* L 5647, 30 germinal, an II.
41. Delon, *La Révolution en Lozère* (1922), p. 575 note.
42. Coutances I, p. 94.
43. p. 46.
44. *Arch. mun. Libourne*, unclassified register of the local club.
45. St. Arnoult, p. 21.

46. *Arch. mun. Avallon* I. 2. 23. 10, 3 ventôse, an II.

47. *Arch. Haute Garonne* L 746, 14 April 1793.

48. p. 361; p. 399.

49. p. 205, note 2.

50. xv, p. 146.

51. x, p. 16.

52. Bibl. Bordeaux, MSS. 1037 f. 23.

53. p. 340.

54. p. 121.

55. *Arch. Seine Inférieure* L 5641, 27 June 1791.

56. Beaufort-en-Vallée, p. 18.

57. *Ved.*, no. 9, 20 pluviôse, an II.

58. *Jour. A.-C.*, no. 20, 12 April 1791.

59. p. 259.

60. Marechal, *La Révolution dans la Haute Saône* (1903), p. 589. See also Bordeaux, pp. 340 ff.

61. *Jour. rép. R. & L.*, nos. 29 and 31, 18 and 22 ventôse, an II.

62. *Arch. Seine Inférieure*, L 5644, 30 brumaire, an II.

63. Vaulry, p. 51.

64. p. 320.

65. Creyssac, pp. 180-182. Were it not for the word *épanchements* at the very end, one might suspect these Jacobins of a true conviviality inconsistent with what we have called their Puritanism; and no doubt many Jacobins did enjoy themselves, here and elsewhere. But *épanchements* are obviously too literary and humanitarian to have a place in real dissipation; and the scale of the thing was too large. There is in such feasts an unmistakable touch of the trumped up conviviality of the Sunday school picnic, the class reunion or club banquet. The Jacobin clubs never in the least resembled the Abbaye de Thélème.

66. *Ved.*, no. 8, 18 pluviôse, an II.

67. p. 79.

68. Guéret, pp. 394-396.

69. p. 187.

70. p. 40.

71. p. 138.

72. Crepin-Leblond and Renaud, *Ephémérides moulinoises*, p. 393 note.

73. *Arch. mun Beauvais* D 6, 12 prairial, an III.

CHAPTER VII

1. xiii, p. 218.
2. *Ved.*, no. 9, 4 Dec. 1792.
3. p. 316.
4. p. 465.
5. *Bibl. Bordeaux* MSS. 1037 f. 16.
6. p. 345.
7. *Arch. Yonne* 1140 f. 75.
8. Some of the questions at Avallon are interesting in their search after detail:

> 4. At the news of Capet's departure in June, what was your conduct?
>
> 5. At the fall of Longwy, Verdun, Valenciennes, and other strongholds delivered to the enemy by the treason of our generals, what did you say or do?
>
> 12. What public positions have you held since the Revolution?
>
> 13. Have you filled them with the zeal and integrity of a good citizen?
>
> 15. Have you ever spoken against the *sociétés populaires* and have you ever done anything to disturb their meetings?

All this of course, with "tu" instead of "vous." *Arch. mun. Avallon* I 2. 23. 10, 28 nivôse, an II.

9. xiii, p. 538.
10. p. 220.
11. *Ved.*, no 10, 23 pluviôse, an II.
12. *Jour. rep. R. & L.*, no. 7, 4 nivôse, an II.
13. p. 753.
14. III, p. 967.
15. *Arch. Seine Inférieure* L 5600.
16. As a final example of how what may easily appear the more vulgar forms of emotion dominated these *épurations,* and gave them a maudlin tone shocking to conservative tastes, we may cite from the Paris club. Citizen Petit was accused of something unjacobin, and expelled. His son, a boy of twelve, who was weeping in a corner of the room "rushes to the tribune and declares that his father is a good patriot, who has brought him up in accordance with the purest principles of the Revo-

lution. The father is taken back, the son is embraced by the
president, and given a card of entrance to the society." Paris
I, v, p. 545.
17. p. 468.
18. Paris I, ii, p. 265.
19. *Arch. Meurthe-et-Moselle* L 3137.
20. p. 260.
21. p. 258.
22. *Arch. Seine Inférieure* L 5644, 10 Sept. 1793.
23. *Arch. Yonne* L 1140 f. 166 and f. 367.
24. *Arch. Haute Saône* 359. 1. f. 7.
25. Prévost, A., *Histoire du diocèse de Troyes pendant la Révolution* (1908), ii, p. 589.
26. Buffenoir, H., "L'image de J.-J. Rousseau dans les sociétés de
province," *Révolution française*, lxxi, p. 51.
27. x, p. 14.
28. p. 72.
29. Basses-Pyrénées, p. 496.
30. Marechal, *La Révolution dans la Haute Saône*, p. 592.
31. Limoges, p. 209.
32. Paris I, iii, p. 68.
33. *Ibid.*, i, p. 397.
34. *Arch. Allier* L 904.
35. *De l'influence de la liberté sur les moeurs; discours prononcé
par le républicain Fronsard, deputé de la société populaire
épurée de Clermont-Ferrand* (Clermont-Ferrand, n.d.).
36. I, i, p. 46.
37. p. 2.
38. *Arch Aveyron*, L unclassified register of the club of Sauveterre.
39. p. 43.
40. xiv, p. 113.
41. Paris I, ii, p. 103.
42. *Jour. Déb. Jac.*, no. 8, June 1791.
43. Paris I, iii, p. 214.
44. *Ibid.*, ii, p. 235.
45. Limoges, pp. 246, 169.
46. p. 347.
47. p. 118.
48. *Arch. Haute Garonne* L 746, 19 April 1793.
49. *Arch. Oise* L IV, unclassified papers of the club of Beauvais.

50. *Arch. Seine Inférieure* L 5647, 24 germinal, an II.
51. *La Ved.*, no. 68, 29 June 1792.
52. I, p. 52.
53. I, ii, p. 189.
54. xiv, p. 544.
55. p. 326.
56. Limoges, p. 243.
57. *Arch. Allier* L 901.
58. I, iii, p. 313.
59. I, v, p. 618.
60. St. Jean-de-Maurienne, p. 70.
61. p. 45.
62. Provins, p. 123.
63. La Garde-Freinet, p. 155.
64. p. 170.
65. p. 181.
66. p. 446.
67. *Arch. Seine Inférieure* L 5644, 19 Sept. 1793.
68. *Ved.*, no. 54, 11 May 1792.
69. *Arch. Yonne* L 1140, 18 Aug. 1793.
70. *Arch. Oise* L IV, unclassified papers of the club of Gerberoy.
71. p. 205.

CHAPTER VIII

1. p. 71.
2. *Ved.*, no. 33, 28 Feb. 1792.
3. p. 166.
4. Guéret, p. 418.
5. Chaumont, p. 28.
6. p. 476.
7. Gray, p. 92.
8. p. 159.
9. p. 194.
10. p. 494.
11. II, p. 16.
12. Rouen, p. 225.
13. ii, p. 18.
14. Montignac, p. 151.
15. I, p. 161.

16. At Moulins, for instance, the society as purified by Boisset in the autumn of 1794 had 99 *fonctionnaires* out of a membership of 183. *Arch. Allier* L 904.

17. Cochin, A., "La crise de l'histoire révolutionnaire" in *Les Sociétés de pensée et la démocratie* (1921).

18. Jacobin virtue, for instance, is not attainable by ordinary human beings.

APPENDICES

APPENDIX I

The following list of references is intended, not as a complete bibliography of the Jacobin Clubs, but as a key to the footnotes used in this book, and to the sources for the statistical material used in Appendix II.

Under each place-name will be found first a reference to the printed work, or works, referred to in text and footnotes. Where there is more than one work used for a single town, these works are designated by *large* Roman numerals: thus, for instance, a footnote in the form Paris IV, p. 63, refers to Bouchard, A., *Le Club Breton* (1920), page 63. Where the name of the town occurs unambiguously in the text, the reference in the footnote gives merely page, and where necessary, volume, the latter in *small* Roman numerals.

There follow under each place name references where necessary to sources used for: (a) lists of members with professions, ages, etc.; (b) population of town about 1790; (c) tax-rolls about 1790; (d) lists of buyers of *biens nationaux;* (e) lists of terrorists drawn up after thermidor.

Arch. = Archives départementales
Arch. mun. = Archives municipales
Arch. nat. = Archives nationales
Bibl. = Bibliothèque
Jour. A. C. = Journal des Amis de la Constitution
Jour. Déb. Jac. = Journal des Débats de la Société des Amis de la Constitution séante à Paris
Jour. rép. R. & L. = Journal républicain des deux Départements de Rhône et de Loire
Ved. = La Vedette, ou Journal du Département du Doubs
Place of publication of separate works—as opposed to articles in periodicals—is Paris unless otherwise given.

Agen (Lot-et-Garonne)
Azéma, C., "Les sans-culottes agenais de l'an II," *Revue de l'Agenais* (1901), xxxiv, 150-155.

Aiguesmortes (Gard)

Falgairolle, E., "La Société populaire d'Aiguesmortes," *Revue rétrospective* (1898), viii, 121-144, 193-216, 214-288, 313-342.

Aix (Bouches du Rhône)

Ponteil, F., "La Société populaire des Antipolitiques d'Aix," *Revue historique de la Révolution française* (1918-1923), xiii, 30-47, 266-290, 454-474, 577-589; xiv, 40-45, 263-271; xv, 16-26, 146-161.

Alban (Tarn)

(a) Arch. Tarn L unclassified; (c) Arch. Tarn C 577.

Albi (Tarn)

(a) Arch. Tarn L unclassified; (b) Arch. Tarn L 353; (c) Arch. Tarn C 577; (e) Arch. Tarn L 706 f. 129.

Allassac (see Donzenac)

Angoulême (Charente)

Morel, C., "Adresse de la Société populaire d'Angoulême aux habitants de la campagne en 1792," *Bulletin de la Société . . . . de la Charente* (1919), x, pp. xcviii-cvix.

Ars-en-Ré (Charente Inférieure)

de Richemond, M., "Délibérations de la Société des Amis de la Liberté et de l'Egalité d'Ars-en-Ré," *Archives historiques de la Saintonge et de l'Aunis* (1904), xxxiv, 1-253.

Artonne (Puy de Dôme)

Martin, F., *Les Jacobins au village* (Clermont-Ferrand, 1902).

Auch (Gers)

I. Brégail, F., "La Société populaire d'Auch," *Bulletin du comité des travaux historiques* (1911) 143-220.

II. Dellas, "La Société populaire d'Auch sous la Révolution," *Revue de Gascogne* (1898), xxxix, 29-37.

Auterive (Haute Garonne)

(c) Arch. Haute Garonne C 534; (e) Arch. Haute Garonne L 2229.

Auxerre (Yonne)

(e) Arch. Yonne L 1405 f. 52.

Avallon (Yonne)

(a) Arch. mun. Avallon I 2. 23. 9-10; (e) Arch. Yonne L 1406 f. 54.

Avranches (Manche)

Le Grin, "Lectures: la Société populaire d'Avranches," *Revue de l'Avranchin* (1910), xvi, 150-155.

Bacqueville (Seine Inférieure)

(a) Arch. Seine Inférieure L 5600; (c) Arch. Seine Inférieure C 1740.

Bar-le-Duc (Meuse)

· Bister, E., "Adresse de la Société des Amis de la Constitution de Bar-le-Duc à ses frère les citoyens des campagnes," *Mémoires de la Société . . . . de Bar-le-Duc* (1909), vii, pp. xxxvi-xl.

Bayeux (Calvados)

Anquetil, E., "Le cavalier jacobin de la Société populaire," *Bulletin de la Société . . . . de Bayeux* (1907). ix, 47-64.

Beaufort-en-Vallée (Maine-et-Loire)

Hatreux, G., *Voyage à travers un vieux registre* (Angers, 1907).

Beaulieu-sur-Dordogne (Corrèze)

(a) Arch. Corrèze L 756; (b) Arch. Corrèze C 208; (c) Arch. Corrèze C 208.

Beaumont (Dordogne)

Testut, L., "Adresse de la Société populaire de Beaumont," *Bulletin de la Société . . . . du Périgord* (1922), xlix, 235-240.

Beauvais (Oise)

I. Moreau, E., "Du rôle des citoyennes de Beauvais dans la Société des Amis de la Constitution," *Bulletin de la Société d'études de l'Oise* (1905), i, 120-127.

II. Bordez, F., "La Société des Amis de la Constitution de Beauvais," *Bulletin de la Société d'études de l'Oise* (1906), ii, 137-172.

III. Thiot, L., "Les Sociétés populaires de Beauvais," *Bulletin de la Société d'études de l'Oise* (1908), iv, 515-548, 962-997.

(a) Arch. Oise L IV unclassified; (b) Arch. mun. Beauvais F 1; (c) Arch. mun. Beauvais G 2, 4, 6, 8; (d) Arch. Oise Q unclassified; (e) Arch. mun. Beauvais D 6.

Beauvoisin (Gard)

(a) Arch. Gard L 11.1; (b) Arch. Gard L 4.4.36; (c) Arch. Gard L 4.4.5.

Belfort (Territoire de Belfort)

D. R., "La Société populaire de Belfort," *Bulletin de la Société belfortaine d'émulation* (1906), xxv, 61-68.

(a) Arch. Haut Rhin L unclassified.

Bénévent (see Creuse)

Bergerac (Dordogne)

Labroue, H., *La Société populaire de Bergerac* (1915).

284 THE JACOBINS

(a) Labroue, H., *Liste des membres de la Société populaire de Bergerac* (1914); (b) Delfau, G., *Annuaire statistique de la Dordogne* (Périgueux, an XII); (c) Arch. mun. Bergerac unclassified.

Bergues (Nord)

Looten, C., "Bouchotte et la Société populaire de Bergues," *Annales du comité flamand de France* (1908), xxix, 80-104.

Beynat (Corrèze)

(a) Arch. Corrèze L 757.

Béziers (Hérault)

Soucaille, A., "Historique de la Société populaire de Béziers," *Bulletin de la Société . . . de Béziers* (1890), xv, 226-326.

Billac (Corrèze)

(a) Arch. Corrèze L 758.

Blagnac (Haute Garonne)

(c) Arch. Haute Garonne C 537; (e) Arch. Haute Garonne L 2227.

Blois (Loir-et-Cher)

Dufay, P., *Les Sociétés populaires et l'armée* (1913).

Bordeaux (Gironde)

Flottes, "Le club des Jacobins de Bordeaux," *Révolution française* (1916) lxix, 337-362.

(a) Arch. Gironde L 2108, 2118; (b) Arch. Gironde L 1258; (c) Arch. Gironde L 844-845; (e) Arch. Gironde L 1248.

Boulogne (Pas de Calais)

Unsigned, "Séances de la Société populaire de Boulogne le 25 et le 26 thermidor, an II," *Bulletin de la Société académie de Boulogne* (1904), vii, 257-274.

Bourges (Cher)

(a) Arch. Cher L 924; (b) Arch. Cher L 175; (c) Arch. Cher C 204, Bibl. Bourges CC 90; (e) Lemas, T., *Études sur le Cher pendant la Révolution* (1887), 25.

Bourgoin (Isère)

Fochier, L., *Souvenirs historiques sur Bourgoin: Extraits pris sur les registres de la Société populaire* (Vienne, 1880).

Breteuil (Eure)

Anchel, R., "Les Jacobins de Breteuil," *Révolution française* (1913), lxv, 481-495.

Brive (Corrèze)

(a) Arch. Corrèze L 760.

Caen (Calvados)

Renard, C., *Notice sur les Carabots de Caen* (Caen, 1858).

Callas (Var)

Poupé, E., "La Société populaire de Callas," *Révolution française* (1902) xliii, 482-503.

Carcassonne (Aude)

Mandoul, J., "Le club des Jacobins de Carcassonne," *Révolution française* (1893), xxv, 153-169, 232-260, 308-336.

Castelnau-Rivière-Basse (Hautes Pyrénées)

Dufour-Clarac, L., "La Société républicaine et montagnarde de Castelnau" *Société académique des Hautes Pyrénées, Bulletin local*, i, 78-88, 323-328; ii, 178-180, 390-468.

Castres (Tarn)

Dupéron, C., "La Société populaire de Castres," *Bulletin de la section des sciences économiques et sociales* (1897), 393-398.

(a) Arch. Tarn L unclassified; (d) Arch. Tarn Q 140.

Caussade (Tarn-et-Garonne)

Campagnac, E., "L impôt sur le revenu dans les statuts d'une Société populaire en 1793," *Annales révolutionnaires* (1910), iii, 242-244.

Chablis (Yonne)

(a) Arch. Yonne L 1140; (d) Arch. Yonne Q 249.

Châlons-sur-Marne (Marne)

de Barthélemy, E., "Une Société populaire . . . pendant la Révolution," *Revue de Champagne et de Brie* (1889), i, 260-270.

Charnècles (Isère)

Vernay, F., "La Société populaire de Charnècles," *Le Dauphiné*, 5, 12, 19, 26 October; 2 November 1919.

Charost (Cher)

(a) Arch. Cher L 925; (b) Arch. Cher L 175; (c) Arch. Cher C 252.

Châteauneuf-sur-Cher (Cher)

(a) Arch. Cher L 944; (c) Arch. Cher C 247.

Châteauroux (Indre)

Jouet, A., "La Société populaire de Châteauroux," *Revue archéologique, historique et scientifique du Berry* (1896), 33-123.

Château-Thierry (Aisne)

I. Rollet, J., "Les procès-verbaux de la Société populaire de Château-Thierry en l'an II," *Annales de la Société historique et archéologique de Château-Thierry* (1881), 180-269.

II. Corlieu, A., "La Société populaire de Château-Thierry," *Annales de la Société historique et archéologique de Château-Thierry* (1903), 210-221.

Chaumont (Haute Marne)

Forestier, L., *La Société populaire de Chaumont* (Chaumont, 1892).

Chauny (Aisne)

Fleury, E., *Un club à Chauny en 1794* (Laon, 1849).

Cherbourg (Manche)

Galland, A., "La Société populaire de Cherbourg," *Bulletin du comité des travaux historiques* (Paris, 1906), 330-343; (1908), 381-397.

Cognac (Charente)

Le Gallo, E., "Les Jacobins de Cognac," *Révolution française* (1902-1905), xliii, 238-255; xlvii, 409-435; xlviii, 234-248.

Colmar (Haut Rhin)

Leuillot, P., *Les Jacobins de Colmar* (Strasbourg, 1923).

(a) *Ibid.;* (b) Scherlen, A., *Topographie de Colmar* (Colmar, 1925); (c) Arch. mun. Colmar, tax-register, 1789; (d) Arch. Haut Rhin L 866.

Cordes (Tarn)

(a) Arch. Tarn L unclassified; (c) Arch Tarn C 577.

Cosnac (Corrèze)

(a) Arch. Corrèze L 764.

Coutances (Manche)

I. Sarot, C., *Les Sociétés populaires de Coutances* (Coutances, 1880).

II. Dommanget, M., "La Société populaire de Coutances et le problème de l'éducation," *Annales révolutionnaires* (1921), xiii, 144-147.

(a) Sarot, C., *L'organisation . . . de la Manche pendant la Révolution* (Coutances, 1880).

Crest (Drôme)

Chevalier, J., "Procès-verbaux des séances de la Société populaire de Crest," *La Révolution à Die* (Valence, 1905).

Creuse (Department of the)

Lacrocq, L., "Notes sur les Sociétés populaires dans la Creuse," *Mémoires de la Société des sciences naturelles et archéologiques de la Creuse* (1903-1905), viii, 197-205; ix, 378-431; x, 307-370; xi, 87-127.

Creyssac (Dordogne)
    Durand de Ramfort, "Une fête civique à Creyssac pendant la Ré-
    volution," *Bulletin de la Société . . . du Périgord* (1918), xlv, 179-
    182.
Dieuze (Moselle)
    (a) Arch. Meurthe-et-Moselle L 3127.
Digne (Basses Alpes)
    Hubert, A., "Les Amis de la Constitution à Digne," *Révolution
    française* (1887), xii, 420-426.
Dijon (Côte d'Or)
    Hugueney, L., *Les clubs dijonnais sous la Révolution* (Dijon, 1905)
    (a) Arch. Côte d'Or L IVb.9.2; (b) Hugueney, *op. cit.;* (c) Arch.
    Côte d'Or C 5910; (d) Arch. Côte d'Or Q 241-245; (e) Arch.
    Côte d'Or L police générale, prairial, an III.
Donzenac (Corrèze)
    Ulry, A., "Les clubs révolutionnaires de Donzenac et d'Allassac"
    Bulletin de la Société . . . de la Corrèze (1921), xlii, 153-177.
Dreux (Eure-et-Loir)
    Champagne, G., *La Société populaire de Dreux* (Dreux, 1908).
Epinal (Vosges)
    Philippe, A., "La Société populaire d'Epinal," *La Révolution dans
    les Vosges,* iv, 129-144; 225-240; v, 33-48, 81-102.
Ervy (Aube)
    Destainville, H., "Les Sociétés populaires du district d'Ervy," *An-
    nales historiques de la Révolution française* (1924), i, 440.
Estang (Gers)
    Tallez, P., "Une Société populaire en Bas Armagnac," *Revue de
    Gascogne* (1920), xv, 97-112.
Eymoutiers (Haute Vienne)
    Granier, E., "Un club limousin" *Annales révolutionnaires* (1923),
    xv, 296.
Faverney (Haute Saône)
    (a) Arch. Haute Saône L 358.1; (b) Arch. Haute Saône L 13.1;
    (c) Arch. Haute Saône L 21.24; (d) Arch. Haute Saône Q 128.
Ferté-Milon, la (Aisne)
    Dommanget, M., "La Société populaire de la Ferté-sur-Ourcq,"
    La Révolution dans le canton de Neuilly-St.-Front (1913).
Fleurance (Gers)
    Cadéot, N., "La Société montagnarde de Fleurance," *Bulletin de la
    Société . . . du Gers* (1912), 65-85.

Fleurey-les-Faverney (Haute Saône)

(a) Arch. Haute Saône L 359.1; (b) Arch. Haute Saône L 13.2.

Fontainebleau (Seine-et-Marne)

Constant, C., "Un club des Jacobins en province," *Le Correspondant* (1876), cii, 747-769.

Fousseret, le (Haute Garonne)

Vié, L., "La Société populaire du Fousseret," *Revue de Comminges* (1906), xxi, 129-135.

Frouzins (Haute Garonne)

(c) Arch. Haute Garonne C 1901; (e) Arch. Haute Garonne L 2229.

Gaillefontaine (Seine Inférieure)

(a) Arch. Seine Infèrieure L 5632.

Garde-Freinet, la (Var)

Labroue, H., "La Société populaire de la Garde-Freinet," *Révolution française* (1908), liv, 42-64; 131-157.

Gerberoy (Oise)

Dommanget, M., "La Société populaire de Gerberoy," *Annales révolutionnaires* (1920), xii, 507-510.

Gers (Department of the)

I. Brégail, "Deux grands congrès des Sociétés populaires dans le Gers," *Bulletin de la Société . . . du Gers* (1900), 126-133.
II. Barada, J., "Les Sociétés populaires de diverses communes du Gers," *Bulletin de la Société . . . du Gers* (1920), 45-57.

Giromagny (Territoire de Belfort)

(a) Arch. Haut Rhin L unclassified.

Givet (Ardennes)

Unsigned, "Le club patriotique de Givet," *Revue historique de l'Ardennes* (1898), 86-89.

Gray (Haute Saône)

Godard, C., "Les Sociétés populaires de Gray," *Bulletin de la Société grayloise d'émulation* (1911), 57-108.

Grenoble (Isère)

Tissot, R., *La Société populaire de Grenoble*, (Grenoble, 1910). (a) Tissot, *op. cit.*, 190-204; (b) Arch. Isère L 304; (c) Arch. Isère L 363, C 535; (e) Tissot, *op. cit.*, 205.

Guéret (See Creuse)

Haudivillers (Oise)

(a) Dommanget, M., "La Société populaire d'Haudivillers," *Annales révolutionnaires* (1916), viii, 709-712.

Havre, le (Seine Inférieure)

(a) Arch. Seine Inférieure L 5640-5648; (b) Arch. Seine Inférieure, *Inventaire sommaire de la série* L; (c) Arch. Seine Inférieure C 542; (d) Arch. Seine Inférieure Q unclassified, register of sales of *biens nationaux*, district of Montivilliers.

Honfleur (Calvados)

I. Blossier, A., "Taveau, . . . sa correspondance politique avec la municipalité et la Société populaire de Honfleur," *Bulletin du comité des travaux historiques* (1908) 371-381.

II. Blossier, A., "Claude Fauchet . . . et la Société de Honfleur," *Révolution française* (1904), xlvii, 513-542.

Indre-et-Loire (Department of the)

Faye, H., "Les Sociétés populaires dans le département de l'Indre-et-Loire," *Revue de la Révolution* (1887-1888), ix, 367-384, 481-492; x, 24-42.

Indes françaises

Castonnet-Desfosses, H., "La Révolution et les clubs dans l'Inde française," *Revue de la Révolution* (1883-1884), i, 233-248, 333-337, 383-392, ii, 91-97.

Jussey (Haute Saône)

(a) Arch. Haute Saône L 363.1; (b) Arch. Haute Saône L 13.1; (c) Arch. Haute Saône L 21.28; (d) Arch. Haute Saône Q 128.

Larche (Corrèze)

Blusson, R., and Marchant A., *La Société populaire du canton de Larche* (Tulle, 1905).

Largentière (Ardèche)

Mazon, A., "La Société populaire de Largentière," *Revue . . . du Vivarais* (1903), xi, 248-281, 305-314.

Laval (Mayenne)

Galland A., "Les Sociétés populaires de Laval et de Mayenne," *Bulletin de la commission historique et archéologique de la Mayenne* (1902), xviii, 15-40.

Lavalette (Haute Garonne)

(c) Arch. Haute Garonne C 1111; (e) Arch. Haute Garonne L 2227.

Lescar (Basses Pyrénées)

Annat, J., "La Société populaire de Lescar," *Revue du Béarn* (1912) iii, 481-492, 542-550.

Lescure (Tarn)

(a) Arch. Tarn L unclassified; (b) Arch. Tarn L 353; (c) Arch. Tarn C 578.

Libourne (Gironde)

Corbineau, M., "Documents . . . des Sociétés populaires de Libourne," *Archives historiques du département de la Gironde* (1910), xlv, 351-428.

(a) Arch. mun. Libourne, unclassified registers of Jacobin clubs; (b) Arch. Gironde L 1876; (c) Arch. Gironde L 842.

Ligny-en-Barrois (Meuse)

Braye, L., "Le club de Ligny," *Mémoires de la Société* . . . *de Bar-le-Duc* (1909), 34-39.

Lille (Nord)

Leleu, E., *La Société populaire de Lille* (Lille, 1919).

(a) Leleu, *op. cit.*, typewritten appendix in copy at Bibl. Nat.; (b) Dieudonné, C., *Statistique du département du Nord* (Douai, 1804); (c) Arch. mun. Lille 253; (e) Arch. Nord L 844-845.

Limoges (Haute Vienne)

Fray-Fournier, A., *Le club des Jacobins de Limoges* (Limoges, 1903).

Londinières (Seine Inférieure)

(a) Arch. Seine Inférieure L 5567.

Lons-le-Saunier (Jura)

Libois, H., "Délibérations de la Société populaire de Lons-le-Saunier," *Mémoires de la Société d'émulation du Jura* (1896), 19-483.

Lorient (see Morbihan)

Louhans (Saône-et-Loire)

Guillemant, L., *Une petite ville pendant la Terreur* (Louhans, 1902).

Lunéville (Meurthe-et-Moselle)

Baumont, H., "La Société populaire de Lunéville," *Annales de l'Est* (1889), iii, 337-376.

(a) Arch. Meurthe-et-Moselle L 3130.

Mainz (Germany)

Bockenheimer, K., Die Mainzer Klubisten der Jahren 1792-1793 (Mainz, 1896).

Mamers (Sarthe)

(a) Fleury, G., *La ville et le district de Mamers pendant la Révolution* (1911); (b) *Ibid.*

Manneville-la Goupil (Seine Inférieure)

(a) Arch. Seine Inférieure L 5672; (d) Arch. Seine Inférieure Q, unclassified register of sales of *biens nationaux*, district of Montivilliers.

Mareuil (Cher)
(a) Arch. Cher L 925.
Marmande (Lot-et-Garonne)
Bonnat, R., "La Société populaire de Marmande," *Revue de l'Agenais* (1903), xxx, 507-514.
Mayenne (see Laval)
Melun (Seine-et-Marne)
I. Leroy, G., "Le club des Jacobins de Melun," *Révolution française* (1901), xli, 439-446.
II. Noiriel, E., "La Société des Amis de la Constitution de Melun," *Révolution française* (1904), xlvi, 323-345.
Metz (Moselle)
Bultingaire, L., *Le Club des Jacobins de Metz* (1906).
(a) *Ibid.*, 94-99.
Millau (Aveyron)
Constans, L., "La Société populaire de Millau," *Révolution française* (1888), xiv, 769-803.
Miramont (Lot-et-Garonne)
Dupin, G., "Les Jacobins de Miramont," *Révolution française* (1888), xiv, 920-928.
Monpazier (Dordogne)
de Cardenal, L., *Les Sociétés populaires de Monpazier* (Lille, 1924).
Montaigut-en-Combrailles (Puy de Dôme)
Dorey, L., "La Société populaire et républicaine de Montaigut," *Révolution française* (1910), lix, 533-551.
Montauban (Tarn-et-Garonne)
Galabert, F., "Le club jacobin de Montauban," *Revue d'histoire moderne*, (1899, 1908), i, 124-168, 235-258, 457-474; x, 5-27, 273-317.
Montbard (Côte d'Or)
(a) Arch. Côte d'Or, L IVb.2.14; (c) Arch. Côte d'Or C 7337.
Montignac (Dordogne)
Le Roy, E., *La Société populaire de Montignac*, 1791-1795 (Bordeaux, 1888).
Montjoire (Haut Garonne)
(c) Arch. Haute Garonne C 1193; (e) Arch. Haute Garonne L 2227.
Montpellier (Herault)
Chobaut, H., "Une pétition du club de Montpellier," *Annales historiques de la Révolution française* (1927), iv, 547-563.

Morbihan (Department of the)

Muller, P., "Clubs et clubistes du Morbihan," *Revue de la Révolution* (1885-1886), v, 233-241, 257-266, 461-470; vi, 122-129, 183-196, 263-272, 359-380.

Moulins (Allier)

(a) Arch. Allier L 900-904; Faure, H., *Histoire de Moulins*, (Moulins, 1900), ii, 676; (c) Arch. mun. Moulins 380.

Nancy (Meurthe-et-Moselle)

I. Mansuy, A., "Les Sociétés populaires à Nancy," *Annales de l'Est* (1899), xiii, 432-448.

II. Poulet, H., "Le sans-culotte Philip, président de la Société populaire de Nancy," *Annales de l'Est et du Nord* (1906), 248-283, 321-266, 501-529.

(e) Arch. Meurthe-et-Moselle L 1486 ff. 87-92.

Nantes (Loire Inférieure)

I. Lallié, A., "Les Sociétés populaires à Nantes," *Revue de Bretagne et de Vendée* (1890), iv, 255-271, 335-352.

II. Muller, P., "Mémoires de Blanchard; . . . Les clubs et clubistes de Nantes," *Revue de la Révolution* (1884), iv, 74-84, 107-117, 156-160.

III. Martin, G., "Les chambres littéraires de Nantes," *Annales de Bretagne* (1926), xxxvii, 347-365.

Neuilly-St.-Front (see la Ferté-Milon)

Nevers (Nièvre)

Charrier, J., "La vie d'une Société populaire pendant la Révolution," *Revue des questions historiques* (1924), ci, 371-379.

Nice (Alpes Maritimes)

Combet, J., *La Société populaire de Nice* (Nice, 1911).

Nîmes (Gard)

(a) Arch. Gard L 11.3; (c) Arch. Gard C 1072-1073; (e) Rouvière, F., *La Révolution dans le Gard* (Nîmes, 1887-1889), iv, 360-362.

Nomény (Meurthe-et-Moselle)

(a) Arch. Meurthe-et-Moselle L 3135; (b) Arch. Meurthe-et-Moselle L 1898; (c) Arch. Meurthe-et-Moselle L 1887; (d) Arch. Meurthe-et-Moselle Q 16.

Noviant-aux-Prés (Meurthe-et-Moselle)

(a) Arch. Meurthe-et-Moselle L 3124; (b) Arch. Meurthe-et-Moselle L 1898; (c) Arch. Meurthe-et-Moselle L 1887; (d) Arch. Meurthe-et-Moselle Q 16.

Noyon (Oise)

Cozette, P., "La Société populaire de Noyon à ses frères les habitants des campagnes," *Bulletin du comité des travaux historiques* (1904), 419-429.

Nuits-St. Georges (Côte d'Or)

(a) Arch. Côte d'Or L IVb. 14bis.5.

Orthez (Basses Pyrénées)

Planté, A., "Déliberations de la Société des Amis de la Constitution d'Orthez," *Bulletin de la Société* . . . *de Pau* (1901), xxix, 1-263.

Paris (Seine)

I. Aulard, A., *La Société des Jacobins* (1889-1897).

II. Stern, A., "Le club des patriotes suisses à Paris," *Revue historique* (1889), xxxix, 282-322.

III. Mathiez, A., "Un club révolutionnaire inconnu: le club de la Réunion," *Revue historique* (1925), cxlviii, 63-72.

IV. Bouchard, A., *Le Club Breton* (1920).

V. Fribourg, A., *Le Club des Jacobins en 1790* (1910).

VI. Kuhlmann, C., "On the Conflict of Parties in the Jacobin Club," *University of Nebraska Studies* (1905).

VII. Kuhlmann, C., "The Relation between the Jacobins and the Army, the National Guard, and Lafayette," *ibid.* (1906).

VIII. Mathiez, A., *Le Club des Cordeliers pendant la crise de Varennes* (1910).

IX. Bougeart, A., *Les Cordeliers* (Caen, 1891).

X. Challamel, E., *Les clubs contre-révolutionnaires* (1895).

(a) Aulard, *op. cit.*, i, pp. xxxiv-lxxvii.

Pau (Basses Pyrénées)

Laborde, J., "Un club féminin pendant la Révolution," *Revue du Béarn* (1911), ii, 337-351, 397-411, 453-470.

Pechbonnieu (Haute Garonne)

Also for the surrounding villages of Montbéron, Labastide-St.-Sernin, St. Loup, St. Geniest and le Fossat.

(a) Arch. Haute Garonne L 3166; (c) Arch. Haute Garonne C 1238, 1212, 1173, 1288, 1266, 1152.

Périgueux (Dordogne)

Poumeau, E., *La Société populaire de Périgueux* (Périgueux, 1907).

Poitiers (Vienne)

de Roux, "La Révolution à Poitiers," *Mémoires de la Société des antiquités de l'Ouest* (1910).

Pont-à-Mousson (Meurthe-et-Moselle)

    (a) Arch. Meurthe-et-Moselle L 3137; (d) Arch. Meurthe-et-Moselle Q 16.

Porrentruy (Switzerland)

    Gautherot, *La Révolution française à Bâle* (1908).

Pouilly-sur-Loire (see Nevers)

Provins (Seine-et-Marne)

    Bellanger, J., *Les Jacobins peints par eux-mêmes* (1908).

Pyrénées, Basses (Department of the)

    Annat, J., "Les Sociétés populaires dans les Basses Pyrénées," *Revue du Béarn* (1911), ii, 491-497.

Rabastens (Tarn)

    (a) Arch. Tarn L unclassified; (c) Tarn C 783.

Rambouillet (Seine-et-Oise)

    Lorin, F., "La Société populaire de Rambouillet," *Mémoires de la Société . . . de Rambouillet* (1898), xiii, 291-367.

Riceys, les (Aube)

    Ray, L., "La Société des Amis de la Constitution établie aux Riceys," *La Révolution dans l'Aube* (1910), 22-41.

Rieumes (Haute Garonne)

    (c) Arch. Haute Garonne C 1220; (e) Arch. Haute Garonne L 2229.

Rodez (Aveyron)

    Combes de Patris, B., *Procès-verbaux de la Société populaire de Rodez* (Rodez, 1912).

    (a) Combes de Patris, *op. cit.*, appendix; (b) Arch. Aveyron L unclassified, heading *population;* (c) Arch. Aveyron C 597-598; (e) Combes de Patris, *op. cit.*

Romans (Drôme)

    Chevalier, U., *Le comité de surveillance et la Société républico-populaire de Romans* (Valence, 1890).

Rosières-aux-Salines (Meurthe-et-Moselle)

    (a) Arch. Meurthe-et-Moselle L 3138; (b) Arch. Meurthe-et-Moselle L 1588; (c) Arch. Meurthe-et-Moselle L 1598.

Rouen (Seine Inférieure)

    Chardon, E., *Cahiers des procès-verbaux de la Société populaire de Rouen* (Rouen, 1909).

    (e) Arch. Seine Inférieure L 2367.

Ruffec (Charente)

    Chauvet, "Régistre de la Société des Amies des vrais Amis de la

Constitution de Ruffec," *Bulletin du comité des travaux historiques* (1902), 500-530.

Saint-Amand (Nièvre)

Boyer, A., "La Société populaire de St. Amand," *Bulletin de la Société . . . nivernaise* (1905), xx, 429-482.

Saint-Amarin (Haut Rhin)

Arch. Haut Rhin L 119.

Saint-Arnould (Seine Inférieure)

Le Febvre, A., *La Société populaire de St. Arnould* (Rouen, 1914)

Saint-Doulchard (Cher)

(a) Arch. Cher L 925.

Sainte-Marie-aux-Mines (Haut Rhin)

Unsigned, "Procès-verbaux de la Société populaire de Val-aux-Mines," *Bulletin de la société philomathique vosgienne* (1904), xxx, 167-311.

Saint-Jean-de-Luz (Basses Pyrénées)

Annat, J., "La Société populaire de St.-Jean-de-Luz," *Revue du Béarn* (1910), 71-76, 118-129, 168-175, 200-213.

Saint-Jean-de-Maurienne (Savoie)

Gros, A., *Le club des Jacobins de St. Jean-de-Maurienne* (St. Jean-de-Maurienne, 1908).

Saint-Omer (Pas de Calais)

Bled, O., *Les Sociétés populaires de St. Omer pendant la Révolution* (St. Omer, 1910).

Saint-Saëns (Seine Inférieure)

(a) Arch. Seine Inférieure L 5719.

Saint-Servan (Ille-et-Vilaine)

Haize, J., "La Société populaire de St. Servan," *Annales de la Société historique de St. Malo* (1906), 61-79.

Saint-Zacharie (Var)

Poupé, E., "Les papiers de la Société populaire de St. Zacharie," *Bulletin de la société d'études de Draguignan* (1905), xxv, 59-74.

Sauveterre (Aveyron)

(a) Arch. Aveyron L unclassified; (c) Arch. Aveyron C 574.

Saverne (Bas Rhin)

Fischer, D., "La Société populaire de 'Saverne," *Revue d'Alsace* (1869), xx, 23-34, 73-84, 121-131, 180-190.

Sedan (Ardennes)

Unsigned, "Bouchotte et la Société des Amis de la Constitution de Sedan," *Revue historique de l'Ardennes* (1905), xii, 229-231.

Sisteron (Basses Alpes)

Cauvin, C., *La formation de la Société populaire de Sisteron* (Digne, 1901).

Soissons (Aisne)

Pécheur, Abbe, "Notice sur les clubs de Soissons," *Bulletin de la Société . . . de Soissons* (1891), i, 183-195.

Strasbourg (Bas Rhin)

Heitz, F., *Les Sociétés politiques de Strasbourg pendant les années 1790 à 1795* (Strasbourg, 1863).

Tain (Drôme)

Bellet, C., "La Société populaire de Tain," *Bulletin de la Société . . . . du Drôme* (1921), iv, 365-393.

Thann (Haut Rhin)

Poulet, H., "L'esprit publique à Thann pendant la Révolution," *Revue historique de la Révolution française* (1918-1923), xiii, 5-29, 214-248, 367-396, 529-549; xiv, 33-39, 108-118, 187-192, 272-284; xv, 27-40, 162-173, 298-303, 367-420.

Thonon (Haute Savoie)

Mugnier, F., "La Société populaire de Thonon," *Mémoires de la Société savoisienne* (1898), xxxvii, 5-243.

Tonneins (Lot-et-Garonne)

Bresson, L., "Une petitie ville du sud-ouest en l'an II," *Révolution française* (1882), iii, 173-175, 231-240.

Toul (Meurthe-et-Moselle)

Denis, A., *Le club des Jacobins de Toul* (Nancy, 1895).

(a) *Ibid.*, appendix; (b) Arch. Meurthe-et-Moselle L 2406; (c) Arch. Meurthe-et-Moselle L 2406; (d) Arch. Meurthe-et-Moselle Q 224-225.

Toulon (Var)

Labroue, H., "Le club jacobin de Toulon," *Annales de la Société d'études provençales* (1907), 1-51.

Toulouse (Haute Garonne)

(a) Arch. Haute Garonne L 746-751; (b) Arch. mun. Toulouse 1F 100 bis.

(o) Arch. mun. Toulouse, registers of the *capitation* for the *capitoulats* of Daurade (1790), Dalbade (1788), Pont Vieux (1790), La Pierre (1789) and St. Pierre (1790); CC 1733; (e) Arch. Haute Garonne L 2228.

Tours (see Indre-et-Loire)

Trets (Bouches-du-Rhône)

Teissère, V., "Un discours dans un club en 1791," *Annales de la Société d'études provençales* (1905), ii, 219-224.

Trévoux (Ain)

Berard, A., "Un document de l'époque révolutionnaire," *Annales de la Société d'émulation de l'Ain* (1903), xxxvi, 5-24.

Tulle (Corrèze)

Forot, V., *Le club des Jacobins de Tulle* (Tulle, 1912).

(a) *Ibid.*, 569-605; (c) Arch. Corrèze C 144; (d) Arch. Corrèze Q 483; (e) Forot, V., *Les thermidoriens tullois* (Tulle, 1908).

Turenne (Corrèze)

(a) Arch. Corrèze, L 789; (b) Arch. Corrèze C 220; (c) Arch. Corrèze C 220.

Vannes (Morbihan)

Bliard, P., "Un club en province," *Revue des questions historiques* (1902), lxxii, 489-537.

Vaulry (Haute Vienne)

Maurat-Bellange, A., "Registre de la Société populaire de Vaulry," *Bulletin de la Société archéologique et historique du Limousin* (1910), lx, 44-63.

Vauvert (Gard)

(a) Arch. Gard 11 L 3; (c) Arch. Gard 4 L 4.36.

Ventes d'Eawy (Seine Inférieure)

(a) Arch. Seine Inférieure L 5736; (c) Arch. Seine Inférieure C 1943.

Verfeil (Haute Garonne)

(a) Arch. Haute Garonne L 3166; (c); (c) Arch. Haute Garonne C 1298.

Vermenton (Yonne)

(a) Arch. Yonne L 208; (d) Arch. Yonne Q 249.

Vesoul (Haute Saône)

Cousin, M., *L'esprit publique dans le baillage d'Amont pendant la Révolution* (Dijon, 1922).

(a) Arch. Haute Saône L 366.2 (b) Cousin, *op. cit.* (c) Arch. Haute Saône L 21.28; (d) Arch. Haute Saône Q 128.

Villecroze (Var)

Poupé, E., "La Société populaire de Villecroze," *Révolution française* (1901), xl, 132-152.

Villemur (Haute-Garonne)

(a) Arch. Haute Garonne L 3166.

Villenauxe-la-Grande (Aube)

Bardet, A., "La Société républicaine et montagnarde des sans-culottes de Villenauxe," *Annales de l'Aube* (1893), 43-71.

Villeneuve-sur-Yonne)

Prevost, G., "La Société des Amis de la Constitution de Villeneuve," *Bulletin de la Société . . . de l'Yonne* (1913), lxviii, 465-525.
(a) *Ibid*. (d) Arch. Yonne Q 249.

Vilquiers (Cher)

(a) Arch. Cher L 925.

Vire (Calvados)

Butet-Hamel, "La Société populaire de Vire," *Bulletin du comité des travaux historiques* (1906), 269-329.

Vouneuil-sur-Vienne (Vienne)

Unsigned, "La Société populaire de Vouneuil, registre de ses dé-liberations," *Révolution française* (1906), l, 144-162, 239-258.

APPENDIX II

The sources for all material in these tables will be found under the place-names in Appendix I. It is to be noted that the total membership even of the same club will vary in difference tables, according to the bases of these tables. Thus, for instance, in considering occupations, all members are included; in considering tax-assessments, only resident members. Moreover, there are always gaps in the best of these records; complete information for every member—name, Christian names, occupation, age, birthplace, residence before and after 1789, date of elections to membership, government positions held—is not to be found for a single club.

TABLE I

TOTAL MEMBERSHIP RESIDENT AND NON-RESIDENT, OVER WHOLE PERIOD
1789-1795

PLACE	NUMBER IN CLUB	POPULATION	PERCENTAGE OF JACOBINS
Beaufort-en-Vallée	150	5,990	2.5
Beauvais	390	12,136	3.2
Bergerac	901	8,552	10.5
Colmar	1,037	13,360	7.8
Gray	700	5,100	13.7
Grenoble	432	16,584	2.6
Libourne	429	9,500	6.6
Lille	1,092	55,980	2.0
Montauban	1,396	21,950	6.4
Moulins	384	12,844	3.0
Nuits-St.-Georges	206	2,541	8.1
Rodez	680	6,060	11.2
Toulon	1,239	22,000	5.6
Tulle	364	9,362	3.9
Totals	9,400	201,959	4.2

TABLE II
MEMBERSHIP DURING THE PERIOD 1793-1795

PLACE	NUMBER IN CLUB	POPULATION	PERCENTAGE OF JACOBINS
Albi	326	10,272	3.2
Beauvais	141	12,136	1.2
Belfort	133	4,400	3.0
Bergerac	338	8,552	4.0
Bourges	226	15,000	1.5
Brive	295	5,762	5.1
Castres	461	15,171	3.0
Châteauroux	125	8,049	1.6
Colmar	302	13,360	2.3
Coutances	264	8,507	3.1
Dijon	679	19,800	3.4
Dreux	290	5,437	5.3
Epinal	106	7,321	1.4
Gray	300	5,100	5.9
Grenoble	326	16,584	2.0
Le Havre	355	25,000	1.4
Lunéville	308	10,436	3.0
Mamers	101	5,382	1.9
Moulins	356	12,844	2.8
Nîmes	350	39,594	0.9
Provins	147	5,500	2.7
St. Omer	258	20,100	1.3
La Souterraine	228	2,665	8.5
Toulouse	731	52,961	1.4
Vesoul	293	4,800	6.1
Totals	7,439	334,733	2.2

TABLE III
MEMBERSHIP DURING THE PERIOD 1793-1795

PLACE	NUMBER IN CLUB	POPULATION	PERCENTAGE OF JACOBINS
Beauvoisin	156	812	19.2
Charost	45	848	5.3
Cosnac	76	811	9.4
Faverney	133	1,204	11.0
Fleurey-les-Faverney	53	354	15.0
Gaillefontaine	53	1,481	3.6
Gerberoy	59	365	16.2
Haudivillers	26	275	9.5
Jussey	258	2,700	9.6
Lescure	62	1,720	3.6
Nomény	59	1,392	4.2
Noviant	27	384	7.0
Sauveterre	68	816	8.3
Vauvert	317	3,202	9.9
Totals	1,392	16,364	8.5

TABLE IV

Total Membership, 1789-1795

Place	Date of List	Law	Clergy	Other Liberal Professions	Merchants	Petty Tradesmen	Artisans	Peasants	Officers	Soldiers	Civil Servants	No Profession Given	Total
Colmar	1791-95	24	37	50	48	96	113	34	25	110	95	405	1037
Grenoble	1789-95	18	13	29	52	65	66	5	15	2	22	145	432
Lille	1790-95	36	30	80	102	145	139	4	179	77	90	210	1092
Limoges	1790-95	21	9	17	24	11	13	3	3	..	36	15	152
Moulins	1790-94	44	36	33	30	27	35	5	5	5	111	53	384
Nuits-Saint-Georges	1791-95	11	2	8	11	42	69	46	1	3	..	13	206
Rodez	1790-95	43	26	33	27	51	55	4	4	10	78	349	680
Thann	1791-95	5	6	16	14	40	55	20	5	2	12	65	240
Toul	1790-95	10	17	15	14	12	7	2	8	2	18	37	142
Tulle	1790-95	28	4	27	26	64	102	26	2	11	11	63	364
Vauvert	1791-95	4	2	10	3	38	56	196	1	4	3	..	317
Villemur	1791-95	10	3	22	24	39	162	79	..	5	8	7	359
Totals		254	185	340	375	630	872	424	248	231	484	1362	5405
Per cent		5	3	6	7	12	16	8	5	4	9	25	100
Per cent neglecting category of "no profession"		6	5	8	9	16	22	10	6	6	12	..	100

TABLE V

Memberships, 1789-1792

Place	Date of List	Law	Clergy	Other Liberal Professions	Merchants	Petty Tradesmen	Artisans	Peasants	Officers	Soldiers	Civil Servants	No Profession Given	Total
Avallon	1791	5	..	6	3	4	3	..	..	..	2	13	361
Colmar	1792	23	36	40	37	89	97	25	11	103	35	384	880
Havre, Le	1791	23	14	44	143	156	192	..	22	9	36	214	853
Nuits-Saint-Georges	1791	4	..	1	6	16	26	2	..	2	..	6	63
Paris	1791	122	23	100	33	12	2	6	21	1	36	697	1053
Soissons	1791	3	5	3	3	12	6	..	..	..	..	2	34
Strasbourg	1791	13	8	35	103	5	1	..	39	..	51	60	315
Thann	1791	4	2	5	7	10	14	1	1	..	4	7	55
Tulle	1792	19	4	27	20	51	72	22	2	8	11	53	289
Vauvert	1792	3	2	7	2	24	26	87	..	..	3	..	154
Villemur	1792	6	3	14	12	27	129	56	..	33	4	6	260
Villeneuve s/Yonne	1792	9	6	4	12	4	2	..	..	..	4	4	46
Totals		234	103	286	381	410	570	199	96	126	186	1446	4037
Per cent		6	3	7	9	10	14	5	2	3	5	36	100
Per cent neglecting category of "no profession"		9	4	11	15	16	22	8	4	4	7	..	100

TABLE VI
Memberships, 1793-1795

Place	Date of List	Law	Clergy	Other Liberal Professions	Merchants	Petty Tradesmen	Artisans	Peasants	Officers	Soldiers	Civil Servants	No Profession Given	Total
Alban	1794	2	..	3	4	9	4	4	..	..	2	3	31
Albi	1794	34	11	30	32	101	117	11	3	..	9	13	361
Beaulieu s/Dordogne	1794	5	2	7	4	30	47	24	..	7	2	4	132
Beauvais	1794	17	4	10	24	47	33	5	2	..	11	8	161
Belfort	1795	22	6	16	12	28	20	3	4	5	16	1	133
Beynat	1794	1	..	4	2	4	2	36	..	..	2	:	51
Bourges	1794	28	16	17	16	48	40	16	2	2	28	31	244
Brive	1795	34	4	18	11	62	110	25	..	8	:	23	295
Castres	1795	24	4	33	16	76	172	26	4	8	33	84	480
Chablis	1794	5	1	5	7	15	19	29	..	..	5	:	86
Châlons s/Marne	1794	7	2	6	4	6	10	..	2	..	9	4	50
Charost	1794	3	1	3	2	10	14	14	..	1	3	2	53
Cosnac	1794	1	1	1	2	2	4	64	..	1	:	:	76
Coutances	1794	29	5	21	14	41	32	3	12	1	65	41	264
Dieuze	1795	24	..	9	13	21	31	3	2	..	19	:	122
Dijon	1795	70	26	64	164	156	171	21	3	2	44	62	783
Dreux	1794	8	1	21	19	55	62	12	2	5	22	83	290
Epinal	1794	2	..	1	7	8	7	..	..	..	4	3	32
Gaillefontaine	1794	5	3	5	2	10	14	10	..	..	4	:	53
Gerberoy	1794	4	1	2	4	15	25	4	1	..	2	1	59
Giromagny	1794	4	2	4	3	11	41	10	..	..	3	:	78
Haudivillers	1794	:	..	:	:	3	2	8	1	..	4	8	26
Lorient	1794	4	..	6	4	4	..	..	..	..	9	:	27
Lunéville	1794	32	2	20	30	42	43	10	9	14	22	84	308
Manneville-la-Goupil	1794	1	..	3	3	13	14	2	.•	..	1	6	43

303

TABLE VI (Continued)

PLACE	DATE OF LIST	LAW	CLERGY	OTHER LIBERAL PROFESSIONS	MERCHANTS	PETTY TRADESMEN	ARTISANS	PEASANTS	OFFICERS	SOLDIERS	CIVIL SERVANTS	NO PROFESSION GIVEN	TOTAL
Mareuil	1795	1	:	6	1	8	23	17	1	:	4	6	67
Martres-Tolosane	1794	1	2	5	:	6	28	38	:	1	2	3	86
Metz	1795	9	:	32	17	19	7	:	5	1	30	29	149
Montignac	1794	7	:	4	5	7	5	7	.	.	3	:	38
Nice	1794	6	:	8	15	20	35	2	9	18	39	5	157
Nîmes	1794	:	:	11	20	39	261	9	2	1	2	5	350
Orthez	1793	3	2	2	3	10	6	1	:	.	21	95	143
Perpignan	1794	14	7	15	17	48	58	10	22	6	25	88	310
Rabastens	1794	7	7	8	6	29	214	16	1	1	11	17	317
Rambouillet	1795	12	2	16	18	76	172	38	1	5	3	2	345
Saint Doulchard	1794	:	1	1	:	1	:	45	.	.	:	1	49
Saint Jean-de Maurienne	1794	13	2	8	4	3	2	3	:	:	:	1	36
Saint-Omer	1794	20	.	17	28	39	22	4	2	2	4	9	147
Saint-Saëns	1794	3	1	4	2	26	30	12	:	:	3	:	81
Thonon	1795	15	1	10	5	15	6	3	5	2	2	1	65
Toulouse	1794	24	4	53	87	143	167	4	8	6	52	183	731
Turenne	1794	7	3	7	4	5	14	68	:	1	2	10	121
Ventes d'Eawy	1794	2	:	2	3	4	9	2	:	:	1	:	23
Verfeil	1795	5	7	12	7	27	73	103	5	1	2	15	257
Vesoul	1794	27	5	23	20	53	43	9	7	2	11	74	274
Vilquiers	1794	3	:	3	1	12	9	44	.	.	4	2	78
Totals		545	136	556	662	1407	2218	775	115	101	540	1007	8062
Per cent		7	2	7	8	17	28	10	1	1	7	12	100
Per cent neglecting category "no profession"		8	2	8	9	20	31	11	2	1	8	..	100

TABLE VII

Total Membership, 1789-1795

Place	Date of List	Tax	Date of Roll	Resident Members	Members Paying Tax No.	%	Male Population over 16 Yrs.	Amount Paid by Members (in Livres)	Amount Paid by All Male Inhabitants (in Livres)	Average per Member (in Livres)	Average per Male Inhabitants (in Livres)
Beauvais	1790-95	Contribution foncière	1791	296	180	61	3034	7619	32046	25.74	10.56
Bergerac	1790-95	Capitation	1789	790	308	39	2138	9098	15780	11.52	7.35
Bordeaux*	1790-94	Vingtièmes	1790	827	293	35	25410	39166	377014	42.52	14.84
Colmar	1791-95	Taille & Capitation	1789	719	365	51	3340	12512	42429	16.01	12.70
Grenoble	1789-95	Emprunt forcé	1797	421	166	39	4146	58530	347890	139.03	83.91
Libourne	1790-94	Taille & Capitation	1790	429	228	53	2375	13293	38146	30.98	16.06
Lille	1790-95	Capitation	1790	701	362	52	13995	5836	68397	8.31	4.89
Rodez	1790-95	Impôts ordinaires et vingtièmes	1788-89	580	236	40	1515	11714	30409	20.20	20.07
Totals				4763	2138	45	55953	157768	952111	33.12	17.02

PLACE	DATE OF LIST	TAX	DATE OF ROLL	RESIDENT MEMBERS
Albi	1794	Capitation	1789	326
Beaulieu s/ Dordogne .	1794	Vingtièmes	1787	129
Beauvais ...	1794	Contribution foncière	1791	141
Beauvoisin .	1794	Impôts ordinaires et vingtièmes	1790	156
Bergerac ...	1792-94	Capitation	1789	338
Bordeaux ..	1793-94	Vingtièmes	1790	306
Bourges	1795	Capitation	1789	226
Charost	1794	Vingtièmes	1789	45
Colmar	1794	Taille & Capitation..	1789	209
Dijon	1795	Vingtièmes	1790	679
Faverney ...	1794	Impôts ordinaires ...	1790	133
Grenoble ...	1795	Emprunt forcé	1797	326
Havre, Le ..	1794	Vingtièmes	1789	355
Jussey	1794	Vingtièmes	1790	258
Lescure	1794	Capitation	1789	62
Libourne ...	1792-94	Taille & Capitation..	1790	291
Moulins	1794	Capitation	1789	356
Nomény	1794	Contributions directes	1790	59
Noviant-aux-Prés	1794	Contributions directes	1790	27
Rosières-aux-Salines ...	1794	Contributions directes	1791	64
Sainte-Marie-aux-Mines	1794	Vingtièmes	1789	146
Sauveterre ..	1794	Impôts ordinaires et vingtièmes	1789	68
Toul	1795	Contributions directes	1790	166
Toulouse ...	1792-94	Capitation	1788-90	403
Turenne	1794	Vingtièmes	1790	108
Vesoul	1795	Contributions directes	1790	293
Totals....				5670

VIII
1793-1795

MEMBERS PAYING TAX		MALE POPULATION OVER 16 YRS.	AMOUNT PAID BY MEMBERS (IN LIVRES)	AMOUNT PAID BY ALL MALE INHABITANTS (IN LIVRES)	AVERAGE PER MEMBER (IN LIVRES)	AVERAGE PER MALE INHABITANTS (IN LIVRES)
No.	%					
176	54	2568	1523	6775	4.67	2.64
72	56	375	534	1670	4.14	4.45
83	59	3034	2730	32046	19.36	10.56
119	76	203	2920	4050	18.72	19.95
156	46	2138	5157	15780	15.26	7.35
76	25	25410	8153	377014	26.64	14.84
116	51	3750	1992	20461	8.82	5.49
22	49	212	181	535	4.02	2.55
146	70	3340	5464	42429	26.15	12.70
241	35	4950	9764	54104	14.38	10.93
89	67	301	1490	3551	11.20	11.80
139	43	4146	40680	347890	124.79	83.91
106	30	6250	4983	36252	14.04	5.80
184	71	675	993	2992	3.85	4.43
32	52	430	196	1170	3.17	2.72
141	48	2375	9936	38146	34.15	16.06
194	55	3211	1634	7713	4.59	2.40
52	88	348	903	3602	15.31	10.35
19	70	96	346	1668	12.81	17.16
49	77	565	1630	15598	25.47	27.61
74	51	1615	392	1952	2.51	1.21
41	60	204	1089	5277	16.02	25.33
112	67	1875	4150	43603	25.00	23.26
230	57	7885	3154	46615	7.83	5.91
48	44	313	918	1828	8.49	5.84
194	67	1200	2185	7110	7.46	5.92
2912	51	77469	113097	119831	19.94	14.45

TABLE IX

Membership, 1793-1795

Place		Tax	Date of List	No. Members Paying Tax	No. Non-Members Paying Tax	Amount Paid by Members (in livres)	Amount Paid by Non-Members (in livres)	Average Tax Members (in livres)	Average Tax Non-Members (in livres)
Alban	1794	Capitation	1789	23	431	116.50	1,957.50	5.07	4.54
Bacqueville	1794	Taille & Capitation	1789	31	426	1,561.43	12,764.25	50.37	29.96
Châteauneuf s/Cher	1794	Impôts ordinaires	1790	55	236	1,318.25	2,518.30	23.97	10.67
Cordes	1794	Capitation	1789	86	363	571.50	1,637.60	6.65	4.51
Faverney	1794	Impôts ordinaires	1790	89	200	1,489.63	2,423.64	16.74	12.12
Grenoble	1795	Capitation	1789	201	3,741	1,392.00	13,634.30	6.93	3.64
Pechbonnieu, etc.	1794	Capitation	1789-90	92	245	311.00	761.50	3.38	3.11
Perpignan	1794	Vingtièmes	1788	103	1,799	1,337.85	9,134.50	12.99	5.09
Rosières-aux-Salines	1794	Contribution foncière	1791	49	846	1,629.83	16,196.84	32.26	19.15
Sainte-Marie-aux-Mines	1794	Vingtièmes	1789	74	543	392.05	1,896.00	5.30	3.29
Sauveterre	1794	Impôts ordinaires et vingtièmes	1789	41	211	1,089.00	4,443.00	26.56	21.06
Toul	1794	Contribution directes	1790	102	1,066	4,150.30	45,681.25	40.69	42.85
Tulle	1794	Taille	1789	162	525	1,764.65	3,776.42	10.90	7.00
Ventes d'Eawy	1794	Taille	1789	13	376	826.95	9,993.45	71.30	26.58
Verfeil	1794	Capitation	1790	122	266	627.50	1,262.75	5.14	4.75
Vesoul	1795	Contributions directes	1790	195	1,160	2,185.40	6,090.60	11.21	5.25
Totals				1438	12,434	20,763.84	134,171.90	14.47	10.79

TABLE X
Vingtièmes d'Industrie

Place	Date of List	Date of Roll	No. Members Paying	No. Non-Members Paying	Amount Paid by Members (in Livres)	Amount Paid by Non-Members (in Livres)	Average Tax Members (in Livres)	Average Tax Non-Members (in Livres)
Albi (artisans)	1794	1789	80	526	202.75	755.35	2.53	144.
Albi (merchants)	1794	1789	51	102	617.50	591.00	12.11	5.79–
Bourges	1795	1789	72	524	435.75	1907.35	6.05	3.64
Cordes (weavers)	1794	1789	20	81	78.50	239.10	3.95	2.95
Montbard	1794	1790	31	162	87.35	189.85	2.82	1.17
Rabastens	1795	1789	142	290	601.50	853.35	4.24	2.90
Sainte-Marie-aux-Mines ...	1794	1788	63	336	143.20	334.95	2.27	1.00
Toulouse	1794	1790	53	347	314.65	1,260.70	5.94	3.63
Vauvert	1794	1790	82	105	194.00	138.50	2.37	1.34
Totals			594	2473	2675.20	6270.15	4.47	2.49

TABLE XI

BUYERS OF NATIONAL PROPERTY

PLACE	DATE OF LIST	NUMBER OF RESIDENT MEMBERS	NUMBER OF MEMBERS BUYING	% OF MEMBERS BUYING	NO. OF NON-MEMBERS BUYING	AMOUNT BOUGHT BY MEMBERS (IN LIVRES) *	AMOUNT BOUGHT BY NON-MEMBERS (IN LIVRES)	AVERAGE PURCHASE OF MEMBERS (IN LIVRES)	AVERAGE PURCHASE OF NON-MEMBERS (IN LIVRES)
Castres	1794	461	67	15	48	1,834,305	370,080	27,378	7,918
Colmar	1791-95	719	131	18	133	1,697,550	837,510	12,965	6,297
Faverney	1794	133	12	9	5	27,750	7,925	2,296	1,585
Jussey	1794	258	43	17	9	434,375	37,925	10,102	4,214
Manneville-la-Goupil	1794	43	6	12	2	46,150	5,680	7,692	2,840
Nomeny	1794	59	16	27	4	235,880	1,210	14,743	303
Noviant-aux-Prés	1794	32	8	25	9	57,085	25,170	7,139	2,797
Perpignan	1794	426	98	23	159	832,155	361,775	8,491	2,275
Pont-à-Mousson	1794	230	116	50	108	2,359,170	540,775	20,338	4,590
Toul	1794	166	102	61	253	1,863,660	1,417,750	18,271	5,604
Sainte-Marie-aux-Mines	1794	162	16	10	5	206,195	32,835	12,887	6,297
Tulle	1790-94	576	78	14	34	418,135	175,100	5,361	5,150
Vesoul	1795	293	70	24	48	807,590	801,990	11,537	16,708
Totals		3,558	763	21	817	10,820,000	4,615,725	14,181	5,650

* I have corrected the prices paid in depreciated paper so that the prices given above are the gold prices *at the moment of purchase.* No doubt actual payments were even less in terms of gold as depreciation continued and payment by installments was allowed. But to have worked out this latter figure would have been difficult and even impossible. I have used the tables in Harris, S. E. *The Assignats* (Cambridge, Mass., 1930) to obtain the rates at which the assignats were exchangeable for gold at given periods.

TABLE XII

Buyers of National Property

Place	Date of List	Members of Club	Members Buying	Per Cent
Beauvais	1790-94	296	95	32
Chablis	1794-	86	55	64
Dijon	1795-	783	215	27
Havre, Le	1791-94	912	128	14
Vermenton	1793-	38	9	23
Villeneuve s/Yonne....	1791-	45	15	33
Totals		2160	517	22

TABLE XIII

Membership 1789-1795

Place	Total Members 1789-1795	Members Common to the Periods 1789-92 and 1793-1795
Beauvais	296	39
Bourges	268	149
Libourne	429	209
Moulins	365	109
Nuits-St-Georges	221	151
Tulle	642	330
Totals	2221	987

TABLE XIV

Membership as of Some Date between 1793-1795

(Usually vendemiaire, an III)

Place	Members Elected before January, 1793	Members Elected after January, 1793
Albi	306	57
Belfort	65	57
Castres	110	173
Dieuze	26	104
Grenoble	285	136
Le Havre	131	220
Nîmes	232	105
Rabastens	207	106
Thann	68	183
Vauvert	156	153
Villemur	284	101
Totals	1870	1395

TABLE XV

MEMBERSHIP AS OF SOME DATE
BETWEEN 1793-1795 (USUALLY VENDEMIAIRE, AN III)

PLACE	MEMBERS ELECTED BEFORE JANUARY, 1793		MEMBERS ELECTED AFTER JANUARY, 1793	
	MIDDLE CLASS	WORKING MEN	MIDDLE CLASS	WORKING MEN
Belfort	38	21	36	18
Castres	68	27	58	87
Dieuze	16	7	56	45
Le Havre	251	106	150	101
Rabastens	51	132	23	83
Thann	26	18	55	61
Villemur	73	132	39	38
Totals	523	443	417	433

TABLE XVI

MEMBERSHIP AT SOME PERIOD BETWEEN 1793-1795
(USUALLY VENDEMIAIRE, AN III)

PLACE	AVERAGE TAX PAID. BY MEMBERS ELECTED BEFORE JANUARY, 1793	AVERAGE TAX PAID BY MEMBERS ELECTED AFTER JANUARY, 1793
Albi	8.9 livres	7.8 livres
Bergerac	12.3 "	15.8 "
Bourges	16.2 "	6.9 "
Grenoble	8.7 "	4.7 "
Lille	12.1 "	8.3 "
Moulins	5.8 "	3.7 "
Nîmes	5.5 "	15.3 "
Rabastens	4.5 "	3.2 "
Tulle	13.4 "	6.6 "
Average (each place weighted equally)	15.3 "	14.1 "

INDEX

INDEX

Alais, 113
Alban, 303, 308
Albi, 121, 300, 303, 306, 309, 311, 312
Alençon, 122
Amiens, 98, 123
Angers, 143
Angles, 93
Aiguesmortes, 131, 163
Aix-en-Provence, 91, 188, 189, 194
Aouste, 37
Arnay-sur-Aroux, 144
Arre, 128
Ars-en-Ré, 37, 114, 160, 180, 222
Artonne, 24, 69
assignats, 114, 167
Auch, 14, 33, 113, 193, 220
Augoulême, 93
Aulard, A., 77, 122, 232
Auxerre, 83, 124, 154, 182
Avallon, 43, 84, 98, 110, 191, 302
Avranches, 13

Bacqueville, 35, 208, 308
Bar, 30
Barnave, 143, 220
Bayeux, 63
Beaufort-en-Vallée, 188, 195, 299
Beaulieu-sur-Dordogne, 303, 306
Beauvais, 25, 35, 37, 60, 61, 64, 143, 174, 200, 208, 219, 222, 228, 299, 300, 303, 305, 306, 311
Beauvoisin, 42, 300, 306
Belfort, 300, 311, 312
Bénévent, 173, 182
Bentabole, 123
Bergerac, 14, 62, 78, 83, 88, 116, 153, 194, 195, 211, 219, 255, 299, 300, 305, 306, 312
Bernay, 123
Besançon, 75, 80, 99, 114, 116, 135, 177, 192, 204, 207, 222

Beynat, 303
Blaye, 67, 86, 101, 131
Blois, 65
Boisset, 121, 200
Bordeaux, 65, 66, 68, 82, 87, 108, 194, 205, 305, 306
Boulogne, 181
Bourbon-Lancy, 107
Bourges, 95, 300, 303, 306, 309, 312
Bourgoin, 224
Breteuil, 31
Brissot, 220
Brittany, 12
Brive, 121, 192, 300, 303

Callas, 32
Carcassonne, 124, 135, 220
Cardenal, L. de, 39, 245, 254, 264
Carrier, 124
Castelnau-Rivière-Basse, 25, 126
Castres, 13, 121, 174, 300, 310, 311, 312
Caussade, 32
centralization, 146
Cézy, 109
Chablis, 33, 34, 76, 105, 110, 130, 153, 164, 171, 187, 206, 209, 222, 303, 311
Châlons-sur-Marne, 80, 209, 303
Charnècles, 64
Charost, 42, 300, 303, 306
Châteauneuf-sur-Cher, 308
Châteauroux, 110, 199, 300
Château-Thierry, 190, 191, 225
Chaudron-Rousseau, 124
Cherbourg, 13, 31, 95
Chobaut, H., 39, 249, 250, 253
Clamecy, 122
Clermont-Ferrand, 142, 213
Club Breton, 18, 19, 106, 108
Cochin, A., 10, 12, 69, 232